# The C Book
## Featuring the ANSI C Standard

*SECOND EDITION*

D1323472

# The C Book

## Featuring the ANSI C Standard

*SECOND EDITION*

Mike Banahan
Declan Brady
Mark Doran

 **Addison-Wesley Publishing Company**

Wokingham, England · Reading, Massachusetts · Menlo Park, California · New York
Don Mills, Ontario · Amsterdam · Bonn · Sydney · Singapore
Tokyo · Madrid · San Juan · Milan · Paris · Mexico City · Seoul · Taipei

# the instruction set

The Instruction Set Series
Published in collaboration with The Instruction Set Ltd.

© 1991 The Instruction Set Ltd.
© 1991 Addison-Wesley Publishers Ltd.
© 1991 Addison-Wesley Publishing Company, Inc.

Cover designed by Hybert Design and Type, Maidenhead and printed by The Riverside Printing Co. (Reading) Ltd.
Typeset by CRB Typesetting Services, Ely, Cambs.
Printed in Great Britain by Mackays of Chatham plc, Chatham, Kent.

First edition published 1988. Reprinted 1988.
Second edition printed 1991.

**British Library Cataloguing in Publication Data**
Banahan, M.F. (Michael Francis) 1953–
    The C book : featuring the ANSI C Standard.–2nd. ed.
    1. Computers. Programming languages
    I. Title   II. Brady, Declan   III. Doran, Mark
    005.133I

    ISBN 0-201-54433-4

**Library of Congress Cataloging in Publication Data**
Banahan, Mike.
    The C book, featuring the ANSI C standard / Mike Banahan, Declan Brady, Mark Doran. – 2nd ed.
        p.   cm. – (The Instruction set)
    Rev. ed. of: The C book, featuring the draft ANSI C standard.
    Includes index.
    ISBN 0-201-54433-4
    1. C (Computer program language)   I. Brady, Declan.   II. Doran, Mark.   III. Banahan, Mike. C book, featuring the draft ANSI C standard.   IV. Title.   V. Series.
    QA76.73.C15B36     1991
    005.13'3--dc20
                                                    90-26658
                                                      CIP

# Preface

*About this book*

This book was written with two groups of readers in mind. Whether you are new to C and want to learn it, or already know the older version of the language but want to find out more about the new Standard, we hope that you will find what follows both instructive and at times entertaining too.

This is not a tutorial introduction to programming. The book is designed for programmers who already have some experience of using a modern high-level procedural programming language. As we explain later, C isn't really appropriate for complete beginners – though many have managed to use it – so the book will assume that its readers have already done battle with the notions of statements, variables, conditional execution, arrays, procedures (or subroutines) and so on. Instead of wasting your time by ploughing through tedious descriptions of how to add two numbers together and explaining that the symbol for multiplication is *, the book concentrates on the things that are special to C. In particular, it's the *way* that C is used which is emphasized.

Those who already know C will be interested in the new Standard and how it affects existing C programs. The effect on existing programs might not at first seem to be important to newcomers, but in fact the 'old' and 'new' versions of the language *are* an issue for the beginner too. For some years after the approval of the Standard, programmers will have to live in a world where they can easily encounter a mixture of both the new and the old language, depending on the age of the programs that they are working with. For that reason, the book highlights where the old and new features differ significantly. Some of the old features are no ornament to the language and are well worth avoiding; the Standard goes so far as to consider them obsolescent and recommends that they should not be used. For that reason they are not described in detail, but only far enough to allow a reader to understand what they mean. Anybody who intends to *write* programs using these old-style features should be reading a different book.

This is the second edition of the book, which has been revised to refer to the final, approved version of the Standard. The first edition of the book was based on a draft of the Standard which did contain some differences from the draft that was eventually approved. During the revision we have taken the opportunity to include more summary material and an extra chapter illustrating the use of C and the Standard Library to solve a number of small problems.

### The success of C

C is a remarkable language. Designed originally by one man, Dennis Ritchie, working at AT&T Bell Laboratories in New Jersey, it has increased in use until now it may well be one of the most widely-written computer languages in the world. The success of C is due to a number of factors, none of them key, but all of them important. Perhaps the most significant of all is that C was developed by real practitioners of programming and was designed for practical day-to-day use, not for show or for demonstration. Like any well-designed tool, it falls easily to the hand and feels good to use. Instead of providing constraints, checks and rigorous boundaries, it concentrates on providing you with power and on not getting in your way.

Because of this, it's better for professionals than beginners. In the early stages of learning to program you need a protective environment that gives feedback on mistakes and helps you to get results quickly – programs that run, even if they don't do what you meant. C is not like that! A professional forester would use a chain-saw to cut down trees quickly, aware of the dangers of touching the blade when the machine is running; C programmers work in a similar way. Although modern C compilers do provide a limited amount of feedback when they notice something that is out of the ordinary, you almost always have the option of forcing the compiler to do what you said you wanted and to stop it from complaining. Provided that what you said you wanted was what you really did want, then you'll get the result you expected. Programming in C is like eating red meat and drinking strong rum except your arteries and liver are more likely to survive it.

Not only is C popular and a powerful asset in the armoury of the serious day-to-day programmer, there are other reasons for the success of this language. It has always been associated with the UNIX operating system and has benefited from the increasing popularity of that system. Although it is not the obvious first choice for writing large commercial data processing applications, C has the great advantage of always being available on commercial UNIX implementations. UNIX is written in C, so whenever UNIX is implemented on a new type of hardware, getting a C compiler to work for that system is the first task. As a result it is almost impossible to find a UNIX system without support for C, so the software vendors who want to target the UNIX marketplace find that C is the best bet if they want to get wide coverage of the systems available. Realistically, C is the first choice for portability of software in the UNIX environment.

C has also gained substantially in use and availability from the explosive expansion of the Personal Computer market. C could almost have been designed specifically for the development of software for the PC – developers get not only the readability and productivity of a high-level language, but also the power to get the most out of the PC architecture *without* having to resort to the use of assembly code. C is practically unique in its ability to span two levels of programming; as well as providing high-level control of flow, data structures and procedures – all of the stuff expected in a modern high-level language – it also allows systems programmers to address machine words, manipulate bits and get close to the underlying hardware if they want to. That combination of features is very desirable in the competitive PC software marketplace and an increasing number of software developers have made C their primary language as a result.

Finally, the extensibility of C has contributed in no small way to its popularity. Many other languages have failed to provide the file access and general input/output features that are needed for industrial-strength applications. Traditionally, in these languages I/O is built-in and is actually understood by the compiler. A master-stroke in the design of C (and interestingly, one of the strengths of the UNIX system too) has been to take the view that if you don't know how to provide a complete solution to a generic requirement, instead of providing half a solution (which invariably pleases nobody), you should allow the users to build their own. Software designers the world over have something to learn from this! It's the approach that has been taken by C, and not only for I/O. Through the use of **library functions** you can extend the language in many ways to provide features that the designers didn't think of. There's proof of this in the so-called Standard I/O Library (stdio), which matured more slowly than the language, but had become a sort of standard all of its own before the Standard Committee give it official blessing. It proved that it is possible to develop a model of file I/O and associated features that is portable to many more systems than UNIX, which is where it was first wrought. Despite the ability of C to provide access to low-level hardware features, judicious style and the use of the stdio package results in highly portable programs; many of which are to be found running on top of operating systems that look very different from one another. The nice thing about this library is that if you don't like what it does, but you have the appropriate technical skills, you can usually extend it to do what you *do* want, or bypass it altogether.

### Standards

Remarkably, C achieved its success in the absence of a formal standard. Even more remarkable is that during this period of increasingly widespread use, there has never been any serious divergence of C into the number of dialects that has been the bane of, for example, BASIC. In fact, this is not so surprising. There has always been a 'language reference manual', the widely-known book written by Brian Kernighan and Dennis Ritchie, usually referred to as simply 'K&R':

> D.M. Ritchie and B.W. Kernighan (1978). *The C Programming Language.*
> Englewood Cliffs, New Jersey: Prentice-Hall.

Further acting as a rigorous check on the expansion into numerous dialects, on UNIX systems there was only ever really one compiler for C; the so-called 'Portable C Compiler', originally written by Steve Johnson. This acted as a reference implementation for C – if the K&R reference was a bit obscure then the behaviour of the UNIX compiler was taken as the definition of the language.

Despite this almost ideal situation (a reference manual and a reference implementation are extremely good ways of achieving stability at a very low cost), the increasing number of alternative implementations of C to be found in the PC world did begin to threaten the stability of the language.

The X3J11 committee of the American National Standards Institute started work in the early 1980s to produce a formal standard for C. The committee took as its reference the K&R definition and began its lengthy and painstaking work. The job was to try to eliminate ambiguities, to define the undefined, to fix the most annoying deficiencies of the language and to preserve the spirit of C – all this as well as providing as much compatibility with existing practice as was possible. Fortunately, nearly all of the developers of the competing versions of C were represented on the committee, which in itself acted as a strong force for convergence right from the beginning.

Development of the Standard took a long time, as standards often do. Much of the work is not just technical, although that is a very time-consuming part of the job, but also procedural. It's easy to underrate the procedural aspects of standards work, as if it somehow dilutes the purity of the technical work, but in fact it is equally important. A standard that has no agreement or consensus in the industry is unlikely to be widely adopted and could be useless or even damaging. The painstaking work of obtaining consensus among committee members is critical to the success of a practical standard, even if at times it means compromising on technical 'perfection', whatever that might be. It is a democratic process, open to all, which occasionally results in aberrations just as much as can excessive indulgence by technical purists, and unfortunately the delivery date of the Standard was affected at the last moment by procedural, rather than technical issues. The technical work was completed by December 1988, but it took a further year to resolve procedural objections. Finally, approval to release the document as a formal American National Standard was given on 7 December 1989.

### Hosted and free-standing environments

The dependency on the use of libraries to extend the language has an important effect on the practical use of C. Not only are the Standard I/O Library functions important to applications programmers, but there are a number of other functions that are widely taken almost for granted as being part of the language. String handling, sorting and comparison, character manipulation and similar services are invariably expected in all but the most specialized of applications areas.

Because of this unusually heavy dependency on libraries to do real work, it was most important that the Standard provided comprehensive definitions for the supporting functions too. The situation with the library functions was much more complicated than the relatively simple job of providing a tight definition for the language itself, because the library can be extended or modified by a knowledgeable user and was only partially defined in K&R. In practice, this led to numerous similar but different implementations of supporting libraries in common use. By far the hardest part of the work of the Committee was to reach a good definition of the library support that should be provided. In terms of benefit to the final user of C, it is this work that will prove to be far and away the most valuable part of the Standard.

However, not all C programs are used for the same type of applications. The Standard Library is useful for 'data processing' types of applications, where file I/O and numeric and string oriented data are widely used. There is an equally important application area for C – the 'embedded system' area – which includes such things as process control, real-time and similar applications.

The Standard knows this and provides for it. A large part of the Standard is the definition of the library functions that must be supplied for **hosted environments**. A hosted environment is one that provides the standard libraries. The standard permits both hosted and **freestanding environments** and goes to some length to differentiate between them. Who would want to go without libraries? Well, anybody writing 'stand alone' programs. Operating systems, embedded systems like machine controllers and firmware for instrumentation are all examples of the case where a hosted environment might be inappropriate. Programs written for a hosted environment have to be aware of the fact that the names of *all* the library functions are reserved for use by the implementation. There is no such restriction on the programmer working in a freestanding environment, although it isn't a good idea to go using names that are used in the standard library, simply because it will mislead readers of the program. Chapter 9 describes the names and uses of the library functions.

### *Typographical conventions*

The book tries to keep a consistent style in its use of special or technical terms. Words with a special meaning to C, such as **reserved words** or the names of **library functions**, are printed in a different typeface. Examples are int and printf. Terms used by the book that have a meaning not to C but in the Standard or the text of the book, are **bold** if they have not been introduced recently. They are *not* bold everywhere, because that rapidly annoys the reader. As you have noticed, italics are also used for emphasis from time to time, and to introduce loosely defined terms. Whether or not the name of a function, keyword or so on starts with a capital letter, it is nonetheless capitalized when it appears at the start of a sentence; this is one problem where either solution (capitalize or not) is unsatisfactory. Occasionally quote marks are used around 'special terms' if there is a danger of them being understood in their normal English meaning because of surrounding context. Anything else is at the whim of the authors, or simply by accident.

### *Order of topics*

The order of presentation of topics in this book loosely follows the order that is taught in The Instruction Set's introductory course. It starts with an overview of the essential parts of the language that will let you start to write useful programs quite quickly. The introduction is followed by a detailed coverage of the material that was ignored before, then it goes on to discuss the standard libraries in depth. This means that in principle, if you felt so inclined, you could read the book as far as you like and stop, yet still have learnt a reasonably coherent subset of the language. Previous experience of C will render Chapter 1 a bit slow, but it is still worth persevering with it, if only once.

### *Example programs*

All but the smallest of the examples shown in the text have been tested using a compiler that claims to conform to the Standard. As a result, most of them stand a good chance of being correct, unless our interpretation of the Standard was wrong and the compiler developer made the same mistake. None the less, experience warns that despite careful checking, *some* errors are bound to creep in. Please be understanding with any errors that you may find.

### Deference to higher authority
This book is an attempt to produce a readable and enlightening description of the language defined by the Standard. It sets out to to make interpretations of what the Standard actually means but to express them in 'simpler' English. We've done our best to get it right, but you must never forget that the only place that the language is fully defined is in the Standard itself. It is entirely possible that what we interpret the Standard to mean is at times not what the Standard Committee sought to specify, or that the way we explain it is looser and less precise than it is in the Standard. If you are in any doubt: READ THE STANDARD! It's not meant to be read for pleasure, but it is meant to be accurate and unambiguous; look nowhere else for the authoritative last word.

### Address for the Standard
Copies of the Standard can be obtained from:

> X3 Secretariat,
> CBEMA,
> 311 First Street, NW,
> Suite 500,
> Washington DC 20001-2178,
> USA.
> Phone (+1) (202) 737 8888

*Mike Banahan*
*Declan Brady*
*Mark Doran*

January 1991

# Contents

# CHAPTER 1

# An Introduction to C

## 1.1 The form of a C program

If you're used to the block-structured form of, say, Pascal, then at the outer level the layout of a C program may surprise you. If your experience lies in the FORTRAN camp you will find it closer to what you already know, but the inner level will look quite different. C has borrowed shamelessly from both kinds of language, and from a lot of other places too. The input from so many varied sources has spawned a language a bit like a cross-bred terrier: inelegant in places, but a tenacious brute that the family is fond of. Biologists refer to this phenomenon as 'hybrid vigour'. They might also draw your attention to the 'chimera', an artificial crossbreed of creatures such as a sheep and a goat. If it gives wool and milk, fine, but it might equally well just bleat and stink!

At the coarsest level, an obvious feature is the multi-file structure of a program. The language permits **separate compilation**, where the parts of a complete program can be kept in one or more **source files** and compiled independently of each other. The idea is that the compilation process will produce files which can then be **linked** together using whatever link editor or loader that your system provides. The block structure of the ALGOL-like languages makes this harder by insisting that the whole program comes in one chunk, although there are usually ways of getting around it.

The reason for C's approach is historical and rather interesting. It is supposed to speed things up: the idea is that compiling a program into relocatable **object code** is slow and expensive in terms of resources; compiling is hard work. Using the loader to bind together a number of object code modules should simply be a matter of sorting out the absolute addresses of each item in the modules when combined into a

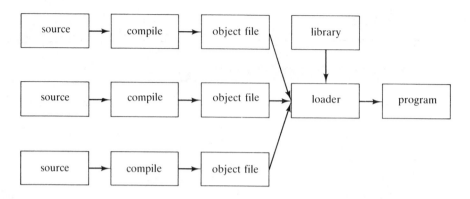

**Figure 1.1** Separate compilation.

complete program. This should be relatively inexpensive. The expansion of the idea to arrange for the loader to scan **libraries** of object modules, and select the ones that are needed, is an obvious one. The benefit is that if you change one small part of a program then the expense of recompiling all of it may be avoided; only the module that was affected has to be recompiled.

All the same, it's true that the more work put on to the loader, the slower it becomes, in fact sometimes it can be the slowest and most resource consuming part of the whole procedure. It is possible that, for some systems, it would be quicker to recompile everything in one go than to have to use the loader: Ada has sometimes been quoted as an example of this effect occurring. For C, the work that has to be done by the loader is not large and the approach is a sensible one. Figure 1.1 shows the way that this works.

This technique is important in C, where it is common to find all but the smallest of programs constructed from a number of separate source files. Furthermore, the extensive use that C makes of libraries means that even trivial programs pass through the loader, although that might not be obvious at the first glance or to the newcomer.

## 1.2 Functions

A C program is built up from a collection of items such as **functions** and what we could loosely call **global variables**. All of these things are given names at the point where they are defined in the program; the way that the names are used to access those items from a given place in the program is governed by rules. The rules are described in the Standard using the term **linkage**. For the moment we only need to concern ourselves with **external linkage** and **no linkage**. Items with external linkage are those that are accessible throughout the program (library functions are a good example); items with no linkage are also widely used but their accessibility is much more restricted. Variables used inside functions are usually 'local' to the function; they have no linkage. Although this book avoids the use of complicated terms like these where it can, sometimes there isn't a plainer way of saying things. **Linkage** is a term that you are going to become familiar with later. The only external linkage that we will see for a while will be when we are using functions.

Functions are C's equivalents of the functions and subroutines in FORTRAN, functions and procedures in Pascal and ALGOL. Neither BASIC in most of its simple mutations, nor COBOL has much like C's functions. The idea of a function is, of course, to allow you to encapsulate one idea or operation, give it a name, then to call that operation from various parts of the rest of your program simply by using the name. The detail of what is going on is not immediately visible at the point of use, nor should it be. In well designed, properly structured programs, it should be possible to change the way that a function does its job (as long as the job itself doesn't change) with no effect on the rest of the program.

In a **hosted environment** there is one function whose name is special; it's the one called main. This function is the first one entered when your program starts running. In a **freestanding environment** the way that a program starts up is **implementation defined**; a term which means that although the Standard doesn't specify what must happen, the actual behaviour must be consistent and documented. When the program leaves the main function, the whole program comes to an end. Here's a simple program containing two functions:

```
#include (stdio.h)

/*
 * Tell the compiler that we intend
 * to use a function called show_message.
 * It has no arguments and returns no value
 * This is the ''declaration''.
 *
 */
void show_message(void);

/*
 * Another function, but this includes the body of
 * the function. This is a ''definition''.
 */
main(){
        int count;

        count = 0;
        while(count < 10){
                show_message();
                count = count + 1;
        }
        return(0);
}
```

```
/*
 * The body of the simple function.
 * This is now a ''definition''.
 */
void
show_message(void){
        printf("hello\n");
}
```
                                                                    (Example 1.1)

## 1.3  A description of Example 1.1

### 1.3.1  What was in it

Even such a small example has introduced a lot of C. Among other things, it contained
two functions, a #include 'statement', and some **comment**. Since comment is the
easiest bit to handle, let's look at that first.

### 1.3.2  Layout and comment

The layout of a C program is not very important to the compiler, although for
readability it is important to use this freedom to carry extra information for the human
reader. C allows you to put space, tab or newline characters practically anywhere in
the program without any special effect on the meaning of the program. All of those
three characters are the same as far as the compiler is concerned and are called
collectively **white space**, because they just move the printing position without causing
any 'visible' printing on an output device. White space can occur practically anywhere
in a program except in the middle of **identifiers**, **strings**, or **character constants**. An
identifier is simply the name of a function or some other object; strings and character
constants will be discussed later – don't worry about them for the moment.
    Apart from the special cases, the only place that white space must be used is to
separate things that would otherwise run together and become confused. In the
example above, the fragment void show_message needs space to separate the two words,
whereas show_message( could have space in front of the ( or not, it would be purely a
matter of taste.
    Comment is introduced to a C program by the pair of characters /*, which
must not have a space between them. From then on, everything found up to and
including the pair of characters */ is gobbled up and the whole lot is replaced by a
single space. In Old C, this was not the case. The rule used to be that comment
could occur anywhere that space could occur: the rule is now that comment *is*
space. The significance of the change is minor and eventually becomes apparent in
Chapter 7 where we discuss the **preprocessor**. A consequence of the rule for
the end of comment is that you can't put a piece of comment inside another piece,

because the *first* */ pair will finish all of it. This is a minor nuisance, but you learn to live with it.

It is common practice to make a comment stand out by making each line of multi-line comment always start with a *, as the example illustrates.

### 1.3.3 Preprocessor statements

The first statement in the example is a **preprocessor directive**. In days gone by, the C compiler used to have two phases: the **preprocessor**, followed by the real compiler. The preprocessor was a **macro processor**, whose job was to perform simple textual manipulation of the program before passing the modified text on to be compiled. The preprocessor rapidly became seen as an essential aspect of the compiler and so has now been defined as part of the language and cannot be bypassed.

The preprocessor only knows about *lines* of text; unlike the rest of the language it is sensitive to the end of a line and though it is possible to write multi-line preprocessor directives, they are uncommon and a source of some wonder when they are found. Any line whose first visible character is a # is a preprocessor directive.

In Example 1.1 the preprocessor directive #include causes the line containing it to be replaced completely by the contents of another file. In this case the filename is found between the ⟨ and ⟩ brackets. This is a widely used technique to incorporate the text of standard **header files** into your program without having to go through the effort of typing it all yourself. The ⟨stdio.h⟩ file is an important one, containing the necessary information that allows you to use the standard library for input and output. If you want to use the I/O library you *must* include ⟨stdio.h⟩. Old C was more relaxed on this point.

### *Define statements*
Another of the preprocessor's talents which is widely exploited is the #define statement. It is used like this:

```
#define IDENTIFIER      replacement
```

which says that the name represented by IDENTIFIER will be replaced by the text of replacement whenever IDENTIFIER occurs in the program text. Invariably, the identifier is a name in upper-case; this is a stylistic convention that helps the reader to understand what is going on. The replacement part can be any text at all – remember the preprocessor doesn't know C, it just works on text. The most common use of the statement is to declare names for constant numbers:

```
#define PI            3.141592
#define SECS_PER_MIN   60
#define MINS_PER_HOUR  60
#define HOURS_PER_DAY  24
```

and to use them like this

```
circumf = 2 * PI * radius;
if(timer >= SECS_PER_MIN){
        mins = mins + 1;
        timer = timer - SECS_PER_MIN;
}
```

the output from the preprocessor will be as if you had written this:

```
circumf = 2 * 3.141592 * radius;
if(timer >= 60){
        mins = mins + 1;
        timer = timer - 60;
}
```

☐  **SUMMARY**

○ Preprocessor statements work on a line-by-line basis, the rest of C does not.

○ #include statements are used to read the contents of a specified file, typically to facilitate the use of library functions.

○ #define statements are typically used to give names for constants. By convention, the names are in upper case (capitalized).

### 1.3.4 Function declaration and definition

*Declaration*
After the ⟨stdio.h⟩ file is included comes a **function declaration**; it tells the compiler that show_message is a function which takes no arguments and returns no values. This demonstrates one of the changes made by the Standard: it is an example of a **function prototype**, a subject which Chapter 4 discusses in detail. It isn't always necessary to declare functions in advance – C will use some (old) default rules in such cases – but it is now strongly recommended that you *do* declare them in advance. The distinction between a **declaration** and a **definition** is that the former simply describes the type of the function and any arguments that it might take, the latter is where the body of a function is provided. These terms become more important later.

By declaring show_message before it is used, the compiler is able to check that it is used correctly. The declaration describes three important things about the function: its name, its type, and the number and type of its arguments. The void show_message( part indicates that it is a function and that it returns a value of type void, which is discussed in a moment. The second use of void is in the declaration of the function's argument list, (void), which indicates that there are *no* arguments to this function.

### Definition

Right at the end of the program is the function definition itself; although it is only four lines long, it usefully illustrates a complete function.

In C, functions perform the tasks that some other languages split into two parts. Most languages use a function to return a value of some sort, typical examples being perhaps trigonometric functions like sin, cos, or maybe a square root function; C is the same in this respect. Other similar jobs are done by what look very much like functions but which don't return a value: FORTRAN uses **subroutines**, Pascal and ALGOL call them **procedures**. C simply uses functions for all of those jobs, with the *type* of the function's return value specified when the function is defined. In the example, the function show_message doesn't return a value so we specify that its type is void.

The use of void in that way is either crashingly obvious or enormously subtle, depending on your viewpoint. We could easily get involved here in an entertaining (though fruitless) philosophical side-track on whether void really is a value or not, but we won't. Whichever side of the question you favour, it's clear that you can't *do* anything with a void and that's what it means here – 'I don't want to do anything with any value this function might or might not return'.

The type of the function is void, its name is show_message. The parentheses () following the function name are needed to let the compiler know that at this point we are talking about a function and not something else. If the function did take any arguments, then their names would be put between the parentheses. This one doesn't take any, which is made explicit by putting void between the parentheses.

For something whose essence is emptiness, abnegation and rejection, void turns out to be pretty useful.

The body of the function is a **compound statement**, which is a sequence of other statements surrounded by curly brackets {}. There is only one statement in there, but the brackets are still needed. In general, C allows you to put a compound statement anywhere that the language allows the use of a single simple statement; the job of the brackets being to turn several statements in a row into what is effectively a single statement.

It is reasonable to ask whether or not the brackets are strictly needed, if their only job is to bind multiple statements into one, yet all that we have in the example is a single statement. Oddly, the answer is yes – they *are* strictly needed. The only place in C where you can't put a single statement but *must* have a compound statement is when you are defining a function. The simplest function of all is therefore the empty function, which does nothing at all:

```
void do_nothing(void){}
```

The statement inside show_message is a call of the library function printf. Printf is used to format and print things, this example being one of the simplest of its uses. Printf takes one or more arguments, whose values are passed forward from the point of the call into the function itself. In this case the argument is a **string**. The contents of the string are interpreted by printf and used to control the way the values of the other arguments are printed. It bears a little resemblance to the FORMAT statement in FORTRAN; but not enough to predict how to use it.

☐  **SUMMARY**

    ○ **Declarations** are used to introduce the name of a function, its return type and the type (if any) of its arguments.

    ○ A function **definition** is a declaration with the body of the function given too.

    ○ A function returning no value should have its type declared as void. For example, `void func(/* list of arguments */);`

    ○ A function taking no arguments should be declared with void as its argument list. For example, `void func(void);`

## 1.3.5 Strings

In C, strings are a sequence of characters surrounded by quote marks:

```
"like this"
```

Because a string is a single element, a bit like an identifier, it is not allowed to continue across a line – although space or tab characters are permitted inside a string.

```
"This is a valid string"
"This has a newline in it
and is NOT a valid string"
```

To get a very long string there are two things that you can do. You could take advantage of the fact that absolutely everywhere in a C program, the sequence 'backslash end-of-line' disappears totally.

```
"This would not be valid but doesn't have \
a newline in it as far as the compiler is concerned"
```

The other thing you could do is to to use the string joining feature, which says that two adjacent strings are considered to be just one.

```
"All this " "comes out as "
"just one string"
```

Back to the example. The sequence '\n' in the string is an example of an **escape sequence** which in this case represents 'newline'. Printf simply prints the contents of the string on the program's output file, so the output will read 'hello', followed by a new line.

To support people working in environments that use character sets which are 'wider' than US ASCII, such as the shift-JIS representation used in Japan, the Standard now allows **multibyte characters** to be present in strings and comments. The Standard defines the 96 characters that are the alphabet of C (see Chapter 2). If your system supports an extended character set, the only place that you may use these extended characters is in strings, character constants, comment and the names of **header files**. Support for extended character sets is an implementation defined feature, so you will have to look it up in your system's documentation.

### 1.3.6 The `main` function

In Example 1.1 there are actually two functions, `show_message` and `main`. Although `main` is a bit longer than `show_message` it is obviously built in the same shape: it has a name, the parentheses () are there, followed by the opening bracket { of the compound statement that must follow in a function definition. True, there's a lot more stuff too, but right at the end of the example you'll find the matching closing bracket } that goes with the first one to balance the numbers.

This is a much more realistic function now, because there are several statements inside the function body, not just one. You might also have noticed that the function is *not* declared to be `void`. There is a good reason for this: it returns a proper value. Don't worry about its arguments yet; they are discussed in Chapter 10.

The most important thing about `main` is that it is the first function to be called. In a hosted environment your C language system arranges, magically, for a call on the `main` function (hence its name) when the program is first started. When the function is over, so is the program. It's obviously an important function. Equally important is the stuff *inside* `main`'s compound statement. As mentioned before, there can be several statements inside a compound statement, so let's look at them in turn.

### 1.3.7 Declarations

The first statement is this:

```
int count;
```

which is not an instruction to do anything, but simply introduces a variable to the program. It declares something whose name is `count`, and whose type is 'integer'; in C the keyword that declares integers is unaccountably shortened to `int`. C has an idiosyncratic approach to these keywords with some having their names spelled in full and some being shortened like `int`. At least `int` has a meaning that is more or less intuitive; just wait until we get on to `static`.

As a result of that declaration the compiler now knows that there is something that will be used to store integral quantities, and that its name is count. In C, all variables must be declared before they are used; there is none of FORTRAN's implicit declarations. In a compound statement, all the declarations must come first; they must precede any 'ordinary' statements and are therefore somewhat special.

(Note for pedants: unless you specifically ask, the declaration of a variable like count is also a **definition**. The distinction will later be seen to matter.)

### 1.3.8  Assignment statement

Moving down the example we find a familiar thing, an **assignment statement**. This is where the first value is assigned to the variable count; in this case the value assigned is a constant whose value is zero. Prior to the assignment, the value of count was undefined and unsafe to use. You might be a little surprised to find that the assignment symbol (strictly speaking an **assignment operator**) is a single = sign. This is not fashionable in modern languages, but hardly a major blemish.

So far then, we have declared a variable and assigned the value of zero to it. What next?

### 1.3.9  The while statement

Next is one of C's loop control statements, the while statement. Look carefully at its form. The formal description of the while statement is this:

```
while(expression)
        statement
```

Is that what we have got? Yes it is. The bit that reads

```
count < 10
```

is a **relational expression**, which is an example of a valid expression, and the expression is followed by a compound statement, which is a form of valid statement. As a result, it fits the rules for a properly constructed while statement.

What it does must be obvious to anyone who has written programs before. For as long as the relationship count < 10 holds true, the body of the loop is executed and the comparison repeated. If the program is ever to end, then the body of the loop must do something that will eventually cause the comparison to be false: of course it does.

There are just two statements in the body of the loop. The first one is a function call, where the function show_message is invoked. A function call is indicated by the name of the function followed by the parentheses () which contain its argument list – if it takes no arguments, then you provide none. If there were any arguments, they would be put between the parentheses like this:

```
/* call a function with several arguments */
function_name(first_arg, second_arg, third_arg);
```

and so on. The call of printf is another example. More is explained in Chapter 4.

The last statement in the loop is another assignment statement. It adds one to the variable count, so that the requirement for the program to stop will eventually be met.

## 1.3.10 The return statement

The last statement that is left to discuss is the return statement. As it is written, it looks like another function call, but in fact the rule is that the statement is written

> return *expression;*

where the *expression* is optional. The example uses a common stylistic convention and puts the *expression* into parentheses, which has no effect whatsoever.

The return causes a value to be returned from the current function to its caller. If the expression is missing, then an unknown value is passed back to the caller – this is almost certainly a mistake unless the function returns void. Main wasn't declared with any type at all, unlike show_message, so what type of value does it return? The answer is int. There are a number of places where the language allows you to declare things by default: the default type of functions is int, so it is common to see them used in this way. An equivalent declaration for main would have been

```
int main(){
```

and exactly the same results would have occurred.

You can't use the same feature to get a default type for variables because their types must be provided explicitly.

What does the value returned from main mean, and where does it go? In Old C, the value was passed back to the operating system or whatever else was used to start the program running. In a UNIX-like environment, the value of 0 meant 'success' in some way, any other value (often -1) meant 'failure'. The Standard has enshrined this, stating that 0 stands for correct termination of the program. This *does not* mean that 0 is to be passed back to the host environment, but the appropriate 'success' value for that system will be. Because there is sometimes confusion around this, you may prefer to use the defined values EXIT_SUCCESS and EXIT_FAILURE instead, which are defined in the header file ⟨stdlib.h⟩. Returning from the main function is the same as calling the library function exit with the return value as an argument. The difference is that exit may be called from *anywhere* in the program, and terminates it at that point, after doing some tidying up activities. If you intend to use exit, you *must* include the header file ⟨stdlib.h⟩. From now on, we shall use exit rather than returning from main.

☐   **SUMMARY**

○ The main function returns an int value.

○ Returning from main is the same as calling the exit function, but exit can be called from anywhere in a program.

○ Returning 0 or EXIT_SUCCESS is the way of indicating success, anything else indicates failure.

### 1.3.11  Progress so far

This example program, although short, has allowed us to introduce several important language features, amongst them:

- Program structure
- Comment
- File inclusion
- Function definition
- Compound statements
- Function calling
- Variable declaration
- Arithmetic
- Looping

although of course none of this has been covered rigorously.

## 1.4  Some more programs

While we're still in the informal phase, let's look at two more examples. You will have to work out for yourself what some of the code does, but as new or interesting features appear, they will be explained.

### 1.4.1  A program to find prime numbers

```
/*
 *
 * Dumb program that generates prime numbers.
 */
#include ⟨stdio.h⟩
#include ⟨stdlib.h⟩
```

```
main(){
        int this_number, divisor, not_prime;

        this_number = 3;

        while(this_number < 10000){
                divisor = this_number / 2;
                not_prime = 0;
                while(divisor > 1){
                        if(this_number % divisor == 0){
                                not_prime = 1;
                                divisor = 0;
                        }
                        else
                                divisor = divisor - 1;
                }

                if(not_prime == 0)
                        printf("%d is a prime number\n", this_number);
                this_number = this_number + 1;
        }
        exit(EXIT_SUCCESS);
}
```
                                                           (Example 1.2)

What was interesting in there? A few new points, perhaps. The program works in a really stupid way: to see if a number is prime, it divides that number by all the numbers between half its value and two – if any divide without remainder, then the number isn't prime. The two operators that you haven't seen before are the remainder operator %, and the equality operator, which is a double equal sign ==. That last one is without doubt the cause of more bugs in C programs than any other single factor.

The problem with the equality test is that wherever it can appear it is also legal to put the single = sign. The first, ==, compares two things to see if they are equal, and is generally what you need in fragments like these:

```
if(a == b)
while (c == d)
```

The assignment operator = is, perhaps surprisingly, also legal in places like those, but of course it assigns the value of the right-hand expression to whatever is on the left. The problem is particularly bad if you are used to the languages where comparison for equality is done with what C uses for assignment. There's nothing that you can do to help, so start getting used to it now. (Modern compilers do tend to produce warnings when they think they have detected 'questionable' uses of assignment operators, but that is a mixed blessing when your choice was deliberate.)

There is also the introduction for the first time of the if statement. Like the while statement, it tests an expression to see if the expression is true. You might have noticed that also like the while statement, the expression that controls the if statement is in parentheses. That is always the case: all of the conditional control of flow statements require a parenthesized expression after the keyword that introduces them. The formal description of the if statement goes like this:

```
if(expression)
        statement

if(expression)
        statement
else
        statement
```

showing that it comes in two forms. Of course, the effect is that if the expression part is evaluated to be true, then the following statement is executed. If the evaluation is false, then the following statement is not executed. When there is an else part, the statement associated with it is executed only if the evaluation gives a false result.

If statements have a famous problem. In the following piece of code, is the *statement-2* executed or not?

```
if(1 > 0)
        if(1 < 0)
                statement-1
else statement-2
```

The answer is that it *is*. Ignore the indentation (which is misleading). The else could belong to either the first or second if, according to the description of the if statement that has just been given, so an extra rule is needed to make it unambiguous. The rule is simply that an else is associated with the nearest else-less if above it. To make the example work the way that the indentation implied, we have to invoke a compound statement:

```
if(1 > 0){
        if(1 < 0)
                statement-1
}
else
        statement-2
```

Here, at least, C adheres to the practice used by most other languages. In fact a lot of programmers who are used to languages where the problem exists have never even realized that it is there – they just thought that the disambiguating rule was 'obvious'. Let's hope that everyone feels that way.

### 1.4.2 The division operators

The division operators are the division operator /, and the remainder operator %. Division does what you would expect, except that when it is applied to integer operands it give a result that is truncated towards zero. For example, 5/2 gives 2, 5/3 gives 1. The remainder operator is the way to get the truncated remainder. 5%2 gives 1, 5%3 gives 2. The signs of the remainder and quotient depend on the divisor and dividend in a way that is defined in the Standard and shown in Chapter 2.

### 1.4.3  An example performing input

It's useful to be able to perform input as well as to write programs that print out more or less interesting lists and tables. The simplest of the library routines (and the only one that we'll look at just now) is called getchar. It reads single characters from the program's input and returns an integer value. The value returned is a coded representation for that character and can be used to print the same character on the program output. It can also be compared against character constants or other characters that have been read, although the only test that makes sense is to see if both characters are the same. Comparing for greater or less than each other is not portable in general; there is no guarantee that 'a' is less than 'b', although on most common systems that would be the case. The only guarantee that the Standard makes is that the codes for '0' through to '9' will always be consecutive. Here is one example.

```
#include <stdio.h>
#include <stdlib.h>

main(){
        int ch;

        ch = getchar();
        while(ch != 'a'){
                if(ch != '\n')
                        printf("ch was %c, value %d\n", ch, ch);
                ch = getchar();
        }
        exit(EXIT_SUCCESS);
}
```
                                                                (Example 1.3)

There are two interesting points in there. The first is to notice that at the end of each line of input read, the character represented by

```
'\n'
```

(a character constant) will be seen. This is just like the way that the same symbol results in a new line when printf prints it. The model of I/O used by C is not based on a line by line view of the world, but character by character instead; if you choose to think in a line-oriented way, then '\n' allows you to mark the end of each 'line'. Second is the way that %c is used to output a character by printf, when it appears on the output as a character. Printing it with %d prints the same variable, but displays the integer value used by your program to represent the character.

If you try that program out, you may find that some systems do not pass characters one by one to a program, but make you type a whole line of input first. Then the whole line is made available as input, one character at a time. Beginners have been known to be confused: the program is started, they type some input, and nothing comes back. This behaviour is nothing to do with C; it depends on the computer and operating system in use.

### 1.4.4 Simple arrays

The use of **arrays** in C is often a problem for the beginner. The declaration of arrays isn't too difficult, especially the one-dimensional ones, but a constant source of confusion is the fact that their indices always count from 0. To declare an array of 5 ints, the declaration would look like this:

```
int something[5];
```

In array declarations C uses square brackets, as you can see. There is no support for arrays with indices whose ranges do not start at 0 and go up; in the example, the valid array elements are something[0] to something[4]. Notice very carefully that something[5] is *not* a valid array element.

This program reads some characters from its input, sorts them into the order suggested by their representation, then writes them back out. Work out what it does for yourself; the algorithm won't be given much attention in the explanation which follows.

```
#include 〈stdio.h〉
#include 〈stdlib.h〉

#define ARSIZE  10

main(){
        int ch_arr[ARSIZE], count1;
        int count2, stop, lastchar;

        lastchar = 0;
        stop = 0;
        /*
         * Read characters into array.
         * Stop if end of line, or array full.
         */
        while(stop != 1){
                ch_arr[lastchar] = getchar();
                if(ch_arr[lastchar] == '\n')
                        stop = 1;
                else
                        lastchar = lastchar + 1;
                if(lastchar == ARSIZE)
                        stop = 1;
        }
        lastchar = lastchar - 1;
```

```
/*
 * Now the traditional bubble sort.
 */
count1 = 0;
while(count1 < lastchar){
        count2 = count1 + 1;
        while(count2 <= lastchar){
                if(ch_arr[count1] > ch_arr[count2]){
                        /* swap */
                        int temp;
                        temp = ch_arr[count1];
                        ch_arr[count1] = ch_arr[count2];
                        ch_arr[count2] = temp;
                }
                count2 = count2 + 1;
        }
        count1 = count1 + 1;
}

count1 = 0;
while(count1 <= lastchar){
        printf("%c\n", ch_arr[count1]);
        count1 = count1 + 1;
}
exit(EXIT_SUCCESS);
}
```
                                                        (Example 1.4)

You might note that the defined constant ARSIZE is used everywhere instead of the actual array size. Because of that, to change the maximum number of characters that can be sorted by this program simply involves a change to one line and then re-compiling. Not so obvious but critical to the safety of the program is the detection of the array becoming full. Look carefully; you'll find that the program stops when element ARSIZE - 1 has been filled. That is because in an N element array, only elements 0 through to N - 1 are available (giving N in total).

Unlike some other languages it is unlikely that you will be told if you 'run off' the end of an array in C. It results in what is known as **undefined behaviour** on the part of your program, this generally being to produce obscure errors in the future. Most skilled programmers avoid this happening by rigorous testing to make sure either that it can't happen given the particular algorithm in use, or by putting in an explicit test before accessing a particular member of an array. This is a common source of run-time errors in C; you have been warned.

☐   **SUMMARY**

   ○  Arrays always number from 0; you have no choice.

   ○  A n-element array has members which number from 0 to n - 1 only. Element n does not exist and to access it is a big mistake.

## 1.5 Terminology

In C programs there are two distinct types of things: things used to hold values and things that are functions. Instead of having to refer to them jointly with a clumsy phrase that maintains the distinction, we think that it's useful to call them both loosely 'objects'. We do quite a lot of that later, because it's often the case that they follow more or less the same rules. Beware though, that this isn't quite what the Standard uses the term to mean. In the Standard, an 'object' is explicitly a region of allocated storage that is used to represent a value and a function is something different; this leads to the Standard often having to say '. . . functions and objects . . .'. Because we don't think that it leads to too much confusion and does improve the readability of the text in most cases, we will continue to use our looser interpretation of object to include functions and we will explicitly use the terms 'data objects' and 'functions' when the distinction is appropriate.

Be prepared to find this slight difference in meaning if you do read the Standard.

## ■ 1.6 SUMMARY

This chapter has introduced many of the basics of the language although informally. Functions, in particular, form the basic building block for C. Chapter 4 provides a full description of these fundamental objects, but you should by now understand enough about them to follow their informal use in the intervening material.

Although the idea of library functions has been introduced, it has not been possible to illustrate the extent of their importance to the C application programmer. The Standard Library, described in Chapter 9, is *extremely* important, both in the way that it helps to improve the portability of programs intended for general use and also in the aid to productivity that these useful functions can provide.

The use of variables, expressions and arithmetic are soon to be described in great detail. As this chapter has shown, at a simple level, C differs little from most other modern programming languages.

Only the use of structured data types still remains to be introduced, although arrays have had a very brief airing.

## EXERCISES

1.1   Type in and test Example 1.1 on your system.

1.2   Using Example 1.2 as a pattern, write a program that prints prime pairs – a pair of prime numbers that differ by 2, for example 11 and 13, 29 and 31. (If you can detect a pattern between such pairs, congratulations! You are either a genius or just wrong.)

**1.3**   Write a function that returns an integer: the decimal value of a string of digits that it reads using getchar. For example, if it reads 1 followed by 4 followed by 6, it will return the number 146. You may make the assumption that the digits 0–9 are consecutive in the computer's representation (the Standard says so) and that the function will only have to deal with valid digits and newline, so error checking is not needed.

**1.4**   Use the function that you just wrote to read a sequence of numbers. Put them into an array declared in main, by repeatedly calling the function. Sort them into ascending numerical order, then print the sorted list.

**1.5**   Again using the function from Exercise 1.3, write a program that will read numbers from its input, then print them out in binary, decimal and hexadecimal form. You should not use any features of printf apart from those mentioned in this chapter (especially the hexadecimal output format!). You are expected to work out what digits to print by calculating each one in turn and making sure that they are printed in the right order. This is not particularly difficult, but it is not trivial either.

# CHAPTER 2

# Variables and Arithmetic

## 2.1  Some fundamentals

Here is where we start to look in detail at the bits that the last chapter chose to sweep under the carpet while it did its 'Instant C' introduction. The problem is, of course, the usual one of trying to introduce enough of the language to let you get a feel for what it's all about, without drowning beginners in a froth of detail that isn't essential at the time.

Because this is a lengthy chapter, and because it deliberately chooses to cover some subtle problems that are often missed out in introductory texts, you should make sure that you are in the right mood and proper frame of mind to read it.

The weary brain may find that the breaks for exercises are useful. We strongly recommend that you do actually attempt the exercises on the way through. They help to balance the weight of information, which otherwise turns into an indigestible lump.

It's time to introduce some of the fundamentals.

## 2.2  The alphabet of C

This is an interesting area; alphabets are important. All the same, this is the one part of this chapter that you can read superficially first time round without missing too

**Table 2.1**   The alphabet of C.

```
a b c d e f g h i j k l m n o p q r s t u v w x y z
A B C D E F G H I J K L M N O P Q R S T U V W X Y Z
0 1 2 3 4 5 6 7 8 9
! " # % & ' ( ) * + , - . /
: ; < = > ? [ \ ] ^ _ { | } ~
space, horizontal and vertical tab
form feed, newline
```

much. Read it to make sure that you've seen the contents once, and make a mental note to come back to it later on.

### 2.2.1 Basic alphabet

Few computer languages bother to define their alphabet rigorously. There's usually an assumption that the English alphabet augmented by a sprinkling of more or less arbitrary punctuation symbols will be available in every environment that is trying to support the language. The assumption is not always borne out by experience. Older languages suffer less from this sort of problem, but try sending C programs by Telex or restrictive e-mail links and you'll understand the difficulty.

The Standard talks about two different character sets: the one that programs are written in and the one that programs execute with. This is basically to allow for different systems for compiling and execution, which might use different ways of encoding their characters. It doesn't actually matter a lot except when you are using character constants in the preprocessor, where they may not have the same value as they do at execution time. This behaviour is implementation-defined, so it must be documented. Don't worry about it yet.

The Standard requires that an alphabet of 96 symbols is available for C as shown in Table 2.1. It turns out that most of the commonly used computer alphabets contain all the symbols that are needed for C with a few notorious exceptions. The C alphabetic characters shown below are missing from the International Standards Organisation ISO 646 standard 7-bit character set, which is a subset of all the widely used computer alphabets.

> # [ \ ] ^ { | } ~

To cater for systems that can't provide the full 96 characters needed by C, the Standard specifies a method of using the ISO 646 characters to represent the missing few; the technique is the use of **trigraphs**.

### 2.2.2 Trigraphs

Trigraphs are a sequence of three ISO 646 characters that get treated as if they were one character in the C alphabet; all of the trigraphs start with two question marks ??

**Table 2.2**    Trigraphs.

| C character | Trigraph |
|-------------|----------|
| #           | ??=      |
| [           | ??(      |
| ]           | ??)      |
| {           | ??<      |
| }           | ??>      |
| \           | ??/      |
| \|          | ??!      |
| ~           | ??-      |
| ^           | ??'      |

which helps to indicate that 'something funny' is going on. Table 2.2 shows the trigraphs defined in the Standard. As an example, let's assume that your terminal doesn't have the # symbol. To write the preprocessor line

```
#define MAX      32767
```

isn't possible; you must use trigraph notation instead:

```
??=define MAX      32767
```

Of course trigraphs will work even if you do have a # symbol; they are there to help in difficult circumstances more than to be used for routine programming.

The ? 'binds to the right', so in any sequence of repeated ?s, only the two at the right could possibly be part of a trigraph, depending on what comes next – this disposes of any ambiguity.

It would be a mistake to assume that programs written to be highly portable would use trigraphs 'in case they had to be moved to systems that only support ISO 646'. If your system can handle all 96 characters in the C alphabet, then that is what you should be using. Trigraphs will only be seen in restricted environments, and it is extremely simple to write a character-by-character translator between the two representations. However, all compilers that conform to the Standard will recognize trigraphs when they are seen.

Trigraph substitution is the very first operation that a compiler performs on its input text.

### 2.2.3 Multibyte characters

Support for multibyte characters is new in the Standard. Why?

A very large proportion of day-to-day computing involves data that represents text of one form or another. Until recently, the rather chauvinist computing industry has assumed that it is adequate to provide support for about a hundred or so printable characters (hence the 96 character alphabet of C), based on the requirements of the

English language – not surprising, since the bulk of the development of commercial computing has been in the US market. This alphabet (technically called the **repertoire**) fits conveniently into seven or eight bits of storage, which is why the US ASCII character set standard and the architecture of mini and microcomputers both give very heavy emphasis to the use of 8-bit bytes as the basic unit of storage.

C also has a byte-oriented approach to data storage. The smallest individual item of storage that can be directly used in C is the byte, which is defined to be at least eight bits in size. Older systems or architectures that are not designed explicitly to support this may incur a performance penalty when running C as a result, although there are not many that find this a big problem.

Perhaps there was a time when the English alphabet was acceptable for data processing applications worldwide – when computers were used in environments where the users could be expected to adapt – but those days are gone. Nowadays it is absolutely essential to provide for the storage and processing of textual material in the native alphabet of whoever wants to use the system. Most of the US and Western European language requirements can be squeezed together into a character set that still fits in eight bits per character, but Asian and other languages simply cannot.

There are two general ways of extending character sets. One is to use a fixed number of bytes (often two) for every character. This is what the **wide character** support in C is designed to do. The other method is to use a shift-in shift-out coding scheme; this is popular over 8-bit communication links. Imagine a stream of characters that looks like:

    a b c ⟨SI⟩ a b g ⟨SO⟩ x y

where ⟨SI⟩ and ⟨SO⟩ mean 'switch to Greek' and 'switch back to English' respectively. A display device that agreed to use that method might well then display a, b, c, alpha, beta, gamma, x and y. This is roughly the scheme used by the shift-JIS Japanese standard, except that once the shift-in has been seen, *pairs* of characters together are used as the code for a single Japanese character. Alternative schemes exist which use more than one shift-in character, but they are less common.

The Standard now allows explicitly for the use of extended character sets. Only the 96 characters defined earlier are used for the C part of a program, but in comments, strings, character constants and header names (these are really data, not part of the program as such) extended characters are permitted if your environment supports them. The Standard lays down a number of pretty obvious rules about how you are allowed to use them which we will not repeat here. The most significant one is that a byte whose value is zero is interpreted as a **null character** irrespective of any shift state. That is important, because C uses a null character to indicate the end of strings and many library functions rely on it. An additional requirement is that multibyte sequences must start and end in the initial shift state.

The char type is specified by the Standard as suitable to hold the value of all of the characters in the 'execution character set', which will be defined in your system's documentation. This means that (in the example above) it could hold the value of 'a' or 'b' or even the 'switch to Greek' character itself. Because of the shift-in shift-out mechanism, there would be no difference between the value stored in a char that was intended to represent 'a' or the Greek 'alpha' character. To make them different would mean using a different representation – probably needing more than eight bits, which on many systems would be too big for a char. That is why the Standard introduces the wchar_t type. To use this, you must include the ⟨stddef.h⟩ header, because wchar_t is simply defined as an alternative name for one of C's other types. We discuss it further in Section 2.8.

☐   **SUMMARY**

○ C requires at least 96 characters in the source program character set.

○ Not all character sets in common use can stretch to 96 characters, trigraphs allow the basic ISO 646 character set to be used (at a pinch).

○ Multibyte character support has been added by the Standard, with support for

– Shift-encoded multibyte characters, which can be squeezed into 'ordinary' character arrays, so still have char type.

– Wide characters, each of which may use more storage than a regular character. These usually have a different type from char.

## 2.3  The textual structure of programs

### 2.3.1  Program layout

The examples so far have used the sort of indentation and line layout that is common in languages belonging to the same family as C. They are 'free format' languages and you are expected to use that freedom to lay the program out in a way that enhances its readability and highlights its logical structure. Space (including horizontal tab) characters can be used for indentation anywhere except in identifiers or keywords without any effect on the meaning of the program. New lines work in the same way as space and tab *except* on preprocessor command lines, which have a line-by-line structure.

If a line is getting too long for comfort there are two things you can do. Generally it will be possible to replace one of the spaces by a newline and simply use two lines instead, as this example shows.

```
/* a long line */
a = fred + bill * ((this / that) * sqrt(3.14159));
/* the same line */
a = fred + bill *
        ((this / that) *
        sqrt(3.14159));
```

If you're unlucky it may not be possible to break the lines like that. The preprocessor suffers most from the problem, because of its reliance on single-line 'statements'. To help, it's useful to know that the sequence 'backslash newline' becomes invisible to the C translation system. As a result, the sequence is valid even in unusual places such as the middle of identifiers, keywords, strings and so on. Only trigraphs are processed before this step.

```
/*
 * Example of the use of line joining
 */
#define IMPORTANT_BUT_LONG_PREPROCESSOR_TEXT \
printf("this is effectively all ");\
printf("on a single line ");\
printf("because of line-joining\n");
```

The only time that you might want to use this way of breaking lines (outside of preprocessor control lines) is to prevent long strings from disappearing off the right-hand side of a program listing. New lines are *not* permitted inside strings and character constants, so you might think that the following is a good idea.

```
/* not a good way of folding a string */
printf("This is a very very very\
long string\n");
```

That will certainly work, but for strings it is preferable to make use of the string-joining feature introduced by the Standard:

```
/* This string joining will not work in Old C */
printf("This is a very very very"
       "long string\n");
```

The second example allows you to indent the continuation portion of the string without changing its meaning; adding indentation in the first example would have put the indentation into the string.

Incidentally, both examples contain what is probably a mistake. There is no space in front of the 'long' in the continuation string, which will contain the sequence 'verylong' as a result. Did you notice?

### 2.3.2 Comment

Comment, as has been said already, is introduced by the character pair /* and terminated by */. It is translated into a single space wherever it occurs and so it follows exactly the same rules that spaces do. It's important to realize that it doesn't simply disappear, which it used to do in Old C, and that it is not possible to put comment into strings or character constants. Comment in such a place becomes part of the string or constant:

```
/*"This is comment"*/
"/*The quotes mean that this is a string*/"
```

Old C was a bit hazy about what the deletion of comment implied. You could argue that

```
int/**/egral();
```

should have the comment deleted and so be taken by the compiler to be a call of a function named integral. The Standard C rule is that comment is to be read as if were a space, so the example must be equivalent to

```
int egral();
```

which declares a function egral that returns type int.

### 2.3.3 Translation phases

The various character translation, line joining, comment recognition and other early phases of translation must be specified to occur in a certain order. The Standard says that the translation is to proceed as if the phases occurred in this order (there are more phases, but these are the important ones):

(1) Trigraph translation.
(2) Line joining.
(3) Translate comment to space (but not in strings or character constants). At this stage, multiple white spaces may optionally be condensed into one.
(4) Translate the program.

Each stage is completed before the next is started.

## 2.4 Keywords and identifiers

After covering the underlying alphabet, we can look at more interesting elements of C. The most obvious of the language elements are **keywords** and **identifiers**; their forms are identical (although their meanings are different).

### 2.4.1 Keywords

C keeps a small set of **keywords** for its own use. These keywords cannot be used as identifiers in the program – a common restriction with modern languages. Where

**Table 2.3**   Keywords.

| | | | |
|---|---|---|---|
| auto | double | int | struct |
| break | else | long | switch |
| case | enum | register | typedef |
| char | extern | return | union |
| const | float | short | unsigned |
| continue | for | signed | void |
| default | goto | sizeof | volatile |
| do | if | static | while |

users of Old C may be surprised is in the introduction of some new keywords; if those names were used as identifiers in previous programs, then the programs will have to be changed. It will be easy to spot, because it will provoke your compiler into telling you about invalid names for things. Table 2.3 lists the keywords used in Standard C; you will notice that none of them uses upper case letters.

The new keywords that are likely to surprise old programmers are: const, signed, void and volatile (although void has been around for a while). Eagle-eyed readers may have noticed that some implementations of C used to use the keywords entry, asm, and fortran. These are not part of the Standard, and few will mourn them.

### 2.4.2 Identifiers

**Identifier** is the fancy term used to mean 'name'. In C, identifiers are used to refer to a number of things: we've already seen them used to name variables and functions. They are also used to give names to some things we haven't seen yet, amongst which are **labels** and the 'tags' of **structures**, **unions**, and **enums**.

The rules for the construction of identifiers are simple: you may use the 52 upper and lower case alphabetic characters, the 10 digits and finally the underscore '_', which is considered to be an alphabetic character for this purpose. The only restriction is the usual one; identifiers *must* start with an alphabetic character.

Although there is no restriction on the length of identifiers in the Standard, this is a point that needs a bit of explanation. In Old C, as in Standard C, there has *never* been any restriction on the length of identifiers. The problem is that there was never any guarantee that more than a certain number of characters would be checked when names were compared for equality – in Old C this was eight characters, in Standard C this has changed to 31.

So, practically speaking, the new limit is 31 characters – although identifiers *may* be longer, they must differ in the first 31 characters if you want to be sure that your programs are portable. The Standard allows for implementations to support longer names if they wish to, so if you do use longer names, make sure that you don't rely on the checking stopping at 31.

One of the most controversial parts of the Standard is the length of **external identifiers**. External identifiers are the ones that have to be visible outside the current source code file. Typical examples of these would be library routines or functions which have to be called from several different source files.

The Standard chose to stay with the old restrictions on these external names: they are not guaranteed to be different unless they differ from each other in the first *six* characters. Worse than that, upper and lower case letters may be treated the same!

The reason for this is a pragmatic one: the way that most C compilation systems work is to use operating system specific tools to bind library functions into a C program. These tools are outside the control of the C compiler writer, so the Standard has to impose realistic limits that are likely to be possible to meet. There is nothing to prevent any specific implementation from giving better limits than these, but for maximum portability the six monocase characters must be all that you expect. The Standard warns that it views both the use of only one case and any restriction on the length of external names to less than 31 characters as obsolescent features. A later standard may insist that the restrictions are lifted; let's hope that it is soon.

## 2.5 Declaration of variables

You may remember that in Chapter 1 we said that you have to declare the names of things before you can use them (the only exceptions to this rule are the names of functions returning int, because they are declared by default, and the names of **labels**). You can do it either by using a **declaration**, which introduces just the name and type of something but allocates no storage, or go further by using a **definition**, which also allocates the space used by the thing being declared.

The distinction between declaration and definition is an important one, and it is a shame that the two words sound alike enough to cause confusion. From now on they will have to be used for their formal meaning, so if you are in doubt about the differences between them, refer back to this point.

The rules about what makes a declaration into a definition are rather complicated, so they will be deferred for a while. In the meantime, here are some examples and rule-of-thumb guidelines which will work for the examples that we have seen so far, and will do for a while to come.

```
/*
 * A function is only defined if its body is given
 * so this is a declaration but not a definition
 */

int func_dec(void);

/*
 * Because this function has a body, it is also
 * a definition.
 * Any variables declared inside will be definitions,
 * unless the keyword 'extern' is used.
 * Don't use 'extern' until you understand it!
 */
```

```
int
def_func(void){
        float f_var;          /* a definition */
        int counter;          /* another definition */
        int rand_num(void);   /* declare (but not define) another function */

        return(0);
}
```

## EXERCISES

**2.1**  Why are trigraphs used?

**2.2**  When would you expect to find them in use, and when not?

**2.3**  When is a newline not equivalent to a space or tab?

**2.4**  When would you see the sequence of 'backslash newline' in use?

**2.5**  What happens when two strings are put side by side?

**2.6**  Why can't you put one piece of comment inside another one? (This prevents the technique of 'commenting out' unused bits of program, unless you are careful.)

**2.7**  What are the longest names that may safely be used for variables?

**2.8**  What is a *declaration*?

**2.9**  What is a *definition*?

Now we go on to look at the **type** of variables and expressions.

## 2.6 Real types

It's easier to deal with the real types first because there's less to say about them and they don't get as complicated as the integer types. The Standard breaks new ground by laying down some basic guarantees on the precision and range of the real numbers; these are found in the header file **float.h** which is discussed in detail in Chapter 9. For some users this is extremely important information, but it is of a highly technical nature and is likely only to be fully understood by numerical analysts.

The varieties of real numbers are these:

```
float
double
long double
```

Each of the types gives access to a particular way of representing real numbers in the target computer. If it only has one way of doing things, they might all turn out to be the same; if it has more than three, then C has no way of specifying the extra ones. The type float is intended to be the small, fast representation corresponding to what FORTRAN would call REAL. You would use double for extra precision, and long double for even more.

The main points of interest are that in the increasing 'lengths' of float, double and long double, each type must give at least the same range and precision as the previous type. For example, taking the value in a double and putting it into a long double must result in the same value.

There is no requirement for the three types of 'real' variables to differ in their properties, so if a machine only has one type of real arithmetic, all of C's three types could be implemented in the same way. None the less, the three types would be considered to be different from the point of view of type checking; it would be 'as if' they really were different. That helps when you move the program to a system where the three types really are different – there won't suddenly be a set of warnings coming out of your compiler about type mismatches that you didn't get on the first system.

In contrast to more 'strongly typed' languages, C permits expressions to mix all of the scalar types: the various flavours of integers, the real numbers and also the pointer types. When an expression contains a mixture of arithmetic (integer and real) types there are implicit conversions invoked which can be used to work out what the overall type of the result will be. These rules are quite important and are known as the **usual arithmetic conversions**; it will be worth committing them to memory later. The full set of rules is described in Section 2.8; for the moment, we will investigate only the ones that involve mixing float, double and long double to see if they make sense.

The only time that the conversions are needed is when two different types are mixed in an expression, as in the example below:

```
int
f(void){
        float f_var;
        double d_var;
        long double l_d_var;

        f_var = 1; d_var = 1; l_d_var = 1;
        d_var = d_var + f_var;
        l_d_var = d_var + f_var;
        return(l_d_var);
}
```
                                                          **(Example 2.1)**

There are a lot of forced conversions in that example. Getting the easiest of them out of the way first, let's look at the assignments of the constant value 1 to each of the variables. As the section on constants will point out, that 1 has type int, that is, it is an integer, not a real constant. The assignment converts the integer value to the appropriate real type, which is easy to cope with.

The interesting conversions come next. The first of them is on the line

```
d_var = d_var + f_var;
```

What is the type of the expression involving the + operator? The answer is easy when you know the rules. Whenever two different real types are involved in an expression, the lower precision type is first implicitly converted to the higher precision type and then the arithmetic is performed at that precision. The example involves both a double and a float, so the value of f_var is converted to type double and is then added to the value of the double d_var. The result of the expression is naturally of type double too, so it is clearly of the correct type to assign to d_var.

The second of the additions is a little bit more complicated, but still perfectly OK. Again, the value of f_var is converted and the arithmetic performed with the precision of double, forming the sum of the two variables. Now there's a problem. The result (the sum) is double, but the assignment is to a long double. Once again the obvious procedure is to convert the lower precision value to the higher one, which is done, and then make the assignment.

So we've taken the easy ones. The difficult thing to see is what to do when forced to assign a higher precision result to a lower precision destination. In those cases it may be necessary to lose precision, in a way specified by the implementation. Basically, the implementation must specify whether and in what way it rounds or truncates. Even worse, the destination may be unable to hold the value at all. The Standard says that in these cases loss of precision may occur; if the destination is unable to hold the necessary value – say by attempting to add the largest representable number to itself – then the behaviour is undefined, your program is faulty and you can make no predictions whatsoever about any subsequent behaviour.

It is no mistake to re-emphasize that last statement. What the Standard means by **undefined behaviour** is exactly what it says. Once a program's behaviour has entered the undefined region, absolutely anything can happen. The program might be stopped by the operating system with an appropriate message, or just as likely nothing observable would happen and the program be allowed to continue with an erroneous value stored in the variable in question. It is your responsibility to prevent your program from exhibiting undefined behaviour. Beware!

□ **SUMMARY OF REAL ARITHMETIC**

○ Arithmetic with any two real types is done at the highest precision of the members involved.

○ Assignment involves loss of precision if the receiving type has a lower precision than the value being assigned to it.

○ Further conversions are often implied when expressions mix other types, but they have not been described yet.

## 2.6.1 Printing real numbers

The usual output function, printf, can be used to format real numbers and print them. There are a number of ways to format these numbers, but we'll stick to just one for now. Table 2.4 shows the appropriate format description for each of the real types.

**Table 2.4** Format codes for real numbers.

| Type | Format |
| --- | --- |
| float | %f |
| double | %f |
| long double | %lf |

Here's an example to try:

```
#include ⟨stdio.h⟩
#include ⟨stdlib.h⟩

#define BOILING 212      /* degrees Fahrenheit */

main(){
        float f_var; double d_var; long double l_d_var;
        int i;

        i = 0;
        printf("Fahrenheit to Centigrade\n");
        while(i <= BOILING){
                l_d_var = 5 * (i - 32);
                l_d_var = l_d_var / 9;
                d_var = l_d_var;
                f_var = l_d_var;
                printf("%d %f %f %lf\n", i,
                        f_var, d_var, l_d_var);
                i = i + 1;
        }
        exit(EXIT_SUCCESS);
}
```

(Example 2.2)

Try that example on your own computer to see what results you get.

---

## EXERCISES

---

**2.10**  Which type of variable can hold the largest range of values?

**2.11**  Which type of variable can store values to the greatest precision?

**2.12** Are there any problems possible when assigning a float or double to a double or long double?

**2.13** What could go wrong when assigning, say, a long double to a double?

**2.14** What predictions can you make about a program showing 'undefined behaviour'?

## 2.7 Integral types

The real types were the easy ones. The rules for the integral types are more complicated, but still tolerable, and these rules really should be learnt. Fortunately, the only types used in C for routine data storage are the real and integer types, or **structures** and **arrays** built up from them. C doesn't have special types for character manipulation or the handling of logical (boolean) quantities, but uses the integral types instead. Once you know the rules for the reals and the integers you know them all.

We will start by looking at the various types and then the conversion rules.

### 2.7.1 Plain integers

There are two types (often called 'flavours') of integer variables. Other types can be built from these, as we'll see, but the plain undecorated ints are the base. The most obvious of the pair is the 'signed' int, the less obvious is its close relative, the unsigned int. These variables are supposed to be stored in whatever is the most convenient unit for the machine running your program. The int is the natural choice for undemanding requirements when you just need a simple integral variable, say as a counter in a short loop. There isn't any guarantee about the number of bits that an int can hold, except that it will *always* be 16 or more. The standard header file ⟨limits.h⟩ details the actual number of bits available in a given implementation.

Curiously, Old C had no guarantee whatsoever about the length of an int, but consensus and common practice has always assumed at least 16 bits.

Actually, ⟨limits.h⟩ doesn't quite specify a number of bits, but gives maximum and minimum values for an int instead. The values it gives are 32767 and −32767 which implies 16 bits or more, whether ones or twos complement arithmetic is used. Of course there is nothing to stop a given implementation from providing a greater range in either direction.

The range specified in the Standard for an unsigned int is 0 to at least 65535, meaning that it cannot be negative. More about these shortly.

If you aren't used to thinking about the number of bits in a given variable, and are beginning to get worried about the portability implications of this apparently machine-dependent concern for the number of bits, then you're doing the right thing. C takes portability seriously and actually bothers to tell you what values and ranges are guaranteed to be safe. The bitwise operators encourage you to think about the number of bits in a variable too, because they give direct access to the bits, which you manipulate one by one or in groups. Almost paradoxically, the overall result is that C programmers have a healthy awareness of portability issues which leads to more portable programs. This is *not* to say that you can't write C programs that are horribly non-portable!

## 2.7.2 Character variables

A bit less obvious than int is the other of the plain integral types, the char. It's basically just another sort of int, but has a different application. Because so many C programs do a lot of character handling, it's a good idea to provide a special type to help, especially if the range provided by an int uses up much more storage than is needed by characters. The limits file tells us that three things are guaranteed about char variables: they have at least eight bits, they can store a value of at least +127, and the minimum value of a char is zero or lower. This means that the only guaranteed range is 0–127. Whether or not char variables behave as signed or unsigned types is implementation defined.

In short, a character variable will probably take less storage than an int and will most likely be used for character manipulation. It's still an integer type though, and can be used for arithmetic, as this example shows.

```
#include <limits.h>
#include <stdio.h>
#include <stdlib.h>
main(){
        char c;

        c = CHAR_MIN;
        while(c != CHAR_MAX){
                printf("%d\n", c);
                c = c + 1;
        }
        exit(EXIT_SUCCESS);
}
```

(Example 2.3)

Running that program is left as an exercise for the easily amused. If you are bothered about where CHAR_MIN and CHAR_MAX come from, find limits.h and read it.

Here's a more enlightening example. It uses character constants, which are formed by placing a character in single quotes:

'x'

Because of the rules of arithmetic, the type of this sort of constant turns out to be int, but that doesn't matter since their value is always small enough to assign them to char variables without any loss of precision. (Unfortunately, there is a related version where that guarantee does not hold. Ignore it for the moment.) When a character variable is printed using the %c format with printf, the appropriate character is output. You can use %d, if you like, to see what integer value is used to represent the character. Why %d? Because a char is just another integral type.

It's also useful to be able to read characters into a program. The library function getchar is used for the job. It reads characters from the program's **standard input** and returns an int value suitable for storing into a char. The int value is for one reason only: not only does getchar return all possible character values, but it also returns an *extra* value to indicate that end-of-input has been seen. The range of a char might not be enough to hold this extra value, so the int has to be used.

The following program reads its input and counts the number of commas and full stops that it sees. On end-of-input, it prints the totals.

```c
#include <stdio.h>
#include <stdlib.h>

main(){
        int this_char, comma_count, stop_count;

        comma_count = stop_count = 0;
        this_char = getchar();
        while(this_char != EOF){
                if(this_char == '.')
                        stop_count = stop_count + 1;
                if(this_char == ',')
                        comma_count = comma_count + 1;
                this_char = getchar();
        }
        printf("%d commas, %d stops\n", comma_count,
                        stop_count);
        exit(EXIT_SUCCESS);
}
```
(Example 2.4)

The two features of note in that example were the multiple assignment to the two counters and the use of the defined constant EOF. EOF is the value returned by getchar on end of input (it stands for End Of File), and is defined in <stdio.h>. The multiple assignment is a fairly common feature of C programs.

Another example, perhaps. This will either print out the whole lower case alphabet, if your implementation has its characters stored consecutively, or something even more interesting if they aren't. C doesn't make many guarantees about the ordering of characters in internal form, so this program produces *non-portable* results!

```c
#include <stdio.h>
#include <stdlib.h>

main(){
        char c;
```

```
        c = 'a';
        while(c <= 'z'){
                printf("value %d char %c\n", c, c);
                c = c + 1;
        }
        exit(EXIT_SUCCESS);
}
```

(Example 2.5)

Yet again this example emphasizes that a char is only another form of integer variable and can be used just like any other form of variable. It is *not* a 'special' type with its own rules.

The space saving that a char offers when compared to an int only becomes worthwhile if a lot of them are being used. Most character-processing operations involve the use of not just one or two character variables, but large arrays of them. That's when the saving can become noticeable: imagine an array of 1024 ints. On a lot of common machines that would eat up 4096 8-bit bytes of storage, assuming the common length of four bytes per int. If the computer architecture allows it to be done in a reasonably efficient way, the C implementor will probably have arranged for char variables to be packed one per byte, so the array would only use 1024 bytes and the space saving would be 3072 bytes.

Sometimes it doesn't matter whether or not a program tries to save space; sometimes it does. At least C gives you the option of choosing an appropriate type.

### 2.7.3 More complicated types

The last two types were simple, in both their declaration and subsequent use. For serious systems programming they just aren't adequate in the precision of control over storage that they provide and the behaviour that they follow. To correct this problem, C provides extra forms of integral types, split into the categories of signed and unsigned. (Although both these terms are reserved words, they will also be used as adjectives.) The difference between the two types is obvious. Signed types are those that are capable of being negative, the unsigned types cannot be negative at any time. Unsigned types are usually used for one of two reasons: to get an extra bit of precision, or when the concept of being negative is simply not present in the data that is being represented. The latter is by far the better reason for choosing them.

Unsigned types also have the special property of never overflowing in arithmetic. Adding one to a signed variable that already contains the maximum possible positive number for its type will result in overflow, and the program's behaviour becomes undefined. That can never happen with unsigned types, because they are defined to work 'modulo one greater than the maximum number that they can hold'. What this means is best illustrated by example:

```
#include <stdio.h>
#include <stdlib.h>
```

```
main(){
        unsigned int x;

        x = 0;
        while(x >= 0){
                printf("%u\n", x);
                x = x + 1;
        }
        exit(EXIT_SUCCESS);
}
```
(Example 2.6)

Assuming that the variable x is stored in 16 bits, then its range of values will be 0–65 535 and that sequence will be printed endlessly. The program can't terminate: the test

```
x >= 0
```

must always be true for an unsigned variable.

For both the signed and unsigned integral types there are three subtypes: short, ordinary and long. Taking those into account, here is a list of all of the possible integral types in C, except for the character types:

```
unsigned short int
unsigned int
unsigned long int
signed short int
signed int
signed long int
```

In the last three, the signed keyword is unnecessary because the int types are signed types anyway: you *have* to say unsigned to get anything different. It's also permissible, but not recommended, to drop the int keyword from any of those declarations provided that there is at least one other keyword present – the int will be 'understood' to be present. For example long is equivalent to signed long int. The long and short kinds give you more control over the amount of space used to store variables. Each has its own minimum range specified in ⟨limits.h⟩ which in practice means at least 16 bits in a short and an int, and at least 32 bits in a long, whether signed or unsigned. As always, an implementation can choose to give you more bits than the minimum if it wants to. The only restriction is that the limits must be equalled or bettered, and that you don't get more bits in a shorter type than a longer one (not an unreasonable rule).

The only character types are the signed char and the unsigned char. The difference between char and int variables is that, unless otherwise stated, all ints are signed. The same is not true for chars, which are signed or unsigned depending on the implementor's choice; the choice is presumably taken on efficiency grounds. You can of course explicitly force signed or unsigned with the right keyword. The only time that it is likely to matter is if you are using character variables as extra short shorts to save more space.

☐ **SUMMARY OF INTEGRAL TYPES**

○ The integral types are the short, long, signed, unsigned and plain ints.

○ The commonest is the ordinary int, which is signed unless declared not to be.

○ The char variables *can* be made signed or unsigned, as you prefer, but in the absence of indications to the contrary, they will be allocated the most efficient type.

### 2.7.4 Printing the integral types

Once again you can use printf to print these various types. Character variables work exactly the same way that the other integral variables do, so you can use the standard format letters to print their contents – although the actual numbers stored in them are not likely to be very interesting. To see their contents interpreted as characters, use %c as was done earlier. All of the integral types can be printed as if they were signed decimal numbers by using the %d format, or %ld for long types. Other useful formats are shown in Table 2.5; notice that in every case a letter 'l' is put in front of the normal format letter if a long is to be printed. That's not just there to get the right result printed: the behaviour of printf is undefined if the wrong format is given. A full description of the format codes that you can use with printf is given in Chapter 9.

**Table 2.5**  More format codes.

| Format | Use with |
|---|---|
| %c | char (in character form) |
| %d | decimal signed int, short, char |
| %u | decimal unsigned int, unsigned short, unsigned char |
| %x | hexadecimal int, short, char |
| %o | octal int, short, char |
| %ld | decimal signed long |
| %lu  %lx  %lo | as above, but for longs |

## 2.8 Expressions and arithmetic

Expressions in C can get rather complicated because of the number of different types and operators that can be mixed together. This section explains what happens, but can get deep at times. You may need to reread it once or twice to make sure that you have understood all of the points.

First, a bit of terminology. Expressions in C are built from combinations of **operators** and **operands**, so for example in this expression

```
x = a + b * (-c)
```

we have the operators =, +, * and -. The operands are the variables x, a, b and c. You will also have noticed that parentheses can be used for grouping sub-expressions such as the -c. Most of C's unusually rich set of operators are either **binary operators**, which take two operands, or **unary operators**, which take only one. In the example, the - was being used as a unary operator, and is performing a different task from the binary subtraction operator which uses the same - symbol. It may seem like hair-splitting to argue that they are different operators when the job that they do seems conceptually the same, or at least similar. It's worth doing though, because, as you will find later, some of the operators have both a binary and a unary form where the two meanings bear no relation to each other; a good example would be the binary multiplication operator *, which in its unary form means indirection via a pointer variable!

A peculiarity of C is that operators may appear consecutively in expressions without the need for parentheses to separate them. The previous example could have been written as

```
x = a + b * -c;
```

and still have been a valid expression. Because of the number of operators that C has, and because of the strange way that assignment works, the **precedence** of the operators (and their **associativity**) is of much greater importance to the C programmer than in most other languages. It will be discussed fully after the introduction of the important arithmetic operators.

Before that, we must investigate the type conversions that may occur.

### 2.8.1 Conversions

C allows types to be mixed in expressions, and permits operations that result in type conversions happening implicitly. This section describes the way that the conversions must occur. Old C programmers should read this carefully, because the rules have changed – in particular, the promotion of float to double, the promotions of short integral types and the introduction of **value preserving** rules are genuinely different in Standard C.

Although it isn't directly relevant at the moment, we must note that the integral and the floating types are jointly known as **arithmetic types** and that C also supports other types (notably pointer types). The rules that we discuss here are appropriate only in expressions that have arithmetic types throughout – additional rules come into play when expressions mix pointer types with arithmetic types and these are discussed much later.

There are various types of conversion in arithmetic expressions:

- The **integral promotions**
- Conversions between integral types
- Conversions between floating types
- Conversions between floating and integral types.

Conversions between floating (real) types were discussed in Section 2.6; what we do next is to specify how the other conversions are to be performed, then look at *when* they are required. You will need to learn them by heart if you ever intend to program seriously in C.

The Standard has, among some controversy, introduced what are known as **value preserving** rules, where a knowledge of the target computer is required to work out what the type of an expression will be. Previously, whenever an unsigned type occurred in an expression, you knew that the result had to be unsigned too. Now, the result will only be unsigned if the conversions demand it; in many cases the result will be an ordinary signed type.

The reason for the change was to reduce some of the surprises possible when you mix signed and unsigned quantities together; it isn't always obvious when this has happened and the intention is to produce the 'more commonly required' result.

### Integral promotions

No arithmetic is done by C at a precision shorter than int, so these conversions are implied almost whenever you use one of the objects listed below in an expression. The conversion is defined as follows:

- Whenever a short or a char (or a **bitfield** or **enumeration type** which we haven't met yet) has the integral promotions applied
  - if an int can hold all of the values of the original type then the value is converted to int
  - otherwise, the conversion will be to unsigned int.

This preserves both the value and the sign of the original type. Note that whether a plain char is treated as signed or unsigned is implementation dependent.

These promotions are applied very often – they are applied as part of the **usual arithmetic conversions**, and to the operands of the shift, unary +, -, and ˜ operators. They are also applied when the expression in question is an argument to a function but no type information has been provided as part of a function prototype, as explained in Chapter 4.

### Signed and unsigned integers

A lot of conversions between different types of integers are caused by mixing the various flavours of integers in expressions. Whenever this happens, the integral promotions will already have been done. For all of them, if the new type can hold all of the values of the old type, then the value remains unchanged.

When converting from a signed integer to an unsigned integer whose length is equal to or longer than the original type, then if the signed value was non-negative, its value is unchanged. If the value was negative, then it is converted to the signed form of the longer type and then made unsigned by conceptually adding it to one greater than the maximum that can be held in the unsigned type. In a two's complement system, this preserves the original bit-pattern for positive numbers and guarantees 'sign-extension' of negative numbers.

Whenever an integer is converted into a shorter unsigned type, there can be no 'overflow', so the result is defined to be 'the non-negative remainder on division by the number one greater than the largest unsigned number that can be represented in the shorter type'. That simply means that in a two's complement environment the low-order bits are copied into the destination and the high-order ones discarded.

Converting an integer to a shorter signed type runs into trouble if there is not enough room to hold the value. In that case, the result is implementation defined (although most old-timers would expect that simply the low-order bit pattern is copied).

That last item could be a bit worrying if you remember the integral promotions, because you might interpret it as follows – if I assign a char to another char, then the one on the right is first promoted to one of the kinds of int; could doing the assignment result in converting (say) an int to a char and provoking the 'implementation defined' clause? The answer is no, because assignment is specified not to involve the integral promotions, so you are safe.

### Floating and integral

Converting a floating to an integral type simply throws away any fractional part. If the integral type can't hold the value that is left, then the behaviour is undefined – this is a sort of overflow.

As has already been said, going up the scale from float to double to long double, there is no problem with conversions – each higher one in the list can hold all the values of the lower ones, so the conversion occurs with no loss of information.

Converting in the opposite direction, if the value is outside the range that can be held, the behaviour is undefined. If the value *is* in range, but can't be held exactly, then the result is one of the two nearest values that *can* be held, chosen in a way that the implementation defines. This means that there will be a loss of precision.

### The usual arithmetic conversions

A lot of expressions involve the use of subexpressions of mixed types together with operators such as +, * and so on. If the operands in an expression have different types, then there will have to be a conversion applied so that a common resulting type can be established; these are the conversions:

- If either operand is a long double, then the other one is converted to long double and that is the type of the result.

- Otherwise, if either operand is a double, then the other one is converted to double, and that is the type of the result.

- Otherwise, if either operand is a float, then the other one is converted to float, and that is the type of the result.

- Otherwise the integral promotions are applied to both operands and the following conversions are applied:
  - If either operand is an unsigned long int, then the other one is converted to unsigned long int, and that is the type of the result.
  - Otherwise, if either operand is a long int, then the other one is converted to long int, and that is the type of the result.
  - Otherwise, if either operand is an unsigned int, then the other one is converted to unsigned int, and that is the type of the result.
  - Otherwise, both operands must be of type int, so that is the type of the result.

The Standard contains a strange sentence: 'The values of floating operands and of the results of floating expressions may be represented in greater precision and range than that required by the type; the types are not changed thereby'. This is in fact to allow the Old C treatment of floats. In Old C, float variables were automatically promoted to double, the way that the integral promotions promote char to int. So, an expression involving purely float variables may be done as if they were double, but the type of the result must appear to be float. The only effect is likely to be on performance and is not particularly important to most users.

Whether or not conversions need to be applied, and if so which ones, is discussed at the point where each operator is introduced.

In general, the type conversions and type mixing rules don't cause a lot of trouble, but there is one pitfall to watch out for. Mixing signed and unsigned quantities is fine until the signed number is negative; then its value can't be represented in an unsigned variable and something has to happen. The standard says that to convert a negative number to unsigned, the largest possible number that can be held in the unsigned plus one is added to the negative number; that is the result. Because there can be no overflow in an unsigned type, the result always has a defined value. Taking a 16-bit int for an example, the unsigned version has a range of 0–65535. Converting a signed value of −7 to this type involves adding 65536, resulting in 65529. What is happening is that the Standard is enshrining previous practice, where the bit pattern in the signed number is simply assigned to the unsigned number; the description in the Standard is exactly what would happen if you did perform the bit pattern assignment on a two's complement computer. The one's complement implementations are going to have to do some real work to get the same result.

Putting it plainly, a small magnitude negative number will result in a large positive number when converted to unsigned. If you don't like it, suggest a better solution – it is plainly a mistake to try to assign a negative number to an unsigned variable, so it's your own fault.

Well, it's easy to say 'don't do it', but it can happen by accident and the results can be *very* surprising. Look at this example.

```
#include (stdio.h)
#include (stdlib.h)
```

```
main(){
        int i;
        unsigned int stop_val;

        stop_val = 0;
        i = -10;
        while(i <= stop_val){
                printf("%d\n", i);
                i = i + 1;
        }
        exit(EXIT_SUCCESS);
}
```
(Example 2.7)

You might expect that to print out the list of values from -10 to 0, but it won't. The problem is in the comparison. The variable i, with a value of -10, is being compared against an unsigned 0. By the rules of arithmetic (check them) we must convert both types to unsigned int first, then make the comparison. The -10 becomes at least 65526 (see ⟨limits.h⟩) when it's converted, and is plainly somewhat larger than 0, so the loop is never executed. The moral is to steer clear of unsigned numbers unless you really have to use them, and to be perpetually on guard when they are mixed with signed numbers.

### Wide characters

The Standard, as we've already said, now makes allowances for extended character sets. You can either use the shift-in shift-out encoding method which allows the multibyte characters to be stored in ordinary C strings (which are really arrays of chars, as we explore later), or you can use a representation that uses more than one byte of storage per character for every character. The use of shift sequences only works if you process the characters in strict order; it is next to useless if you want to create an array of characters and access them in non-sequential order, since the actual index of each char in the array and the logical index of each of the encoded characters are not easily determined. Here's the illustration we used before, annotated with the actual and the logical array indices:

```
0 1 2 3   4 5 6 7   8 9 (actual array index)
a b c (SI) a b g (SO) x y
0 1 2     3 4 5       6 7 (logical index)
```

We're still in trouble even if we do manage to use the index of 5 to access the 'correct' array entry, since the value retrieved is indistinguishable from the value that encodes the letter 'g' anyhow. Clearly, a better approach for this sort of thing is to come up with a distinct value for all of the characters in the character set we are using, which may involve more bits than will fit into a char, and to be able to store each one as a separate item without the use of shifts or other position-dependent techniques. That is what the wchar_t type is for.

Although it is always a synonym for one of the other integral types, wchar_t (whose definition is found in ⟨stddef.h⟩) is defined to be the implementation-dependent type that should be used to hold extended characters when you need an array of them. The Standard makes the following guarantees about the values in a wide character:

- A wchar_t can hold distinct values for each member of the largest character set supported by the implementation.
- The null character has the value of zero.
- Each member of the basic character set (see 2.2.1) is encoded in a wchar_t with the same value as it has in a char.

There is further support for this method of encoding characters. Strings, which we have already seen, are implemented as arrays of char, even though they look like this:

```
"a string"
```

To get strings whose type is wchar_t, simply prefix a string with the letter L. For example:

```
L"a string"
```

In the two examples, it is very important to understand the differences. Strings are implemented as arrays and although it might look odd, it is entirely permissible to use array indexing on them:

```
"a string"[4]
L"a string"[4]
```

are both valid expressions. The first results in an expression whose type is char and whose value is the internal representation of the letter 'r' (remember arrays index from zero, not one). The second has the type wchar_t and also has the value of the internal representation of the letter 'r'.

It gets more interesting if we are using extended characters. If we use the notation ⟨a⟩, ⟨b⟩, and so on to indicate 'additional' characters beyond the normal character set which are encoded using some form of shift technique, then these examples show the problems.

```
"abc⟨a⟩⟨b⟩"[3]
L"abc⟨a⟩⟨b⟩"[3]
```

The second one is easier: it has a type of wchar_t and the appropriate internal encoding for whatever ⟨a⟩ is supposed to be – say the Greek letter alpha. The first one is unpredictable. Its type is unquestionably char, but its value is probably the value of the 'shift-in' marker.

As with strings, there are also wide character constants.

'a'

has type char and the value of the encoding for the letter 'a'.

L'a'

is a constant of type wchar_t. If you use a multibyte character in the first one, then you have the same sort of thing as if you had written

'xy'

– multiple characters in a character constant (actually, this is valid but means something funny). A single multibyte character in the second example will simply be converted into the appropriate wchar_t value.

If you don't understand all the wide character stuff, then all we can say is that we've done our best to explain it. Come back and read it again later, when it might suddenly click. In practice it does manage to address the support of extended character sets in C and once you're used to it, it makes a lot of sense.

## EXERCISE

**2.15**  Assuming that chars, ints and longs are respectively 8, 16 and 32 bits long, and that char defaults to unsigned char on a given system, what is the resulting type of expressions involving the following combinations of variables, after the usual arithmetic conversions have been applied?

(a) Simply signed char.
(b) Simply unsigned char.
(c) int, unsigned int.
(d) unsigned int, long.
(e) int, unsigned long.
(f) char, long.
(g) char, float.
(h) float, float.
(i) float, long double.

## Casts

From time to time you will find that an expression turns out not to have the type that you wanted it to have and you would like to force it to have a different type. That is what **casts** are for. By putting a type name in parentheses, for example

(int)

you create a unary operator known as a **cast**. A cast turns the value of the expression on its right into the indicated type. If, for example, you were dividing two integers a / b then the expression would use integer division and discard any remainder. To force the fractional part to be retained, you could either use some intermediate float variables, or a cast. This example does it both ways.

```
#include ⟨stdio.h⟩
#include ⟨stdlib.h⟩


/*
 * Illustrates casts.
 * For each of the numbers between 2 and 20,
 * print the percentage difference between it and the one
 * before
 */
main(){
        int curr_val;
        float temp, pcnt_diff;

        curr_val = 2;
        while(curr_val <= 20){
                /*
                 * % difference is
                 * 1 / (curr_val) * 100
                 */
                temp = curr_val;
                pcnt_diff = 100 / temp;
                printf("Percent difference at %d is %f\n",
                        curr_val, pcnt_diff);
                /*
                 * Or, using a cast:
                 */
                pcnt_diff = 100 / (float)curr_val;
                printf("Percent difference at %d is %f\n",
                        curr_val, pcnt_diff);
                curr_val = curr_val + 1;
        }
        exit(EXIT_SUCCESS);
}
```
                                                      (**Example 2.8**)

The easiest way to remember how to write a cast is to write down exactly what you would use to declare a variable of the type that you want. Put parentheses around the entire declaration, then delete the variable name; that gives you the cast. Table 2.6 shows a few simple examples – some of the types shown will be new to you, but it's the complicated ones that illustrate best how casts are written. Ignore the ones that you don't understand yet, because you will be able to use the table as a reference later.

**Table 2.6**   Casts.

| Declaration | Cast | Type |
|---|---|---|
| int x; | (int) | int |
| float f; | (float) | float |
| char x[30]; | (char [30]) | array of char |
| int *ip; | (int *) | pointer to int |
| int (*f)(); | (int (*)()) | pointer to function returning int |

## 2.8.2 Operators

### The multiplicative operators

Or, put another way, multiplication *, division / and the remainder operator %. Multiplication and division do what is expected of them for both real and integral types, with integral division producing a truncated result. The truncation is towards zero. The remainder operator is only defined to work with integral types, because the division of real numbers supposedly doesn't produce a remainder.

If the division is not exact and neither operand is negative, the result of / is positive and rounded toward zero – to get the remainder, use %. For example,

```
9 / 2 == 4
9 % 2 == 1
```

If either operand is negative, the result of / may be the nearest integer to the true result on either side, and the sign of the result of % may be positive or negative. Both of these features are implementation defined.

It is always true that the following expression is equal to zero:

```
(a / b) * b + a % b - a
```

unless b is zero.

The usual arithmetic conversions are applied to both of the operands.

### Additive operators

Addition + and subtraction - also follow the rules that you expect. The binary operators and the unary operators both have the same symbols, but rather different meanings. For example, the expressions a + b and a - b both use a binary operator (the + or - operators), and result in addition or subtraction. The unary operators with the same symbols would be written +b or -b.

The unary minus has an obvious function – it takes the negative value of its operand; what does the unary plus do? In fact the answer is almost nothing. The unary plus is a new addition to the language, which balances the presence of the unary minus, but doesn't have any effect on the value of the expression. Very few Old C users even noticed that it was missing.

The usual arithmetic conversions are applied to both of the operands of the binary forms of the operators. Only the integral promotions are performed on the operands of the unary forms of the operators.

### The bitwise operators

One of the great strengths of C is the way that it allows systems programmers to do what had, before the advent of C, always been regarded as the province of the assembly code programmer. That sort of code was by definition highly non-portable. As C demonstrates, there isn't any magic about that sort of thing, and into the bargain it turns out to be surprisingly portable. What is it? It's what is often referred to as 'bit-twiddling' – the manipulation of individual bits in integer variables. None of the bitwise operators may be used on real operands because they aren't considered to have individual or accessible bits.

**Table 2.7**   Bitwise operators.

| Operator | Effect | Conversions |
|----------|--------|-------------|
| & | bitwise AND | usual arithmetic conversions |
| \| | bitwise OR | usual arithmetic conversions |
| ^ | bitwise XOR | usual arithmetic conversions |
| << | left shift | integral promotions |
| >> | right shift | integral promotions |
| ~ | one's complement | integral promotions |

There are six bitwise operators, listed in Table 2.7, which also shows the arithmetic conversions that are applied. Only the last, the one's complement, is a unary operator. It inverts the state of every bit in its operand and has the same effect as the unary minus on a one's complement computer. Most modern computers work with two's complement, so it isn't a waste of time having it there.

Illustrating the use of these operators is easier if we can use hexadecimal notation rather than decimal, so now is the time to see hexadecimal constants. Any number written with 0x at its beginning is interpreted as hexadecimal; both 15 and 0xf (or 0XF) mean the same thing. Try running this or, better still, try to predict what it does first and then try running it.

```
#include <stdio.h>
#include <stdlib.h>

main(){
        int x, y;
        x = 0; y = ~0;
```

```
        while(x != y){
                printf("%x & %x = %x\n", x, 0xff, x & 0xff);
                printf("%x | %x = %x\n", x, 0x10f, x | 0x10f);
                printf("%x ^ %x = %x\n", x, 0xf00f, x ^ 0xf00f);
                printf("%x >> 2 = %x\n", x, x >> 2);
                printf("%x << 2 = %x\n", x, x << 2);
                x = (x << 1) | 1;
        }
        exit(EXIT_SUCCESS);
}
```

(Example 2.9)

The way that the loop works in that example is the first thing to study. The controlling variable is x, which is initialized to zero. Every time round the loop it is compared against y, which has been set to a word-length independent pattern of all 1s by taking the one's complement of zero. At the bottom of the loop, x is shifted left once and has 1 ORed into it, giving rise to a sequence that starts 0, 1, 11, 111, ... in binary.

For each of the AND, OR, and XOR (exclusive OR) operators, x is operated on by the operator and some other interesting operand, then the result printed.

The left and right shift operators are in there too, giving a result which has the type and value of their left-hand operand shifted in the required direction a number of places specified by their right-hand operand; the type of both of the operands must be integral. Bits shifted off either end of the left operand simply disappear. Shifting by more bits than there are in a word gives an implementation dependent result.

Shifting left guarantees to shift zeros into the low-order bits.

Right shift is fussier. Your implementation is allowed to choose whether, when shifting signed operands, it performs a logical or arithmetic right shift. This means that a logical shift shifts zeros into the most significant bit positions; an arithmetic shift copies the current contents of the most significant bit back into itself. The position is clearer if an unsigned operand is right shifted, because there is no choice: it must be a logical shift. For that reason, whenever right shift is being used, you would expect to find that the thing being shifted had been declared to be unsigned, or cast to unsigned for the shift, as in the example:

```
int i, j;
i = (unsigned)j >> 4;
```

The second (right-hand) operand of a shift operator does not have to be a constant; any integral expression is legal. Importantly, the rules involving mixed types of operands do not apply to the shift operators. The result of the shift has the same type as the thing that got shifted (after the integral promotions), and depends on nothing else.

Now something different; one of those little tricks that C programmers find helps to write better programs. If for any reason you want to form a value that has 1s in all but its least significant so-many bits, which are to have some other pattern in them, you don't have to know the word length of the machine. For example, to set the low order bits of an int to 0x0f0 and all the other bits to 1, this is the way to do it:

```
int some_variable;
some_variable = ~0xf0f;
```

The one's complement of the desired low-order bit pattern has been one's complemented. That gives exactly the required result and is completely independent of word length; it is a very common sight in C code.

There isn't a lot more to say about the bit-twiddling operators, and our experience of teaching C has been that most people find them easy to learn. Let's move on.

### The assignment operators

No, that isn't a mistake, 'operators' was meant to be plural. C has several assignment operators, even though we have only seen the plain = so far. An interesting thing about them is that they are all like the other binary operators; they take two operands and produce a result, the result being usable as part of an expression. In this statement

```
x = 4;
```

the value 4 is assigned to x. The result has the type of x and the value that was assigned. It can be used like this

```
a = (x = 4);
```

where a will now have the value 4 assigned to it, after x has been assigned to. All of the simpler assignments that we have seen until now (except for one example) have simply discarded the resulting value of the assignment, even though it is produced.

It's because assignment has a result that an expression like

```
a = b = c = d;
```

works. The value of d is assigned to c, the result of that is assigned to b and so on. It makes use of the fact that expressions involving only assignment operators are evaluated from right to left, but is otherwise like any other expression. (The rules explaining what groups right to left and vice versa are given in Table 2.9.)

If you look back to the section describing 'conversions', there is a description of what happens if you convert longer types to shorter types: that is what happens when the left-hand operand of an assignment is shorter than the right-hand one. No conversions are applied to the right-hand operand of the simple assignment operator.

The remaining assignment operators are the compound assignment operators. They allow a useful shorthand, where an assignment containing the same left- and right-hand sides can be compressed; for example

```
x = x + 1;
```

can be written as

```
x += 1;
```

using one of the compound assignment operators. The result is the same in each case.
It is a useful thing to do when the left-hand side of the operator is a complicated
expression, not just a variable; such things occur when you start to use arrays and
pointers. Most experienced C programmers tend to use the form given in the second
example because somehow it 'feels better', a sentiment that no beginner has ever been
known to agree with. Table 2.8 lists the compound assignment operators; you will see
them used a lot from now on. In each case, arithmetic conversions are applied as if the
expression had been written out in full, for example as if a += b had been written
a = a + b.

**Table 2.8**  Compound assignment operators.

| | | |
|---|---|---|
| *= | /= | %= |
| += | -= | |
| &= | \|= | ^= |
| >>= | <<= | |

Reiterating: the result of an assignment operator has both the value and the
type of the object that was assigned to.

### Increment and decrement operators

It is so common to simply add or subtract one in an expression that C has two special
unary operators to do the job. The increment operator ++ adds 1, the decrement --
subtracts 1. They are used like this:

```
x++;
++x;
x--;
--x;
```

where the operator can come either before or after its operand. In the cases shown it
doesn't matter where the operator comes, but in more complicated cases the difference has a definite meaning and must be used properly.

Here is the difference being used.

```
#include (stdio.h)
#include (stdlib.h)

main(){
        int a, b;
        a = b = 5;
```

```
        printf("%d\n", ++a + 5);
        printf("%d\n", a);
        printf("%d\n", b++ + 5);
        printf("%d\n", b);
        exit(EXIT_SUCCESS);
}
```
                                                              **(Example 2.10)**

The results printed were

```
11
6
10
6
```

The difference is caused by the different positions of the operators. If the increment/
decrement operator appears in front of the variable, then its value is changed by one
and the *new* value is used in the expression. If the operator comes after the variable,
then the *old* value is used in the expression and the variable's value is changed
afterwards.

C programmers never add or subtract one with statements like this

```
x += 1;
```

they invariably use one of

```
x++; /*     or     */ ++x;
```

as a matter of course. A warning is in order though: it is not safe to use a variable more
than once in an expression if it has one of these operators attached to it. There is no
guarantee of when, within an expression, the affected variable will actually change
value. The compiler might choose to 'save up' all of the changes and apply them at
once, so an expression like this

```
y = x++ + --x;
```

does not guarantee to assign twice the original value of x to y. It might be evaluated as
if it expanded to this instead:

```
y = x + (x - 1);
```

because the compiler notices that the overall effect on the value of x is zero.

The arithmetic is done exactly as if the full addition expression had been used,
for example x = x + 1, and the usual arithmetic conversions apply.

## EXERCISE

**2.16**   Given the following variable definitions

```
int i1, i2;
float f1, f2;
```

(a)  How would you find the remainder when i1 is divided by i2?

(b)  How would you find the remainder when i1 is divided by the value of f1, treating f1 as an integer?

(c)  What can you predict about the sign of the remainders calculated in the previous two questions?

(d)  What meanings can the - operator have?

(e)  How would you turn off all but the low-order four bits in i1?

(f)  How would you turn on all the low-order four bits in i1?

(g)  How would you turn off only the low-order four bits in i1?

(h)  How would you put into i1 the low-order eight bits in i2, but swapping the significance of the lowest four with the next four up?

(i)  What is wrong with the following expression?

```
f2 = ++f1 + ++f1;
```

## 2.8.3  Precedence and grouping

After looking at the operators we have to consider the way that they work together. For things like addition it may not seem important; it hardly matters whether

```
a + b + c
```

is done as

```
(a + b) + c
```

or

```
a + (b + c)
```

does it? Well, yes in fact it does. If a + b would overflow and c held a value very close to -b, then the second grouping might give the correct answer where the first would cause undefined behaviour. The problem is much more obvious with integer division:

```
a / b / c
```

gives very different results when grouped as

```
a / (b / c)
```

or

```
(a / b) / c
```

If you don't believe that, try it with a = 10, b = 2, c = 3. The first gives 10 / (2 / 3); 2 / 3 in integer division gives 0, so we get 10 / 0 which immediately overflows. The second grouping gives (10 / 2), obviously 5, which divided by 3 gives 1.

The grouping of operators like that is known as **associativity**. The other question is one of **precedence**, where some operators have a higher priority than others and force evaluation of sub-expressions involving them to be performed before those with lower precedence operators. This is almost universal practice in high-level languages, so we 'know' that

```
a + b * c + d
```

groups as

```
a + (b * c) + d
```

indicating that multiplication has higher precedence than addition.

The large set of operators in C gives rise to 15 levels of precedence! Only very boring people bother to remember them all. The complete list is given in Table 2.9, which indicates both precedence and associativity. Not all of the operators have been mentioned yet. Beware of the use of the same symbol for both unary and binary operators: the table indicates which are which.

The question is, what can you do with that information, now that it's there? Obviously it's important to be able to work out both how to write expressions that evaluate in the proper order, and also how to read other people's. The technique is this: first, identify the unary operators and the operands that they refer to. This isn't such a difficult task but it takes some practice, especially when you discover that operators such as unary * can be applied an arbitrary number of times to their operands; this expression

```
a * ****b
```

means a multiplied by *something*, where the something is an expression involving b and several unary * operators.

It's not too difficult to work out which are the unary operators; here are the rules:

(1) ++ and -- are always unary operators.
(2) The operator immediately to the right of an operand is a binary operator unless (1) applies, when the operator to *its* right is binary.
(3) All operators to the left of an operand are unary unless (2) applies.

**Table 2.9**   Operator precedence and associativity.

| Operator | Direction | Notes |
|---|---|---|
| () [] -> . | left to right | 1 |
| ! ~ ++ -- - + (cast) * & sizeof | right to left | all unary |
| * / % | left to right | binary |
| + - | left to right | binary |
| << >> | left to right | binary |
| < <= > >= | left to right | binary |
| == != | left to right | binary |
| & | left to right | binary |
| ^ | left to right | binary |
| \| | left to right | binary |
| && | left to right | binary |
| \|\| | left to right | binary |
| ?: | right to left | 2 |
| = += and all combined assignment | right to left | binary |
| , | left to right | binary |

1. Parentheses are for expression grouping, *not* function call.
2. This is unusual. See Section 3.4.1.

Because the unary operators have very high precedence, you can work out what they do before worrying about the other operators. One thing to watch out for is the way that ++ and -- can be before or after their operands; the expression

```
a + -b++ + c
```

has two unary operators applied to b. The unary operators all associate right to left, so although the - comes first when you read the expression, it really parenthesizes (for clarity) like this:

```
a + -(b++) + c
```

The case is a little clearer if the prefix, rather than the postfix, form of the increment/ decrement operators is being used. Again the order is right to left, but at least the operators come all in a row.

After sorting out what to do with the unary operators, it's easy to read the expression from left to right. Every time you see a binary operator, remember it. Look to the right: if the next binary operator is of a lower precedence, then the operator you just remembered is part of a sub-expression to evaluate before anything else is seen. If the next operator is of the same precedence, keep repeating the procedure as long as equal precedence operators are seen. When you eventually find a lower precedence operator, evaluate the sub-expression on the left according to the associativity rules. If a higher precedence operator is found on the right, forget the previous stuff: the operand to the left of the higher precedence operator is part of a sub-expression separate from anything on the left so far. It belongs to the new operator instead.

If that lot isn't clear don't worry. A lot of C programmers have trouble with this area and eventually learn to parenthesize these expressions 'by eye', without ever using formal rules.

What *does* matter is what happens when you have fully parenthesized these expressions. Remember the 'usual arithmetic conversions'? They explained how you could predict the type of an expression from the operands involved. Now, even if you mix all sorts of types in a complicated expression, the types of the sub-expressions are determined only from the the types of the operands in the sub-expression. Look at this:

```
#include ⟨stdio.h⟩
#include ⟨stdlib.h⟩
main(){
        int i, j;
        float f;

        i = 5; j = 2;
        f = 3.0;

        f = f + j / i;
        printf("value of f is %f\n", f);
        exit(EXIT_SUCCESS);
}
```
**(Example 2.11)**

The value printed is 3.0000, not 3.4000 – which might surprise some, who thought that because a float was involved the whole statement involving the division would be done in that real type.

Of course, the division operator had only int types on either side, so the arithmetic was done as integer division and resulted in zero. The addition had a float and an int on either side, so the conversions meant that the int was converted to float for the arithmetic, and that was the correct type for the assignment, so there were no further conversions.

The previous section on casts showed one way of changing the type of an expression from its natural one to the one that you want. Be careful though:

```
(float)(j / i)
```

would still use integer division, *then* convert the result to float. To keep the remainder, you should use

```
(float)j / i
```

which would force real division to be used.


### 2.8.4 Parentheses

C allows you to override the normal effects of precedence and associativity by the use of parentheses as the examples have illustrated. In Old C, the parentheses had no further meaning, and in particular did *not* guarantee anything about the order of evaluation in expressions like these:

```
int a, b, c;
a + b + c;
(a + b) + c;
a + (b + c);
```

You used to need to use explicit temporary variables to get a particular order of evaluation – something that matters if you know that there are risks of overflow in a particular expression, but by forcing the evaluation to be in a certain order you can avoid it.

Standard C says that evaluation *must* be done in the order indicated by the precedence and grouping of the expression, unless the compiler can tell that the result will not be affected by any regrouping it might do for optimization reasons.

So the expression a = 10 + a + b + 5; cannot be rewritten by the compiler as a = 15 + a + b; unless it can be guaranteed that the resulting value of a will be the same for all combinations of initial values of a and b. That would be true if the variables were both unsigned integral types, or if they were signed integral types but in that particular implementation overflow did not cause a run-time exception and overflow was reversible.

### 2.8.5  Side effects

To repeat and expand the warning given for the increment operators: it is unsafe to use the same variable more than once in an expression if evaluating the expression changes the variable and the new value could affect the result of the expression. This is because the change(s) may be 'saved up' and only applied at the end of the statement. So f = f + 1; is safe even though f appears twice in a value-changing expression, f++; is also safe, but f = f++; is unsafe.

The problem can be caused by using an assignment, use of the increment or decrement operators, or by calling a function that changes the value of an external variable that is also used in the expression. These are generally known as 'side effects'. C makes almost no promise that side effects will occur in a predictable order within a single expression. (The discussion of 'sequence points' in Chapter 8 will be of interest if you care about this.)

## 2.9  Constants

### 2.9.1  Integer constants

The normal integer constants are obvious: things like 1, 1034 and so on. You can put l or L at the end of an integer constant to force it to be long. To make the constant unsigned, one of u or U can be used to do the job.

Integer constants can be written in hexadecimal by preceding the constant with Ox or OX and using the upper or lower case letters a, b, c, d, e, f in the usual way.

Be careful about octal constants. They are indicated by starting the number with 0 and only using the digits 0, 1, 2, 3, 4, 5, 6, 7. It is easy to write 015 by accident, or out of habit, and not to realize that it is *not* in decimal. The mistake is most common with beginners, because experienced C programmers already carry the scars.

The Standard has now invented a new way of working out what type an integer constant is. In the old days, if the constant was too big for an int, it got promoted to a long (without warning). Now, the rule is that a plain decimal constant will be fitted into the first in this list

```
int    long   unsigned long
```

that can hold the value. Plain octal or hexadecimal constants will use this list:

```
int    unsigned int    long    unsigned long
```

If the constant is suffixed by u or U:

```
unsigned int    unsigned long
```

If it is suffixed by l or L:

```
long    unsigned long
```

and finally, if it is suffixed by both u or U and l or L, it can only be an unsigned long.

All that was done to try to give you 'what you meant'; what it does mean is that it is hard to work out exactly what the type of a constant expression is if you don't know something about the hardware. Hopefully, good compilers will warn when a constant is promoted up to another length and the U or L etc. is not specified.

A nasty bug hides here:

```
printf("value of 32768 is %d\n", 32768);
```

On a 16-bit two's complement machine, 32768 will be a long by the rules given above. But printf is only expecting an int as an argument (the %d indicates that). The type of the argument is just wrong. For the ultimate in safety-conscious programming, you should cast such cases to the right type:

```
printf("value of 32768 is %d\n", (int)32768);
```

It might interest you to note that there are no negative constants; writing -23 is an expression involving a positive constant and an operator.

Character constants actually have type int (for historical reasons) and are written by placing a sequence of characters between single quote marks:

```
'a'
'b'
'like this'
```

Wide character constants are written just as above, but prefixed with L:

```
L'a'
L'b'
L'like this'
```

Regrettably it *is* valid to have more than one character in the sequence, giving a machine-dependent result. Single characters are the best from the portability point of view, resulting in an ordinary integer constant whose value is the machine representation of the single character. The introduction of extended characters may cause you to stumble over this by accident; if ⟨a⟩ is a multibyte character (encoded with a shift-in shift-out around it) then '⟨a⟩' will be a plain character constant, but containing several characters, just like the more obvious 'abcde'. This is bound to lead to trouble in the future; let's hope that compilers will warn about it.

To ease the way of representing some special characters that would otherwise be hard to get into a character constant (or hard to read; does ' ' contain a space or a tab?), there is what is called an **escape sequence** which can be used instead. Table 2.10 shows the escape sequences defined in the Standard.

**Table 2.10**   C escape sequences.

| Sequence | Represents |
|----------|------------|
| \a | audible alarm |
| \b | backspace |
| \f | form feed |
| \n | newline |
| \r | carriage return |
| \t | tab |
| \v | vertical tab |
| \\ | backslash |
| \' | quote |
| \" | double quote |
| \? | question mark |

It is also possible to use numeric escape sequences to specify a character in terms of the internal value used to represent it. A sequence of either \ooo or \xhhhh, where the ooo is up to three octal digits and hhhh is any number of hexadecimal digits respectively. A common version of it is '\033', which is used by those who know that on an ASCII based machine, octal 33 is the ESC (escape) code. Beware that the hexadecimal version will absorb any number of valid following hexadecimal digits; if you want a string containing the character whose value is hexadecimal ff followed by a *letter* f, then the safe way to do it is to use the string joining feature:

```
"\xff" "f"
```

The string

```
"\xfff"
```

only contains one character, with all three of the fs eaten up in the hexadecimal sequence.

Some of the escape sequences aren't too obvious, so a brief explanation is needed. To get a single quote as a character constant you type '\'', to get a question mark you may have to use '\?'; not that it matters in that example, but to get two of them in there you can't use '??', because the sequence ??' is a trigraph! You would have to use '\?\?'. The escape \" is only necessary in strings, which will come later.

There are two distinct purposes behind the escape sequences. It's obviously necessary to be able to represent characters such as single quote and backslash unambiguously: that is one purpose. The second purpose applies to the following sequences which control the motions of a printing device when they are sent to it, as follows:

    \a   Ring the bell if there is one. Do not move.
    \b   Backspace.
    \f   Go to the first position on the 'next page', whatever that may mean for the output device.
    \n   Go to the start of the next line.
    \r   Go back to the start of the current line.
    \t   Go to the next horizontal tab position.
    \v   Go to the start of the line at the next vertical tab position.

For \b, \t, \v, if there is no such position, the behaviour is unspecified. The Standard carefully avoids mentioning the physical directions of movement of the output device which are not necessarily the top to bottom, left to right movements common in Western cultural environments.

It is guaranteed that each escape sequence has a unique integral value which can be stored in a char.

### 2.9.2 Real constants

These follow the usual format:

```
1.0
2.
.1
2.634
.125
2.e5
2.e + 5
.125e - 3
2.5e5
3.1E - 6
```

and so on. For readability, even if part of the number is zero, it is a good idea to show it:

```
1.0
0.1
```

The exponent part shows the number of powers of ten that the rest of the number should be raised to, so

```
3.0e3
```

is equivalent in value to the integer constant

```
3000
```

As you can see, the e can also be E. These constants all have type double unless they are suffixed with f or F to mean float or l or L to mean long double.

For completeness, here is the formal description of a real constant:

A real constant is one of:

- A **fractional constant** followed by an optional **exponent**.
- A **digit sequence** followed by an **exponent**.

In either case followed by an optional one of f, l, F, L, where:

- A **fractional constant** is one of:
  - An optional **digit sequence** followed by a decimal point followed by a **digit sequence**.
  - A **digit sequence** followed by a decimal point.
- An **exponent** is one of
  - e or E followed by an optional + or - followed by a **digit sequence**.
- A **digit sequence** is an arbitrary combination of one or more digits.

■ **2.10 SUMMARY**

This has been a lengthy, and perhaps disconcerting, chapter.

The alphabet of C, although of relevance, is not normally a day-to-day consideration of practising programmers, so it has been discussed but can now be largely ignored.

Much the same can be said regarding keywords and identifiers, since the topic is not complicated and simply becomes committed to memory.

The declaration of variables is rarely a problem, although it is worth re-emphasizing the distinction between a declaration and a definition. If that still remains unclear, you might find it of benefit to go back and re-read the description.

Beyond any question, the real complexity lies in what happens when the integral promotions and the arithmetic conversions occur. For beginners, it is often worthwhile to remember that here is a difficult and arduous piece of terrain. Nothing else in the language requires so much attention or is so important to the production of correct, reliable programs. Beginners should *not* try to remember it all, but to go on now and to gain confidence with the rest of the language. After two or three months' practice at using the easier parts of the language, the time really does come when you can no longer afford to ignore Section 2.8 .

Many highly experienced C programmers never bother to learn the different precedences of operators, except for a few important cases. A precedence table pinned above your desk, for easy reference, is a valuable tool.

The Standard has substantially affected parts of the language described in this chapter. In particular, the changes to the conversions and the change from 'unsignedness preserving' to 'value preserving' rules of arithmetic may cause some surprises to experienced C programmers. Even they have some real re-learning to do.

---

## EXERCISE

---

**2.17** First, fully parenthesize the following expressions according to the precedence and associativity rules. Then, replacing the variables and constants with the appropriate type names, show how the type of the expression is derived by replacing the highest precedence expressions with its resulting type.

The variables are:

```
char c;
int i;
unsigned u;
float f;
```

For example: i = u + 1; parenthesizes as (i = (u + 1));
The types are

```
(int = (unsigned + int));
```

then

```
(int = (unsigned)); /* usual arithmetic conversions */
```

then

```
(int); /* assignment */
```

(a)  c = u * f + 2.6L;
(b)  u += --f / u % 3;
(c)  i <<= u * - ++f;
(d)  u = i + 3 + 4 + 3.1;
(e)  u = 3.1 + i + 3 + 4;
(f)  c = (i << - --f) & 0xf;

# CHAPTER 3

---

# Control of Flow and
# Logical Expressions

---

---

## 3.1  The task ahead

In this chapter we look at the various ways that the control of flow statements can be used in a C program, including some statements that haven't been introduced so far. They are almost always used in conjunction with **logical expressions** to select the next action. Examples of logical expressions that have been seen already are some simple ones used in if or while statements. As you might have expected, you can use expressions more complicated than simple comparison (>, <=, == and so on); what may surprise you is the *type* of the result.

### 3.1.1  Logical expressions and relational operators

All of the examples we have used so far have deliberately avoided using complicated logical expressions in the control of flow statements. We have seen expressions like this

```
if(a != 100){...
```

and presumably you have formed the idea that C supports the concept of 'true' and 'false' for these relationships. In a way, it does, but in a way that differs from what is often expected.

All of the relational operators shown in Table 3.1 are used to compare two operands in the way indicated. When the operands are arithmetic types, the usual arithmetic conversions are applied to them.

**Table 3.1** Relational operators.

| Operator | Operation |
|----------|-----------|
| < | less than |
| <= | less than or equal to |
| > | greater than |
| >= | greater than or equal to |
| == | equal to |
| != | not equal to |

Be extra careful of the test for equality, ==. As we have already pointed out, it is often valid to use assignment = where you might have meant == and C can't tell you about your mistake. The results are normally different and it takes a long time for beginners to get used to using == and =.

Now, that usefully introduces the question 'why?'. Why are both valid? The answer is simple. C's concept of 'true' and 'false' boils down to simply 'non-zero' and 'zero', respectively. Where we have seen expressions involving relational operators used to control do and if statements, we have just been using expressions with numeric results. If the expression evaluates to non-zero, then the result is effectively true. If the reverse is the case, then of course the result is false. Anywhere that the relational operators appear, so may any other expression.

The relational operators work by comparing their operands and giving zero for false and (remember this) one for true. The result is of type int. This example shows how they work:

```
#include <stdio.h>
#include <stdlib.h>

main(){
        int i;

        i = -10;
        while(i <= 5){
                printf("value of i is %d, ", i);
                printf("i == 0 = %d, ", i==0 );
                printf("i > -5 = %d\n", i > -5);
                i++;
        }
        exit(EXIT_SUCCESS);
}
```

(Example 3.1)

It produces this on its standard output:

```
value of i is -10, i == 0 = 0, i > -5 = 0
value of i is -9, i == 0 = 0, i > -5 = 0
value of i is -8, i == 0 = 0, i > -5 = 0
value of i is -7, i == 0 = 0, i > -5 = 0
```

```
value of i is -6, i == 0 = 0, i > -5 = 0
value of i is -5, i == 0 = 0, i > -5 = 0
value of i is -4, i == 0 = 0, i > -5 = 1
value of i is -3, i == 0 = 0, i > -5 = 1
value of i is -2, i == 0 = 0, i > -5 = 1
value of i is -1, i == 0 = 0, i > -5 = 1
value of i is 0, i == 0 = 1, i > -5 = 1
value of i is 1, i == 0 = 0, i > -5 = 1
value of i is 2, i == 0 = 0, i > -5 = 1
value of i is 3, i == 0 = 0, i > -5 = 1
value of i is 4, i == 0 = 0, i > -5 = 1
value of i is 5, i == 0 = 0, i > -5 = 1
```

In this probably mistaken piece of code, what do you think happens?

```
if(a = b)...
```

The value of b is assigned to a. As you know, the result has the type of a and whatever value was assigned to a. The if will execute the next statement if the value assigned is not zero. If zero is assigned, the next statement is ignored. So now you understand what happens if you confuse the assignment with the equality operator!

In all of the statements that test the value of an expression, the if, while, do, and for statements, the expression is simply tested to see if its value is zero or not.

We will look at each one in turn.


## 3.2  Control of flow

### 3.2.1  The if statement

The if statement has two forms:

> if(*expression*)  *statement*

> if(*expression*)  *statement1*
> else  *statement2*

In the first form, if (and only if) the *expression* is non-zero, the *statement* is executed. If the *expression* is zero, the *statement* is ignored. Remember that the *statement* can be compound; that is the way to put several statements under the control of a single if.

The second form is like the first except that if the statement shown as *statement1* is selected then *statement2* will not be, and vice versa.

Either form is considered to be a single statement in the syntax of C, so the following is completely legal:

> if(*expression*)
>     if(*expression*)  *statement*

The first if (*expression*) is followed by a properly formed, complete if statement. Since that is legally a statement, the first if can be considered to read

    if(*expression*) *statement*

and is therefore itself properly formed. The argument can be extended as far as you like, but it's a bad habit to get into. It is better style to make the *statement* compound even if it isn't necessary. That makes it a lot easier to add extra statements if they are needed and generally improves readability.

The form involving else works the same way, so we can also write this.

    if(*expression*)
            if(*expression*)
                    *statement*
            else
                    *statement*

As Chapter 1 has said already, this is now ambiguous. It is not clear, except as indicated by the indentation, which of the ifs is responsible for the else. If we follow the rules that the previous example suggests, then the second if is followed by a statement, and is therefore itself a statement, so the else belongs to the first if.

That is *not* the way that C views it. The rule is that an else belongs to the first if above that hasn't already got an else. In the example we're discussing, the else goes with the second if.

To prevent any unwanted association between an else and an if just above it, the if can be hidden away by using a compound statement. To repeat the example in Chapter 1, here it is.

    if(*expression*){
            if(*expression*)
                    *statement*
    }else
            *statement*

Putting in all the compound statement brackets, it becomes this:

    if(*expression*){
            if(*expression*){
                    *statement*
            }
    }else{
            *statement*
    }

If you happen not to like the placing of the brackets, it is up to you to put them where you think they look better; just be consistent about it. You probably need to know that this a subject on which feelings run deep.

### 3.2.2 The while and do statements

The while is simple:

```
while(expression)
        statement
```

The *statement* is only executed if the *expression* is non-zero. After every execution of the *statement*, the *expression* is evaluated again and the process repeats if it is non-zero. What could be plainer than that? The only point to watch out for is that the *statement* may never be executed, and that if nothing in the *statement* affects the value of the *expression* then the while will either do nothing or loop for ever, depending on the initial value of the *expression*.

It is occasionally desirable to guarantee at least one execution of the statement following the while, so an alternative form exists known as the do statement. It looks like this:

```
do
        statement
while(expression);
```

and you should pay close attention to that semicolon – it is not optional! The effect is that the statement part is executed before the controlling expression is evaluated, so this guarantees at least one trip around the loop. It was an unfortunate decision to use the keyword while for both purposes, but it doesn't seem to cause too many problems in practice.

If you feel the urge to use a do, think carefully. It is undoubtedly essential in certain cases, but experience has shown that the use of do statements is often associated with poorly constructed code. Not every time, obviously, but as a general rule you should stop and ask yourself if you have made the right choice. Their use often indicates a hangover of thinking methods learnt with other languages, or just sloppy design. When you *do* convince yourself that nothing else will give you just what is wanted, then go ahead – be daring – use it.

#### *Handy hints*
A *very* common trick in C programs is to use the result of an assignment to control while and do loops. It is so commonplace that, even if you look at it the first time and blench, you've got no alternative but to learn it. It falls into the category of 'idiomatic' C and eventually becomes second nature to anybody who really uses the language. Here is the most common example of all:

```
#include (stdio.h)
#include (stdlib.h)

main(){
        int input_c;
```

```
/* The Classic Bit */
while( (input_c = getchar()) != EOF){
        printf("%c was read\n", input_c);
}
exit(EXIT_SUCCESS);
}
```
                                                                    (Example 3.2)

The clever bit is the expression assigning to input_c. It is assigned to, compared with
EOF (End Of File), and used to control the loop all in one go. Embedding the
assignment like that is a handy embellishment. Admittedly it only saves one line of
code, but the benefit in terms of readability (once you have got used to seeing it) is
quite large. Learn where the parentheses are, too. They're necessary for precedence
reasons – work out why!

Note that input_c is an int. This is because getchar has to be able to return not
only every possible value of a char, but also an extra value, EOF. To do that, a type
longer than a char is necessary.

Both the while and the do statements are themselves syntactically a single
statement, just like an if statement. They occur anywhere that any other single
statement is permitted. If you want them to control *several* statements, then you will
have to use a compound statement, as the examples of if illustrated.

### 3.2.3 The for statement

A very common feature in programs is loops that are controlled by variables used as a
counter. The counter doesn't always have to count consecutive values, but the usual
arrangement is for it to be initialized outside the loop, checked every time around the
loop to see when to finish and updated each time around the loop. There are three
important places, then, where the loop control is concentrated: initialize, check and
update. This example shows them.

```
#include 〈stdio.h〉
#include 〈stdlib.h〉

main(){
        int i;

        /* initialise */
        i = 0;
        /* check */
        while(i <= 10){
                printf("%d\n", i);
                /* update */
                i++;
        }
        exit(EXIT_SUCCESS);
}
```
                                                                    (Example 3.3)

As you will have noticed, the initialization and check parts of the loop are close together and their location is obvious because of the presence of the `while` keyword. What is harder to spot is the place where the update occurs, especially if the value of the controlling variable is used within the loop. In that case, which is by far the most common, the update has to be at the very end of the loop: far away from the initialize and check. Readability suffers because it is hard to work out how the loop is going to perform unless you read the whole body of the loop carefully. What is needed is some way of bringing the initialize, check and update parts into one place so that they can be read quickly and conveniently. That is exactly what the `for` statement is designed to do. Here it is.

for (*initialize*; *check*; *update*) *statement*

The *initialize* part is an expression; nearly always an assignment expression which is used to initialize the control variable. After the initialization, the *check* expression is evaluated: if it is non-zero, the *statement* is executed, followed by evaluation of the *update* expression which generally increments the control variable, then the sequence restarts at the *check*. The loop terminates as soon as the *check* evaluates to zero.

There are two important things to realize about that last description: one, that each of the three parts of the `for` statement between the parentheses are just expressions; two, that the description has carefully explained what they are intended to be used for without proscribing alternative uses – that was done deliberately. You can use the expressions to do whatever you like, but at the expense of readability if they aren't used for their intended purpose.

Here is a program that does the same thing twice, the first time using a `while` loop, the second time with a `for`. The use of the increment operator is exactly the sort of use that you will see in everyday practice.

```
#include (stdio.h)
#include (stdlib.h)

main(){
        int i;

        i = 0;
        while(i <= 10){
                printf("%d\n", i);
                i++;
        }

        /* the same done using ''for'' */
        for(i = 0; i <= 10; i++){
                printf("%d\n", i);
        }
        exit(EXIT_SUCCESS);
}
```

(Example 3.4)

There isn't any difference betweeen the two, except that in this case the for loop is more convenient and maintainable than the while statement. You should always use the for when it's appropriate; when a loop is being controlled by some sort of counter. The while is more at home when an indeterminate number of cycles of the loop are part of the problem. As always, it needs a degree of judgement on behalf of the author of the program; an understanding of form, style, elegance and the poetry of a well written program. There is no evidence that the software business suffers from a surfeit of those qualities, so feel free to exercise them if you are able.

Any of the initialize, check and update expressions in the for statement can be omitted, although the semicolons must stay. This can happen if the counter is already initialized, or gets updated in the body of the loop. If the check expression is omitted, it is assumed to result in a 'true' value and the loop never terminates. A common way of writing never-ending loops is either

```
for(;;)
```

or

```
while(1)
```

and both can be seen in existing programs.

### 3.2.4 A brief pause

The control of flow statements that we've just seen are quite adequate to write programs of any degree of complexity. They lie at the core of C and even a quick reading of everyday C programs will illustrate their importance, both in the provision of essential functionality and in the structure that they emphasize. The remaining statements are used to give programmers finer control or to make it easier to deal with exceptional conditions. Only the switch statement is enough of a heavyweight to need no justification for its use; yes, it can be replaced with lots of ifs, but it does add a lot of readability. The others, break, continue and goto, should be treated like the spices in a delicate sauce. Used carefully they can turn something commonplace into a treat, but a heavy hand will drown the flavour of everything else.

### 3.2.5 The switch statement

This is not an essential part of C. You could do without it, but the language would have become significantly less expressive and less pleasant to use.

It is used to select one of a number of alternative actions depending on the value of an expression, and nearly always makes use of another of the lesser statements: the break. It looks like this:

```
switch (expression){
        case const1:    statements
        case const2:    statements
        default:        statements
}
```

The *expression* is evaluated and its value is compared with all of the *const1* etc. expressions, which must all evaluate to different constant values (strictly they are **integral constant expressions**, see Chapter 6 and below). If any of them has the same value as the *expression* then the statement following the case label is selected for execution. If the default is present, it will be selected when there is no matching value found. If there is no default and no matching value, the entire switch statement will do nothing and execution will continue at the following statement.

One curious feature is that the cases are *not* exclusive, as this example shows:

```
#include ⟨stdio.h⟩
#include ⟨stdlib.h⟩

main(){
        int i;

        for(i = 0; i <= 10; i++){
                switch(i){
                        case 1:
                        case 2:
                                printf("1 or 2\n");
                        case 7:
                                printf("7\n");
                        default:
                                printf("default\n");
                }
        }
        exit(EXIT_SUCCESS);
}
```
(Example 3.5)

The loop cycles with i having values 0-10. A value of 1 or 2 will cause the printing of the message 1 or 2 by selecting the first of the printf statements. What you might not expect is the way that the remaining messages would also appear! It's because the switch only selects one entry point to the body of the statement; after starting at a given point all of the following statements are also executed. The case and default labels simply allow you to indicate *which* of the statements is to be selected. When i has the value of 7, only the last two messages will be printed. Any value other than 1, 2, or 7 will find only the last message.

The labels can occur in any order, but no two values may be the same and you are allowed either one or no default (which doesn't have to be the last label). Several labels can be put in front of one statement and several statements can be put after one label.

The expression controlling the switch can be of any of the integral types. Old C used to insist on *only* int here, and some compilers would forcibly truncate longer types, giving rise on rare occasions to some very obscure bugs.

### The major restriction

The biggest problem with the switch statement is that it doesn't allow you to select mutually exclusive courses of action; once the body of the statement has been entered any subsequent statements within the body will all be executed. What is needed is the break statement. Here is the previous example, but amended to make sure that the messages printed come out in a more sensible order. The break statements cause execution to leave the switch statement immediately and prevent any further statements in the body of the switch from being executed.

```
#include <stdio.h>
#include <stdlib.h>

main(){
        int i;

        for(i = 0; i <= 10; i++){
                switch(i){
                        case 1:
                        case 2:
                                printf("1 or 2\n");
                                break;
                        case 7:
                                printf("7\n");
                                break;
                        default:
                                printf("default\n");
                }
        }
        exit(EXIT_SUCCESS);
}
```
(Example 3.6)

The break has further uses. Its own section follows soon.

### Integral constant expression

Although Chapter 6 deals with constant expressions, it is worth looking briefly at what an integral constant expression is, since that is what must follow the case labels in a switch statement. Loosely speaking, it is any expression that does not involve any value-changing operation (like increment or assignment), function calls or comma operators. The operands in the expression must all be integer constants, character constants, enumeration constants, sizeof expressions and floating-point constants that are the immediate operands of casts. Any cast operators must result in integral types.

Much what you would expect, really.

### 3.2.6 The break statement

This is a simple statement. It only makes sense if it occurs in the body of a switch, do, while or for statement. When it is executed the control of flow jumps to the statement immediately following the body of the statement containing the break. Its use is widespread in switch statements, where it is more or less essential to get the control that most people want.

The use of the break within loops is of dubious legitimacy. It has its moments, but is really only justifiable when exceptional circumstances have happened and the loop has to be abandoned. It would be nice if more than one loop could be abandoned with a single break but that isn't how it works. Here is an example.

```
#include ⟨stdio.h⟩
#include ⟨stdlib.h⟩

main(){
        int i;

        for(i = 0; i < 10000; i++){
                if(getchar() == 's')
                        break;
                printf("%d\n", i);
        }
        exit(EXIT_SUCCESS);
}
```
                                                                        (Example 3.7)

It reads a single character from the program's input before printing the next in a sequence of numbers. If an 's' is typed, the break causes an exit from the loop.

If you want to exit from more than one level of loop, the break is the wrong thing to use. The goto is the only easy way, but since it can't be mentioned in polite company, we'll leave it till last.

### 3.2.7 The continue statement

This statement has only a limited number of uses. The rules for its use are the same as for break, with the exception that it doesn't apply to switch statements. Executing a continue starts the next iteration of the smallest enclosing do, while or for statement immediately. The use of continue is largely restricted to the top of loops, where a decision has to be made whether or not to execute the rest of the body of the loop. In this example it ensures that division by zero (which gives undefined behaviour) doesn't happen.

```
#include ⟨stdio.h⟩
#include ⟨stdlib.h⟩
```

```
main(){
        int i;

        for(i = -10; i < 10; i++){
                if(i == 0)
                        continue;
                printf("%f\n", 15.0/i);
                /*
                 * Lots of other statements .....
                 */
        }
        exit(EXIT_SUCCESS);
}
```

(Example 3.8)

You could take a puritanical stance and argue that, instead of a conditional continue, the body of the loop should be made conditional instead – but you wouldn't have many supporters. Most C programmers would rather have the continue than the extra level of indentation, particularly if the body of the loop is large.

Of course the continue can be used in other parts of a loop, too, where it may occasionally help to simplify the logic of the code and improve readability. It deserves to be used sparingly.

Do remember that continue has no special meaning to a switch statement, where break does have. Inside a switch, continue is only valid if there is a loop that encloses the switch, in which case the next iteration of the loop will be started.

There is an important difference between loops written with while and for. In a while, a continue will go immediately to the test of the controlling expression. The same thing in a for will do two things: first the update expression is evaluated, *then* the controlling expression is evaluated.

### 3.2.8 Goto **and labels**

Everybody knows that the goto statement is a 'bad thing'. Used without care it is a great way of making programs hard to follow and of obscuring any structure in their flow. Dijkstra wrote a famous paper in 1968 called 'Goto Statement Considered Harmful', which everybody refers to and almost nobody has read.

What's especially annoying is that there are times when it is the most appropriate thing to use in the circumstances! In C, it is used to escape from multiple nested loops, or to go to an error handling exit at the end of a function. You will need a **label** when you use a goto; this example shows both.

```
goto L1;
/* whatever you like here */
L1: /* anything else */
```

A label is an identifier followed by a colon. Labels have their own 'name space' so they can't clash with the names of variables or functions. The name space only exists for the function containing the label, so label names can be re-used in different functions. The label can be used before it is declared, too, simply by mentioning it in a goto statement.

Labels *must* be part of a full statement, even if it's an empty one. This usually only matters when you're trying to put a label at the end of a compound statement – like this.

```
label_at_end: ; /* empty statement */
}
```

The goto works in an obvious way, jumping to the labelled statements. Because the name of the label is only visible inside its own function, you can't jump from one function to another one.

It's hard to give rigid rules about the use of gotos but, as with the do, continue and the break (except in switch statements), over-use should be avoided. Think carefully every time you feel like using one, and convince yourself that the structure of the program demands it. More than one goto every 3–5 functions is a symptom that should be viewed with deep suspicion.

☐  **SUMMARY**

○ Now we've seen all of the control of flow statements and examples of their use. Some should be used whenever possible; some are not for use line by line but for special purposes where their particular job is called for. It is possible to write elegant and beautiful programs in C if you are prepared to take the extra bit of care necessary; the specialized control of flow statements give you the chance to add the extra polish that some other languages lack.

All that remains to be done to complete the picture of flow of control in C is to finish off the logical operators.

## 3.3 More logical expressions

This chapter has already shown how C makes no distinction between 'logical' and other values. The relational operators all give a result of 0 or 1 for false and true, respectively. Whenever the control of flow statements demand it, an expression is evaluated to determine what to do next. A 0 means 'don't do it'; anything else means 'do'. It means that the fragments below are all quite reasonable.

```
while(a < b)...
while(a)....
if((c = getchar()) != EOF)...
```

No experienced C programmer would be surprised by any of them. The second of them, `while(a)`, is a common abbreviation for `while(a != 0)`, as you should be able to work out.

What we need now is a way of writing more complicated expressions involving these logical true and false values. So far, it has to be done like this, when we wanted to say `if(a < b AND c < d)`

```
if(a < b){
        if(c < d)...
}
```

It will not be a source of great amazement to find that there is a way of expressing such a statement.

There are three operators involved in this sort of operation: the logical AND `&&`, the logical OR `||` and the NOT `!`. The last is unary, the other two are binary. All of them take expressions as their operands and give as results either 1 or 0. The `&&` gives 1 only when both of its operands are non-zero. The `||` gives 0 only when both operands are zero. The `!` gives 0 if its operand is non-zero and vice versa. Easy really. The results are of type int for all three.

Do not confuse `&` and `|` (the bitwise operators) with their logical counterparts. They are not the same.

One special feature of the logical operators, found in very few of the other operators, is their effect on the sequence of evaluation of an expression. They evaluate left to right (after precedence is taken into account) and every logical expression ceases evaluation as soon as the overall result can be determined. For example, a sequence of `||`s can stop as soon as one operand is found to be non-zero. This next fragment guarantees never to divide by zero.

```
if(a != 0 && b / a > 5)...
/* alternative */
if(a && b / a > 5)
```

In either version `b / a` will only be evaluated if `a` is non-zero. If `a` were zero, the overall result would already have been decided, so the evaluation must stop to conform with C's rules for the logical operators.

The unary NOT is simple. It isn't all that common to see it in use largely because most expresssions can be rearranged to do without it. The examples show how.

```
if(!a)...
/* alternative */
if(a == 0)...

if(!(a > b))
/* alternative */
if(a <= b)
```

```
if(!(a > b && c < d))...
/* alternative */
if(a <= b || c >= d)...
```

Each of the examples and the alternatives serve to show ways of avoiding (or at least doing without) the ! operator. In fact, it's most useful as an aid to readability. If the problem that you are solving has a natural logical relationship inherent in it – say the (b * b - 4 * a * c) > 0 found in quadratic equation solving – then it probably reads better if you write if(!((b * b - 4 * a * c) > 0)) than if((b * b - 4 * a * c) <= 0) – but it's up to you. Pick the one that feels right.

Most expressions using these logical operators work out just about right in terms of the precedence rules, but you can get a few nasty surprises. If you look back to the precedence tables, you will find that there are some operators with lower precedence than the logical ones. In particular, this is a very common mistake:

```
if(a & b == c){...
```

What happens is that b is compared for equality with c, then the 1 or 0 result is anded with a! Some distinctly unexpected behaviour has been caused by that sort of error.

## 3.4 Strange operators

There are two operators left to mention which look decidedly odd. They aren't 'essential', but from time to time do have their uses. Don't ignore them completely. This is the only place where we describe them, so our description includes what happens when they are mixed with pointer types, which makes them look more complicated than they really are.

### 3.4.1 The ?: operator

Like playing the accordion, this is easier to demonstrate than to describe.

*expression1?expression2:expression3*

If *expression1* is true, then the result of the whole expression is *expression2*, otherwise it is *expression3*; depending on the value of *expression1*, only one of them will be evaluated when the result is calculated.

The various combinations of types that are permitted for *expression2* and *expression3* and, based on those, the resulting type of the whole expression, are complicated. A lot of the complexity is due to types and notions that we haven't seen so far. For completeness they are described in detail below, but you'll have to put up with a number of forward references.

The easiest case is when both expressions have arithmetic type (that is, integral or real). The usual arithmetic conversions are applied to find a common type for both expressions and then that is the type of the result. For example

```
a > b ? 1 : 3.5
```

contains a constant (1) of type int and another (3.5) of type double. Applying the arithmetic conversions gives a result of type double.

Other combinations are also permitted.

- If both operands are of compatible structure or union types, then that is the type of the result.
- If both operands have void type, then that is the type of the result.

Various pointer types can be mixed.

- Both operands may be pointers to (possibly **qualified**) compatible types.
- One operand may be a pointer and the other a **null pointer constant**.
- One operand may be a **pointer to an object or incomplete type** and the other a pointer to (possibly qualified) void.

The type of the result when pointers are involved is derived in two separate steps.

(1) If either of the operands is a pointer to a qualified type, the result is a pointer to a type that is qualified by all the qualifiers of both operands.

(2) If one operand is a null pointer constant, then the result has the type of the other operand. If one operand is a pointer to void, the other operand is converted to pointer to void and that is the type of the result. If both operands are pointers to compatible types (ignoring any qualifiers) then the result has the **composite type**.

Qualifiers, composite types and compatible types are all subjects discussed later.

The shortest useful example that we can think of is this one, where the string to be printed by printf is selected using this magical operator.

```
#include ⟨stdio.h⟩
#include ⟨stdlib.h⟩

main(){
        int i;

        for(i = 0; i <= 10; i++){
                printf((i & 1) ? "odd\n" : "even\n");
        }
        exit(EXIT_SUCCESS);
}
```
**(Example 3.9)**

It's cute when you need it, but the first time that they see it most people look very uncomfortable for a while, then recollect an urgent appointment somewhere else.

After evaluating the first operand there is one of the **sequence points** described in Chapter 8.


### 3.4.2 The comma operator

This wins the prize for 'most obscure operator'. It allows a list of expressions to be separated by commas:

*expression-1, expression-2, expression-3, ..., expression-n*

and it goes on as long as you like. The *expressions* are evaluated strictly left to right and their values discarded, except for the last one, whose type and value determine the result of the overall expression. Don't confuse this version of the comma with any of the other uses C finds for it, especially the one that separates function arguments. Here are a couple of examples of it in use.

```c
#include <stdio.h>
#include <stdlib.h>

main(){
        int i, j;

        /* comma used — this loop has two counters */
        for(i = 0, j = 0; i <= 10; i++, j = i * i){
                printf("i %d j %d\n", i, j);
        }

        /*
         * In this futile example, all but the last
         * constant value is discarded.
         * Note use of parentheses to force a comma
         * expression in a function call.
         */
        printf("Overall: %d\n", ("abc", 1.2e6, 4 * 3 + 2));
        exit(EXIT_SUCCESS);
}
```
(Example 3.10)

Unless you are feeling very adventurous, the comma operator is just as well ignored. Be prepared to see it only on special occasions.

After evaluating each operand there is one of the **sequence points** described in Chapter 8.

## ■ 3.5 SUMMARY

This chapter has described the entire range of control of flow available in C. The only areas that cause even moderate surprise are the way in which cases in a switch statement are not mutually exclusive, and the fact that goto cannot transfer control to any function except the one that is currently active. None of this is intellectually deep and it has never been known to cause problems either to beginners or programmers experienced in other languages.

The logical expressions all give integral results. This is perhaps slightly unusual, but once again takes very little time to learn.

Probably the most surprising part about the whole chapter will have been to learn of the conditional and comma operators. A strong case could be made for the abolition of the conditional operator, were it not for compatibility with existing code, but the comma operator does have important uses, especially for automatic generators of C programs.

The Standard has not had much effect on the contents of this chapter. Prospective users of C should ensure that they are completely familiar with all of the topics discussed here (except the conditional and comma operators). They are essential to the practical use of the language, and none of the material is hard.

## EXERCISES

**3.1** What is the type and value of the result of the relational operators?

**3.2** What is the type and value of the result of the logical operators (&&, ||, and !)?

**3.3** What is unusual about the logical operators?

**3.4** Why is break useful in switch statements?

**3.5** Why is continue not very useful in switch statements?

**3.6** What is a possible problem using continue in while statements?

**3.7** How can you jump from one function to another?

# CHAPTER 4

# Functions

## 4.1 Changes

The single worst feature of Old C was that there was no way to declare the number and types of a function's arguments and to have the compiler check that the use of the function was consistent with its declaration. Although it didn't do a lot of damage to the success of C, it did result in portability and maintainability problems that we all could have done without.

The Standard has changed that state of affairs. You can now declare functions in a way that allows their use to be checked, and which is also largely compatible with the old style (so old programs still work, provided they had no errors before). Another useful feature is a portable way of using functions with a variable number of arguments, like printf, which used to be non-portable; the only way to implement it relied upon intimate knowledge of the hardware involved.

The Standard's way of fixing this problem was in large measure to plagiarize from C++, which had already tried out the new ideas in practice. This model has been so successful that lots of 'Old' C compilers adopted it on their way to conforming to the Standard.

The Standard still retains compatibility with Old C function declarations, but that is purely for the benefit of existing programs. Any new programs should make full use of the much tighter checking that the Standard permits and strenuously avoid the old syntax (which may disappear one day).

## 4.2 The type of functions

All functions have a type: they return a value of that type whenever they are used. The reason that C doesn't have 'procedures', which in most other languages are simply functions without a value, is that in C it is permissible (in fact well-nigh mandatory) to discard the eventual value of most expressions. If that surprises you, think of an assignment

```
a = 1;
```

That's a perfectly valid assignment, but don't forget that it has a value too. The value is discarded. If you want a bigger surprise, try this one:

```
1;
```

That is an expression followed by a semicolon. It is a well formed statement according to the rules of the language; nothing wrong with it, it is just useless. A function used as a procedure is used in the same way – a value is *always* returned, but you don't use it:

```
f(argument);
```

is also an expression with a discarded value.

It's all very well saying that the value returned by a function can be ignored, but the fact remains that if the function really *does* return a value then it's probably a programming error not to do something with it. Conversely, if no useful value is returned then it's a good idea to be able to spot anywhere that it is used by mistake. For both of those reasons, functions that don't return a useful value should be declared to be void.

Functions can return any type supported by C (except for arrays and functions), including the pointers, structures and unions which are described in later chapters. For the types that can't be returned from functions, the restrictions can often be sidestepped by using pointers instead.

All functions can be called recursively .

### 4.2.1 Declaring functions

Unfortunately, we are going to have to use some jargon now. This is one of the times that the use of an appropriate technical term really does reduce the amount of repetitive descriptive text that would be needed. With a bit of luck, the result is a shorter, more accurate and less confusing explanation. Here are the terms:

*declaration*
> The point at which a name has a type associated with it.

*definition*
> Also a declaration, but at this point some storage is reserved for the named object. The rules for what makes a declaration into a definition can be complicated, but are easy for functions: you turn a function declaration into a

definition by providing a body for the function in the form of a compound statement.

*formal parameters*
*parameters*

These are the names used inside a function to refer to its arguments.

*actual arguments*
*arguments*

These are the values used as arguments when the function is actually called. In other words, the values that the *formal parameters* will have on entry to the function.

The terms 'parameter' and 'argument' do tend to get used as if they were interchangeable, so don't read too much into it if you see one or the other in the text below.

If you use a function before you declare it, it is implicitly declared to be 'function returning int'. Although this will work, and was widely used in Old C, in Standard C it is bad practice – the use of undeclared functions leads to nasty problems to do with the number and type of arguments that are expected for them. All functions should be fully declared before they are used. For example, you might be intending to use a function in a private library called, say, aax1. You know that it takes no arguments and returns a double. Here is how it should be declared:

```
double aax1(void);
```

and here is how it might be used:

```
main (){
        double return_v, aax1(void);
        return_v = aax1();
        exit(EXIT_SUCCESS);
}
```
                                                                        **(Example 4.1)**

The declaration was an interesting one. It defined return_v, actually causing a variable to come into existence. It also declared aax1 without defining it; as we know, functions only become *defined* when a body is provided for them. Without a declaration in force, the default rules mean that aax1 would have been assumed to be int, even though it really does return a double – which means that your program will have undefined behaviour. Undefined behaviour is disastrous!

The presence of void in the argument list in the declaration shows that the function really takes no arguments. If it had been missing, the declaration would have been taken to give no information about the function's arguments. That way, compatibility with Old C is maintained at the price of the ability of the compiler to check.

To **define** a function you also have to provide a body for it, in the form of a compound statement. Since no function can itself contain the definition of a function, functions are all separate from each other and are only found at the outermost level of the program's structure. Here is a possible definition for the function aax1.

```
double
aax1(void) {
        /* code for function body */
        return(1.0);
}
```

It is unusual for a block-structured language to prohibit you from defining functions inside other functions, but this is one of the characteristics of C. Although it isn't obvious, this helps to improve the run-time performance of C by reducing the housekeeping associated with function calls.

### 4.2.2 The return statement

The return statement is very important. Every function except those returning void should have at least one, each return showing what value is supposed to be returned at that point. Although it is possible to return from a function by falling through the last }, unless the function returns void an unknown value will be returned, resulting in undefined behaviour.

Here is another example function. It uses getchar to read characters from the program input and returns whatever it sees except for space, tab or newline, which it throws away.

```
#include <stdio.h>

int
non_space(void){
        int c;
        while ( (c = getchar ()) == '\t' || c == '\n' || c == ' ')
                ; /* empty statement */
        return(c);
}
```

Look at the way that all of the work is done by the test in the while statement, whose body was an empty statement. It is not an uncommon sight to see the semicolon of the empty statement sitting there alone and forlorn, with only a piece of comment for company and readability. Please, please, never write it like this:

```
while(something);
```

with the semicolon hidden away at the end like that. It's too easy to miss it when you read the code, and to assume that the following statement is under the control of the while.

The type of expression returned must match the type of the function, or be capable of being converted to it as if an assignment statement were in use. For example, a function declared to return double could contain

```
return(1);
```

and the integral value will be converted to double. It is also possible to have just return without any expression – but this is probably a programming error unless the function returns void. Following the return with an expression is *not* permitted if the function returns void.

### 4.2.3 Arguments to functions

Before the Standard, it was not possible to give any information about a function's arguments except in the definition of the function itself. The information was only used in the body of the function and was forgotten at the end. In those bad old days, it was quite possible to define a function that had three double arguments and only to pass it one int when it was called. The program would compile normally, but simply not work properly. It was considered to be the programmer's job to check that the number and the type of arguments to a function matched correctly. As you would expect, this turned out to be a first-rate source of bugs and portability problems. Here is an example of the definition and use of a function with arguments, but omitting for the moment to declare the function fully.

```
#include ⟨stdio.h⟩
#include ⟨stdlib.h⟩

main(){
        void pmax();                    /* declaration */
        int i, j;

        for(i = -10; i <= 10; i++){
                for(j = -10; j <= 10; j++){
                        pmax(i, j);
                }
        }
        exit(EXIT_SUCCESS);
}
/*
 * Function pmax.
 * Returns:     void
 * Prints larger of its two arguments.
 */
void
pmax(int a1, int a2){                    /* definition */
        int biggest;
```

```
        if(a1 > a2){
                biggest = a1;
        }else{
                biggest = a2;
        }
        printf("larger of %d and %d is %d\n",
                a1, a2, biggest);
}                                                    (Example 4.2)
```

What can we learn from this? To start with, notice the careful declaration that pmax returns void. In the function definition, the matching void occurs on the line before the function name. The reason for writing it like that is purely one of style; it makes it easier to find function definitions if their names are always at the beginning of a line.

The function declaration (in main) gave no indication of any arguments to the function, yet the use of the function a couple of lines later involved two arguments. That is permitted by both the old and Standard versions of C, but *must nowadays be considered to be bad practice*. It is much better to include information about the arguments in the declaration too, as we will see. The old style is now an 'obsolescent feature' and may disappear in a later version of the Standard.

Now on to the function definition, where the body is supplied. The definition shows that the function takes two arguments, which will be known as a1 and a2 throughout the body of the function. The types of the arguments are specified too, as can be seen.

In the function definition you don't *have* to specify the type of each argument because they will default to int, but this is bad style. If you adopt the practice of always declaring arguments, even if they do happen to be int, it adds to a reader's confidence. It indicates that you meant to use that type, instead of getting it by accident: it wasn't simply forgotten. The definition of pmax *could* have been this:

```
/* BAD STYLE OF FUNCTION DEFINITION */

void
pmax(a1, a2){
        /* and so on */
```

The proper way to declare and define functions is through the use of **prototypes**.

### 4.2.4 Function prototypes

The introduction of **function prototypes** is the biggest change of all in the Standard.

A function prototype is a function declaration or definition which includes information about the number and types of the arguments that the function takes.

Although you are allowed not to specify any information about a function's arguments in a declaration, it is purely because of backwards compatibility with Old C and should be avoided.

A declaration without any information about the arguments is *not* a prototype.

Here's the previous example 'done right':

```
#include (stdio.h)
#include (stdlib.h)

main(){
        void pmax(int first, int second);     /*declaration*/
        int i, j;

        for(i = -10; i <= 10; i++){
                for(j = -10; j <= 10; j++){
                        pmax(i, j);
                }
        }
        exit(EXIT_SUCCESS);
}

void
pmax(int a1, int a2){                          /*definition*/
        int biggest;

        if(a1 > a2){
                biggest = a1;
        }
        else{
                biggest = a2;
        }
        printf("largest of %d and %d is %d\n",
                a1, a2, biggest);
}
```
                                                                    (Example 4.3)

This time, the declaration provides information about the function arguments, so it's a prototype. The names first and second are not an essential part of the declaration, but they are allowed to be there because it makes it easier to refer to named arguments when you're documenting the use of the function. Using them, we can describe the function simply by giving its declaration

```
void pmax (int xx, int yy );
```

and then say that pmax prints whichever of the arguments xx or yy is the larger. Referring to arguments by their position, which is the alternative (for example, the fifth argument), is tedious and prone to miscounting.

All the same, you can miss out the names if you want to. This declaration is entirely equivalent to the one above.

```
void pmax (int, int);
```

All that is needed is the type names.

For a function that has no arguments the declaration is

```
void f_name (void);
```

and a function that has one `int`, one `double` and an unspecified number of other arguments is declared this way:

```
void f_name (int, double, ...);
```

The ellipsis ( ... ) shows that other arguments follow. That's useful because it allows functions like `printf` to be written. Its declaration is this:

```
int printf (const char *format_string, ...)
```

where the type of the first argument is 'pointer to `const char`'; we'll discuss what that means later.

Once the compiler knows the types of a function's arguments, having seen them in a prototype, it's able to check that the use of the function conforms to the declaration.

If a function is called with arguments of the wrong type, the presence of a prototype means that the actual argument is converted to the type of the formal argument 'as if by assignment'. Here's an example: a function is used to evaluate a square root using Newton's method of successive approximations.

```
#include ⟨stdio.h⟩
#include ⟨stdlib.h⟩

#define DELTA 0.0001

main(){
        double sq_root(double); /* prototype */
        int i;

        for(i = 1; i < 100; i++){
                printf("root of %d is %f\n", i, sq_root(i));
        }
        exit(EXIT_SUCCESS);
}

double
sq_root(double x){        /* definition */
        double curr_appx, last_appx, diff;

        last_appx = x;
        diff = DELTA + 1;
```

```
        while(diff > DELTA){
                curr_appx = 0.5 * (last_appx + x / last_appx);
                diff = curr_appx - last_appx;
                if(diff < 0)
                        diff = -diff;
                last_appx = curr_appx;
        }
        return(curr_appx);
}
```
(Example 4.4)

The prototype tells everyone that sq_root takes a single argument of type double. The argument actually passed in the main function is an int, so it has to be converted to double first. The critical point is that if no prototype had been seen, C would assume that the programmer had meant to pass an int and an int is what would be passed. The Standard simply notes that this results in undefined behaviour, which is as understated as saying that catching rabies is unfortunate. This is a *very serious error* and has led to many, many problems in Old C programs.

The conversion of int to double could be done because the compiler had seen a prototype for the function and knew what to do about it. As you would expect, there are various rules used to decide which conversions are appropriate, so we need to look at them next.

### 4.2.5  Argument conversions

When a function is called, there are a number of possible conversions that will be applied to the values supplied as arguments depending on the presence or absence of a prototype. Let's get one thing clear: although you *can* use these rules to work out what to do if you haven't used prototypes, it is a recipe for pain and misery in the long run. It's so easy to use prototypes that there really is no excuse for not having them, so the only time you will need to use these rules is if you are being adventurous and using functions with a variable number of arguments, using the ellipsis notation in the prototype that is explained in Chapter 9.

The rules mention the **default argument promotions and compatible type**. Where they are used, the default argument promotions are:

- Apply the integral promotions (see Chapter 2) to the value of each argument.
- If the type of the argument is float it is converted to double.

The introduction of prototypes (amongst other things) has increased the need for precision about 'compatible types', which was not much of an issue in Old C. The full list of rules for type compatibility is deferred until Chapter 8, because we suspect that most C programmers will never need to learn them. For the moment, we will simply work on the basis that if two types are the same, they are indisputably compatible.

The conversions are applied according to these rules (which are intended to be guidance on how to apply the Standard, not a direct quote):

(1) At the point of calling a function, if no prototype is in scope, the arguments all undergo the default argument promotions. Furthermore:

- If the number of arguments does not agree with the number of formal parameters to the function, the behaviour is undefined.
- If the function definition was *not* a definition containing a prototype, then the type of the actual arguments after promotion must be **compatible** with the types of the formal parameters in the definition after they too have had the promotions applied. Otherwise the behaviour is undefined.
- If the function definition *was* a definition containing a prototype, and the types of the actual arguments after promotion are not compatible with the formal parameters in the prototype, then the behaviour is undefined. The behaviour is also undefined if the prototype included ellipsis (, ...).

(2) At the point of calling a function, if a prototype *is* in scope, the arguments are converted, as if by assignment, to the types specified in the prototype. Any arguments which fall under the variable argument list category (specified by the ... in the prototype) still undergo the default argument conversions.

It *is* possible to write a program so badly that you have a prototype in scope when you call the function, but for the function definition itself not to have a prototype. Why anyone should do this is a mystery, but in this case, the function that is called must have a type that is **compatible** with the apparent type at the point of the call.

The order of evaluation of the arguments in the function call is explicitly not defined by the Standard.

### 4.2.6 Function definitions

Function prototypes allow the same text to be used for both the declaration and definition of a function. To turn a declaration:

```
double
some_func(int a1, float a2, long double a3);
```

into a definition, we provide a body for the function:

```
double
some_func(int a1, float a2, long double a3){
        /* body of function */
        return(1.0);
}
```

by replacing the semicolon at the end of the declaration with a compound statement.

In either a definition or a declaration of a function, it serves as a prototype if the parameter types are specified; both of the examples above are prototypes.

The Old C syntax for the declaration of a function's formal arguments is still supported by the Standard, although it should not be used by new programs. It looks like this, for the example above:

```
double
some_func(a1, a2, a3)
        int a1;
        float a2;
        long double a3;
{
        /* body of function */
        return(1.0);
}
```

Because no type information is provided for the parameters at the point where they are named, this form of definition does *not* act as a prototype. It declares only the return type of the function; nothing is remembered by the compiler about the types of the arguments at the end of the definition.

The Standard warns that support for this syntax may disappear in a later version. It will not be discussed further.

□  **SUMMARY**

○ Functions can be called recursively.

○ Functions can return any type that you can declare, except for arrays and functions (you can get around that restriction to some extent by using pointers). Functions returning no value should return void.

○ Always use function prototypes.

○ Undefined behaviour results if you call or define a function anywhere in a program unless either
    – a prototype is *always* in scope for *every* call or definition, or
    – you are very, very careful.

○ Assuming that you *are* using prototypes, the values of the arguments to a function call are converted to the types of the formal parameters exactly as if they had been assigned using the = operator.

○ Functions taking no arguments should have a prototype with (void) as the argument specification.

○ Functions taking a variable number of arguments must take at least one named argument; the variable arguments are indicated by ... as shown:
```
int
vfunc(int x, float y, ...);
```
Chapter 9 describes how to write this sort of function.

### 4.2.7 Compound statements and declarations

As we have seen, functions always have a compound statement as their body. It is possible to declare new variables inside any compound statement; if any variables of the same name already exist, then the old ones are hidden by the new ones within the new compound statement. This is the same as in every other block-structured language. C restricts the declarations to the head of the compound statement (or 'block'); once any other kind of statement has been seen in the block, declarations are no longer permitted within that block.

How can it be possible for names to be hidden? The following example shows it happening:

```
int a;              /* visible from here onwards */

void func(void){
        float a;    /* a different 'a' */
        {
                char a; /* yet another 'a' */
        }
                    /* the float 'a' reappears */
}
                    /* the int 'a' reappears */          (Example 4.5)
```

A name declared inside a block hides any outer versions of the same name until the end of the block where it is declared. Inner blocks can also re-declare that name – you can do this for ever.

The **scope** of a name is the range in which it has meaning. Scope starts from the point at which the name is mentioned and continues from there onwards to the end of the block in which it is declared. If it is external (outside of any function) then it continues to the end of the file. If it is internal (inside a function), then it disappears at the end of the block containing it. The scope of any name can be suspended by redeclaring the name inside a block.

Using knowledge of the scope rules, you can play silly tricks like this one:

```
main () {}
int i;
f () {}
f2 () {}
```

Now f and f2 can use i, but main can't, because the declaration of the variable comes later than that of main. This is not an aspect that is used very much, but it is implicit in the way that C processes declarations. It is a source of confusion for anyone reading the file (external declarations are generally expected to precede any function definitions in a file) and should be avoided.

The Standard has changed things slightly with respect to a function's formal parameters. They are now considered to have been declared inside the first compound statement, even though textually they aren't: this goes for both the new and old ways of function definition. So, if a function has a formal parameter with the same name as something declared in the outermost compound statement, this causes an error which will be detected by the compiler.

In Old C, accidental redefinition of a function's formal parameter was a horrible and particularly difficult mistake to track down. Here is what it would look like:

```
/* erroneous redeclaration of arguments */

func(a, b, c){
        int a;  /* AAAAgh! */
}
```

The pernicious bit is the new declaration of a in the body of the function, which hides the parameter called a. Since the problem has now been eliminated we won't investigate it any further.

## 4.3 Recursion and argument passing

So far, we've seen how to give functions a type (how to declare the return value and the type of any arguments the function takes), and how the definition is used to give the body of the function. Next we need to see what the arguments can be used for.

### 4.3.1 Call by value

The way that C treats arguments to functions is both simple and consistent, with no exceptions to the single rule.

When a function is called, any arguments that are provided by the caller are simply treated as expressions. The value of each expression has the appropriate conversions applied and is then used to initialize the corresponding formal parameter in the called function, which behaves in exactly the same way as any other local variables in the function. It's illustrated here:

```
void called_func(int, float);

main(){
        called_func(1, 2 * 3.5);
        exit(EXIT_SUCCESS);
}

void
called_func(int iarg, float farg){
        float tmp;

        tmp = iarg * farg;
}                                                    (Example 4.6)
```

The arguments to called_func in main are two expressions, which are evaluated. The value of each expression is used to initialize the parameters iarg and farg in called_func, and the parameters are indistinguishable from the other local variable declared in called_func, which is tmp.

The initialization of the formal parameters is the last time that any communication occurs between the caller and the called function, except for the return value.

For those who are used to FORTRAN and var arguments in Pascal, where a function *can* change the values of its arguments: forget it. You cannot affect the values of a function's actual arguments by anything that you try. Here is an example to show what we mean:

```
#include ⟨stdio.h⟩
#include ⟨stdlib.h⟩

main(){
        void changer(int);
        int i;

        i = 5;
        printf("before i=%d\n", i);
        changer(i);
        printf("after i=%d\n", i);
        exit(EXIT_SUCCESS);
}

void
changer(int x){
        while(x){
                printf("changer: x=%d\n", x);
                x--;
        }
}
```
(Example 4.7)

The result of running that is:

```
before i = 5
changer: x = 5
changer: x = 4
changer: x = 3
changer: x = 2
changer: x = 1
after i = 5
```

The function changer uses its formal parameter x as an ordinary variable – which is exactly what it is. Although the value of x is changed, the variable i (in main) is unaffected. That is the whole point – the arguments in C are passed into a function by their value only, no changes made by the function are passed back.

## 4.3.2 Call by reference

It is possible to write functions that take **pointers** as their arguments, giving a form of call by reference. This is described in Chapter 5 and *does* allow functions to change values in their callers.

## 4.3.3 Recursion

With argument passing safely out of the way we can look at recursion. Recursion is a topic that often provokes lengthy and unenlightening arguments from opposing camps. Some think it is wonderful, and use it at every opportunity; some others take exactly the opposite view. Let's just say that when you need it, you really *do* need it, and since it doesn't cost much to put into a language, as you would expect, C supports recursion.

Every function in C may be called from any other or itself. Each invocation of a function causes a new allocation of the variables declared inside it. In fact, the declarations that we have been using until now have had something missing: the keyword auto, meaning 'automatically allocated'.

```
/* Example of auto */
main(){
        auto int var_name;
        .
        .
        .
}
```

The storage for auto variables is automatically allocated and freed on function entry and return. If two functions both declare large automatic arrays, the program will only have to find room for both arrays if both functions are active at the same time. Although auto is a keyword, it is never used in practice because it's the default for internal declarations and is invalid for external ones. If an explicit initial value (see Chapter 6) isn't given for an automatic variable, then its value will be unknown when it is declared. In that state, any use of its value will cause undefined behaviour.

The real problem with illustrating recursion is in the selection of examples. Too often, simple examples are used which don't really get much out of recursion. The problems where it really helps are almost always well out of the grasp of a beginner who is having enough trouble trying to sort out the difference between, say, definition and declaration without wanting the extra burden of having to wrap his or her mind around a new concept as well. The chapter on data structures will show examples of recursion where it is a genuinely useful technique.

The following example uses recursive functions to evaluate expressions involving single digit numbers, the operators *, %, /, +, - and parentheses in the same way that C does. (Stroustrop[†], in his book about C++, uses almost an identical example to illustrate recursion. This happened purely by chance.) The whole expression is

[†]Stroustrop B. (1991). *The C++ Programming Language* 2nd edn. Reading, MA: Addison-Wesley

evaluated and its value printed when a character not in the 'language' is read. For simplicity no error checking is performed. Extensive use is made of the ungetc library function, which allows the last character read by getchar to be 'unread' and become once again the next character to be read. Its second argument is one of the things declared in stdio.h.

Those of you who understand BNF notation might like to know that the expressions it will understand are described as follows:

```
⟨primary⟩ ::= digit | (⟨exp⟩)
⟨unary⟩   ::= ⟨primary⟩ | -⟨unary⟩ | +⟨unary⟩
⟨mult⟩    ::= ⟨unary⟩ | ⟨mult⟩ * ⟨unary⟩ |
              ⟨mult⟩ / ⟨unary⟩ | ⟨mult⟩ % ⟨unary⟩
⟨exp⟩     ::= ⟨exp⟩ + ⟨mult⟩ | ⟨exp⟩ - ⟨mult⟩ | ⟨mult⟩
```

The main places where recursion occurs are in the function unary_exp, which calls itself, and at the bottom level where primary calls the top level all over again to evaluate parenthesized expressions.

If you don't understand what it does, try running it. Trace its actions by hand on inputs such as

```
1
1 + 2
1 + 2 * 3 + 4
1 + --4
1 + (2 * 3) + 4
```

That should keep you busy for a while!

```
/*
 * Recursive descent parser for simple C expressions.
 * Very little error checking.
 */
#include ⟨stdio.h⟩
#include ⟨stdlib.h⟩

int expr(void);
int mul_exp(void);
int unary_exp(void);
int primary(void);

main(){
        int val;

        for(;;){
                printf("expression: ");
                val = expr();
                if(getchar() != '\n'){
                        printf("error\n");
                        while(getchar() != '\n')
                                ; /* NULL */
```

```
        } else{
                printf("result is %d\n", val);
        }
    }
    exit(EXIT_SUCCESS);
}

int
expr(void){
    int val, ch_in;

    val = mul_exp();
    for(;;){
        switch(ch_in = getchar()){
        default:
                ungetc(ch_in, stdin);
                return(val);
        case '+':
                val = val + mul_exp();
                break;
        case '-':
                val = val - mul_exp();
                break;
        }
    }
}

int
mul_exp(void){
    int val, ch_in;

    val = unary_exp();
    for(;;){
        switch(ch_in = getchar()){
        default:
                ungetc(ch_in, stdin);
                return(val);
        case '*':
                val = val * unary_exp();
                break;
        case '/':
                val = val / unary_exp();
                break;
        case '%':
                val = val % unary_exp();
                break;
        }
    }
}
```

```
int
unary_exp(void){
        int val, ch_in;

        switch(ch_in = getchar()){
        default:
                ungetc(ch_in, stdin);
                val = primary();
                break;
        case '+':
                val = unary_exp();
                break;
        case '-':
                val = -unary_exp();
                break;
        }
        return(val);
}


int
primary(void){
        int val, ch_in;

        ch_in = getchar();
        if(ch_in >= '0' && ch_in <= '9'){
                val = ch_in - '0';
                goto out;
        }
        if(ch_in == '('){
                val = expr();
                getchar();        /* skip closing ')' */
                goto out;
        }
        printf("error: primary read %d\n", ch_in);
        exit(EXIT_FAILURE);
out:
        return(val);
}
```

(Example 4.8)

## 4.4 Linkage

Although the simple examples have carefully avoided the topic, we now have to look into the effects of scope and linkage, terms used to describe the accessibility of various objects in a C program. Why bother? It's because realistic programs are built up out of multiple files and of course libraries. It is clearly crucial that functions in one file should be able to refer to functions (or other objects) in other files and libraries; naturally there are a number of concepts and rules that apply to this mechanism.

If you are relatively new to C, there are more important subjects to cover first. Come back to this stuff later instead.

There are essentially two types of object in C: the internal and external objects. The distinction between external and internal is to do with functions: anything declared outside a function is external, anything inside one, including its formal parameters, is internal. Since no function can be defined inside another, functions themselves are always external. At the outermost level, a C program is a collection of **external objects**.

Only external objects participate in this cross-file and library communication.

The term used by the Standard to describe the accessibility of objects from one file to another, or even within the same file, is **linkage**. There are three types of linkage: **external linkage**, **internal linkage** and **no linkage**. Anything internal to a function – its arguments, variables and so on – *always* has no linkage and so can only be accessed from inside the function itself. (The way around this is to declare something inside a function but prefix it with the keyword extern which says 'it isn't really internal', but we needn't worry about that just yet.)

Objects that have external linkage are all considered to be located at the outermost level of the program; this is the default linkage for functions and anything declared outside of a function. *All instances of a particular name with external linkage refer to the same object in the program.* If two or more declarations of the same name have external linkage but incompatible types, then you've done something very silly and have undefined behaviour. The most obvious example of external linkage is the printf function, whose declaration in ⟨stdio.h⟩ is

```
int printf(const char *, ...);
```

From that we can tell that it's a function returning int and with a particular prototype – so we know everything about its type. We also know that it has external linkage, because that is the default for every external object. As a result, everywhere that the name printf is used with external linkage, we are referring to this function.

Quite often, you want to be able to declare functions and other objects within a single file in a way that allows them to reference each other but *not* to be accessible from outside that file. This is often necessary in the modules that support library functions, where the additional framework that makes those functions work is not interesting to the user and would be a positive nuisance if the names of those things became visible outside the module. You do it through the use of **internal linkage**.

Names with internal linkage only refer to the same object within a single source file. You do this by prefixing their declarations with the keyword static, which changes the linkage of external objects from external linkage to internal linkage. It is also possible to declare internal objects to be static, but that has an entirely different meaning which we can defer for the moment.

It's confusing that the types of linkage and the types of object are both described by the terms 'internal' and 'external'; this is to some extent historical. C archaeologists may know that at one time the two were equivalent and one implied the other – for us it's unfortunate that the terms remain but the meanings have diverged. Linkage and accessibility are summarized in Table 4.1.

**Table 4.1**   Linkage and accessibility.

| Type of linkage | Type of object | Accessibility |
| --- | --- | --- |
| external | external | throughout the program |
| internal | external | a single file |
| none | internal | local to a single function |

Finally, before we see an example, it is important to know that all objects with external linkage must have one and only one definition, although there can be as many compatible declarations as you like. Here's the example.

```
/* first file */

int i; /* definition */
main () {
        void f_in_other_place (void);   /* declaration */
        i = 0;
}
/* end of first file */

/* start of second file */

extern int i; /* declaration */
void
f_in_other_place (void){                /* definition */
        i++;
}
/* end of second file */
```
                                                                **(Example 4.9)**

Although the full set of rules is a bit more complex, the basic way of working out what constitutes a definition and a declaration is not hard:

- A function declaration without a body for the function is just a declaration.
- A function declaration with a body for the function is a definition.
- At the external level, a declaration of an object (like the variable i) is a definition unless it has the keyword extern in front of it, when it is a declaration only.

Chapter 8 revisits the definition and declaration criteria to a depth that will cause decompression sickness when you surface.

In the example it's easy to see that each file is able to access the objects defined in the other by using their names. Just from that example alone you should be able to work out how to construct programs with multiple files and functions and variables declared or defined as appropriate in each of them.

Here's another example, using static to restrict the accessibility of functions and other things.

```
/* example library module */
/* only 'callable' is visible outside */
static int buf [100];
static int length;
static void fillup(void);

int
callable (){
        if(length == 0){
                fillup();
        }
        return(buf[length--]);
}

static void
fillup (void){
        while(length < 100){
                buf[length++] = 0;
        }
}
```
                                                                    (Example 4.10)

A user of this module can safely re-use the names declared here, length, buf, and fillup, without any danger of surprising effects. Only the name callable is accessible outside this module.

A very useful thing to know is that any external object that has no other initializer (and except for functions we haven't seen any initializers yet) is always set to the value of zero before the program starts. This is widely used and relied on – the previous example relies on it for the initial value of length.

*Effect of scope*

There's one additional complicating factor beyond simply linkage. Linkage allows you to couple names together on a per-program or a per-file basis, but scope determines the visibility of the names. Fortunately, the rules of scope are completely independent of anything to do with linkage, so you don't have to remember funny combinations of both.

What introduces the complexity is the dreaded extern keyword. The nice regular block structure gets blown to pieces with this, which although at a first glance is simple and obvious, does some very nasty things to the fabric of the language. We'll leave its nasty problems to Chapter 8, since they only rear up if you deliberately start to do perverse things with it and then say 'what does this mean'? We've already seen it used to ensure that the declaration of something at the outer block level (the external level) of the program is a declaration and not a definition (but beware: you can still override the extern by, for example, providing an **initializer** for the object).

Unless you prefix it with `extern`, the declaration of any data object (not a function) at the outer level is also a definition. Look back to Example 4.9 to see this in use.

All function declarations implicitly have the `extern` stuck in front of them, whether or not you put it there too. These two ways of declaring `some_function` are equivalent and are always declarations:

```
void some_function(void);

extern void some_function(void);
```

The thing that mysteriously turns those declarations into definitions is that when you also provide the body of the function, that is effectively the initializer for the function, so the comment about initializers comes into effect and the declaration becomes a definition. So far, no problem.

Now, what is going on here?

```
void
some_function(void){
        int i_var;
        extern float e_f_var;
}

void
another_func(void){
        int i;

        i = e_f_var;    /* scope problem*/
}
```

What happened was that although the declaration of `e_f_var` declares that something called `e_f_var` is of type `float` and is accessible throughout the entire program, the *scope* of the name disappears at the end of the function that contains it. That's why it is meaningless inside `another_func` – the name of `e_f_var` is out of scope, just as much as `i_var` is.

So what use is that? It's sometimes handy if you only want to make use of an external object from within a single function. If you followed the usual practice and declared it at the head of the particular source file, then there is no easy way for the reader of that file to see which functions actually use it. By restricting the access and the scope of the name to the place where it is needed, you do communicate to a later reader of the program that this is a very restricted use of the name and that there is no intention to make widespread use of it throughout the file. Of course, any half-way decent cross-reference listing would communicate that anyway, so the argument is a bit hard to maintain.

Chapter 8 is the place to find out more. There's a set of guidelines for how to get the results that are most often wanted from multi-file construction, and a good deal more detail on what happens when you mix extern, static and internal and external declarations. It isn't the sort of reading that you're likely to do for pleasure, but it does answer the 'what if' questions.

*Internal* static

You are also allowed to declare internal objects as static. Internal variables with this attribute have some interesting properties: they are initialized to zero when the program starts, they retain their value between entry to and exit from the statement containing their declaration and there is only one copy of each one, which is shared between all recursive calls of the function containing it.

Internal statics can be used for a number of things. One is to count the number of times that a function has been called; unlike ordinary internal variables whose value is lost after leaving their function, statics are convenient for this. Here's a function that always returns a number between 0 and 15, but remembers how often it was called.

```
int
small_val (void) {
        static unsigned count;
        count++;
        return (count % 16);
}
```
(Example 4.11)

They can help detect excessive recursion:

```
void
r_func (void){
        static int depth;

        depth++;
        if(depth > 200){
                printf ("excessive recursion\n");
                exit (EXIT_FAILURE);
        }
        else {
                /* do usual thing,
                 * not shown here.
                 * This last action
                 * occasionally results in another
                 * call on r_func()
                 */
                x_func();
        }
        depth--;
}
```
(Example 4.12)

**Table 4.2** Summary of linkage.

| Declaration | Keyword | Resulting linkage | Accessibility | Note |
|---|---|---|---|---|
| external | none | external | entire program | 2 |
| external | extern | external | entire program | 2 |
| external | static | internal | a single file | 2 |
| internal | none | none | a single function | |
| internal | extern | external | entire program | 1 |
| internal | static | none | a single function | 2 |

1. Although the accessibility of internal declarations prefixed with extern is program-wide, watch out for the scope of the name.
2. External (or internal static) objects are initialized once only, at program start-up. The absence of explicit initialization is taken to be a default initialization of zero.

## ■ 4.5 SUMMARY

With the appropriate declarations, you can have names that are visible throughout the program or limited to a single file or limited to a single function, as appropriate.

Table 4.2 shows the combinations of the use of the keywords, the types of declarations and the resulting linkage.

There are a few golden rules for the use of functions that are worth re-stating too.

- To use a function returning other than int, a declaration or definition must be in scope.
- Do not return from a function by falling out of its body unless its type is void.

A declaration of the types of arguments that a function takes is not mandatory, but it is extremely strongly recommended.

Functions taking a variable number of arguments can be written portably if you use the methods described in Section 9.9.

Functions are the cornerstone of C. Of all the changes to the language, the Standard has had by far its most obvious effect by introducing function prototypes. This change has won widespread approval throughout the user community and should help to produce a substantial improvement in reliability of C programs, as well as opening the possibility of optimization by compilers in areas previously closed to them.

The use of call-by-value is sometimes surprising to people who have used languages that prefer a different mechanism, but at least the C approach is the 'safest' most of the time.

The attempts by the Standard to remove ambiguity in the scope and meaning of declarations are interesting, but frankly have explored an obscure region which rarely caused any difficulties in practice.

From the beginner's point of view, it is important to learn thoroughly everything discussed in this chapter, perhaps with the exception of the linkage rules. They can be deferred for a more leisurely inspection at some later time.

## EXERCISES

If you skipped the section on linkage, then Exercises 4.2, 4.3 and 4.4 will cause you problems; it's up to you whether or not you want to read it and then try them.

Write a function and the appropriate declaration for the following tasks:

**4.1**    A function called abs_val that returns int and takes an int argument. It returns the absolute value of its argument, by negating it if it is negative.

**4.2**    A function called output that takes a single character argument and sends it to the program output with putchar. It will remember the current line number and column number reached on the output device – the only values passed to the function are guaranteed to be alphanumeric, punctuation, space and newline characters.

**4.3**    Construct a program to test output, where that function is in a separate file from the functions that are used to test it. In the same file as output will be two functions called current_line and current_column which return the values of the line and column counters. Ensure that those counters are made accessible only from the file that contains them.

**4.4**    Write and test a recursive function that performs the admittedly dull task of printing a list of numbers from 100 down to 1. On entry to the function it increments a static variable. If the variable has a value below 100, it calls itself again. Then it prints the value of the variable, decrements it and returns. Check that it works.

**4.5**    Write functions to calculate the sine and cosine of their input. Choose appropriate types for both argument and return value. The series (given below) can be used to approximate the answer. The function should return when the value of the final term is less than 0.000001 of the current value of the function.

```
sin x = x - pow(x, 3) / fact(3) + pow(x, 5) / fact(5)...
cos x = 1 - pow(x, 2) / fact(2) + pow(x, 5) / fact(5)...
```

Note the fact that the sign in front of each term alternates (-+-+-+...). pow (x, n) returns x to the $n$th power, fact(n) factorial of n $(1 * 2 * 3 * \ldots * n)$. You will have to write such functions. Check the results against published tables.

# CHAPTER 5

# Arrays and Pointers

## 5.1  Opening shots

### 5.1.1  So why is this important?

The arithmetic data types and operators of C are interesting but hardly riveting. They show, collectively, a certain imagination and spirit that has stamped C with a special flavour, but they form the sauce, not the meat, of this particular dish. For most users, it's functions and the parts of the language covered in this chapter that provide the real feel of C.

For the new reader, this is the part of the language that causes the biggest problems. Most beginners with C are at least familiar with the use of arithmetic, functions and arrays; those are not the problem areas. The difficulties arise when we get on to the structured types (structures and unions), and the way that C just wouldn't be C without the use of pointers.

Pointers aren't a feature that you can choose to ignore. They're used everywhere; their influence affects the whole language and must be the single most noticeable feature of all but the simplest C programs. If you think that this is one of the bits you can skip because it's hard and doesn't look too important, you are wrong! Most of the examples used so far in this book have had pointers used in them (although not obviously), so you might as well accept the inevitable and learn how to use them properly.

The most natural way to introduce the use of pointers is by looking into arrays first. C intertwines arrays and pointers so closely that they are hard to separate. Since you are expected to be familiar with the use of arrays, their treatment will be brief and aimed at using them to illustrate the use of pointers when they are seen later.

### 5.1.2 Effect of the Standard

The new Standard has left very little mark on the contents of this chapter; a lot of it would be nearly word for word the same even if it only talked about Old C. The inference to be drawn is that nothing was wrong with the old version of the language, and that there was nothing to be gained by fixing what wasn't broken. This may be received with some relief by those readers who already knew this part of the old language and who, like the Committee, felt that it was good enough to leave alone.

Even so, the introduction of **qualified types** by the Standard does add some complexity to this chapter. The rules about exactly how the various arithmetic and relational operators work when they are applied to pointers have been clarified, which adds bulk to the text but has not changed things substantially. In the early examples we do not pay a lot of attention to them, but after that they are introduced gradually and where appropriate.

## 5.2 Arrays

Like other languages, C uses arrays as a way of describing a collection of variables with identical properties. The group has a single name for all of the members, with the individual members being selected by an **index**. Here's an array being declared:

```
double ar[100];
```

The name of the array is `ar` and its members are accessed as `ar[0]` through to `ar[99]` inclusive, as Figure 5.1 shows. Each of the hundred members is a separate variable whose type is `double`. Without exception, all arrays in C are numbered from 0 up to one less than the bound given in the declaration. This is a prime cause of surprise to beginners – watch out for it. For simple examples of the use of arrays, look back at earlier chapters where several problems are solved with their help.

One important point about array declarations is that they don't permit the use of varying subscripts. The numbers given must be constant expressions which can be

**Figure 5.1**   100 element array.

evaluated at compile time, not run time. For example, this function incorrectly tries to use its argument in the size of an array declaration:

```
f(int x){
        char var_sized_array[x];        /* FORBIDDEN */
}
```

It's forbidden because the value of x is unknown when the program is compiled; it's a run-time, not a compile-time, value.

To tell the truth, it would be easy to support arrays whose *first* dimension is variable, but neither Old C nor the Standard permits it, although we do know of one Very Old C compiler that used to do it.

### 5.2.1 Multidimensional arrays

Multidimensional arrays can be declared like this:

```
int three_dee[5][4][2];
int t_d[2][3]
```

The use of the brackets gives a clue to what is going on. If you refer to the precedence table given in Section 2.8.3 (Table 2.9), you'll see that [] associates left to right and that, as a result, the first declaration gives us a five-element array called three_dee. The members of that array are each a four-element array whose members are an array of two ints. We have declared arrays of arrays, as Figure 5.2 shows for two dimensions.

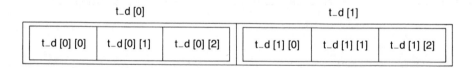

**Figure 5.2**  Two-dimensional array, showing layout.

In the diagram, you will notice that t_d[0] is one element, immediately followed by t_d[1] (there is no break). It so happens that both of those elements are themselves arrays of three integers. Because of C's storage layout rules, t_d[1][0] is immediately after t_d[0][2]. It would be possible (but very poor practice) to access t_d[1][0] by making use of the lack of array-bound checking in C, and to use the expression t_d[0][3]. That is not recommended – apart from anything else, if the declaration of t_d ever changes, then the results will be likely to surprise you.

That's all very well, but does it really matter in practice? Not much, it's true; but it is interesting to note that in terms of actual machine storage layout the rightmost subscript 'varies fastest'. This has an impact when arrays are accessed via pointers. Otherwise, they can be used just as would be expected; expressions like these are quite in order:

```
three_dee[1][3][1] = 0;
three_dee[4][3][1] += 2;
```

The second of those is interesting for two reasons. First, it accesses the very last member of the entire array – although the subscripts were declared to be [5][4][2], the highest usable subscript is always one less than the one used in the declaration. Second, it shows where the combined assignment operators are a real blessing. For the experienced C programmer it is much easier to tell that only one array member is being accessed, and that it is being incremented by two. Other languages would have to express it like this:

```
three_dee[4][3][1] = three_dee[4][3][1] + 2;
```

It takes a conscious effort to check that the same array member is being referenced on both sides of the assignment. It makes things easier for the compiler too: there is only one array indexing calculation to do, and this is likely to result in shorter, faster code. (Of course a clever compiler would notice that the left- and right-hand sides look alike and would be able to generate equally efficient code – but not all compilers are clever and there are lots of special cases where even clever compilers are unable to make use of the information.)

It may be of interest to know that although C offers support for multidimensional arrays, they aren't particularly common to see in practice. One-dimensional arrays are present in most programs, if for no other reason than that's what strings are. Two-dimensional arrays are seen occasionally, and arrays of higher order than that are most uncommon. One of the reasons is that the array is a rather inflexible data structure, and the ease of building and manipulating other types of data structures in C means that they tend to replace arrays in the more advanced programs. We will see more of this when we look at pointers.

## 5.3 Pointers

Using pointers is a bit like riding a bicycle. Just when you think that you'll never understand them – suddenly you do! Once learned the trick is hard to forget. There's no real magic to pointers, and a lot of readers will already be familiar with their use. The only peculiarity of C is how heavily it relies on the use of pointers, compared with other languages, and the relatively permissive view of what you can do with them.

### 5.3.1 Declaring pointers

Of course, just like other variables, you have to declare pointers before you can use them. Pointer declarations look much like other declarations: but don't be misled.

When pointers are declared, the keyword at the beginning (c int, char and so on) declares the type of variable that the pointer will point to. The pointer itself is *not* of that type, it is of type *pointer to that type*. A given pointer only points to one particular type, not to all possible types. Here's the declaration of an array and a pointer:

```
int ar[5], *ip;
```

We now have an array and a pointer (see Figure 5.3).

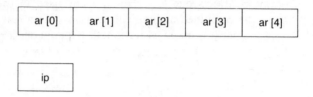

**Figure 5.3** An array and a pointer.

The * in front of ip in the declaration shows that it is a pointer, not an ordinary variable. It is of type pointer to int, and can only be used to refer to variables of type int. It's still uninitialized, so to do anything useful with it, it has to be made to point to something. You can't just stick some integer value into it, because integer values have the type int, not pointer to int, which is what we want. (In any case, what would it mean if this fragment were valid:

```
ip = 6;
```

What would ip be pointing to? In fact it could be construed to have a number of meanings, but the simple fact is that, in C, that sort of thing is just wrong.)

Here is the right way to initialize a pointer:

```
int ar[5], *ip;
ip = &ar[3];
```

In that example, the pointer is made to point to the member of the array ar whose index is 3, that is, the fourth member. This is important. You can assign values to pointers just like ordinary variables; the difference is simply in what the value means. The values of the variables that we have now are shown in Figure 5.4 (?? means uninitialized).

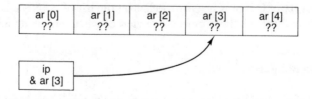

**Figure 5.4** Array and initialized pointer.

You can see that the variable ip has the value of the expression &ar[3]. The arrow indicates that, when used as a pointer, ip points to the variable ar[3].

What is this new unary &? It is usually described as the 'address-of' operator, since on many systems the pointer will hold the store address of the thing that it points to. If you understand what addresses are, then you will probably have more trouble than those who don't: thinking about pointers as if they were addresses generally leads to grief. What seems a perfectly reasonable address manipulation on processor X can almost always be shown to be impossible on manufacturer Y's washing machine controller which uses 17-bit addressing when it's on the spin cycle, and reverses the order of odd and even bits when it's out of bleach. (Admittedly, it's unlikely that *anyone* could get C to work on an architecture like that. But you should see some of the ones it *does* work on; they aren't much better.)

We will continue to use the term 'address of' though, because to invent a different one would be even worse.

Applying the & operator to an operand returns a pointer to the operand:

```
int i;
float f;
        /* ''&i'' would be of type pointer to int */
        /* ''&f'' would be of type pointer to float */
```

In each case the pointer would point to the object named in the expression.

A pointer is only useful if there's some way of getting at the thing that it points to; C uses the unary * operator for this job. If p is of type 'pointer to something', then *p refers to the thing that is being pointed to. For example, to access the variable x via the pointer p, this would work:

```
#include ⟨stdio.h⟩
#include ⟨stdlib.h⟩

main(){
        int x, *p;

        p = &x;          /* initialise pointer */
        *p = 0;          /* set x to zero */
        printf("x is %d\n", x);
        printf("*p is %d\n", *p);

        *p += 1;         /* increment what p points to */
        printf("x is %d\n", x);

        (*p)++;          /* increment what p points to */
        printf("x is %d\n", x);

        exit(EXIT_SUCCESS);
}
```

(**Example 5.1**)

You might be interested to note that, since & takes the address of an object, returning a pointer to it, and since * means 'the thing pointed to by the pointer', the & and * in the combination *& effectively cancel each other out. (But be careful. Some things, constants for example, don't have addresses and the & operator cannot be applied to them; &1.5 is not a pointer to anything, it's an error.) It's also interesting to see that C is one of the few languages that allows an expression on the left-hand side of an assignment operator. Look back at the example: the expression *p occurs twice in that position, and then the amazing (*p)++; statement. That last one is a great puzzle to most beginners – even if you've managed to wrap your mind around the concept that *p = 0 writes zero into the thing pointed to by p, and that *p += 1 adds one to where p points, it still seems a bit much to apply the ++ operator to *p.

The precedence of (*p)++ deserves some thought. It will be given more later, but for the moment let's work out what happens. The brackets ensure that the * applies to p, so what we have is 'post-increment the thing pointed to by p'. Looking at Table 2.9, it turns out that ++ and * have equal precedence, but they associate *right to left*; in other words, without the brackets, the implied operation would have been *(p++), whatever that would mean. Later on you'll be more used to it – for the moment, we'll be careful with brackets to show the way that those expressions work.

So, provided that a pointer holds the address of something, the notation *pointer is equivalent to giving the name of the something directly. What benefit do we get from all this? Well, straight away it gets round the call-by-value restriction of functions. Imagine a function that has to return, say, two integers representing a month and a day within that month. The function has some (unspecified) way of determining these values; the hard thing to do is to return two separate values. Here's a skeleton of the way that it can be done:

```
#include ⟨stdio.h⟩
#include ⟨stdlib.h⟩
void date(int *, int *);      /* declare the function */

main(){
        int month, day;
        date (&day, &month);
        printf("day is %d, month is %d\n", day, month);
        exit(EXIT_SUCCESS);
}

void
date(int *day_p, int *month_p){
        int day_ret, month_ret;
        /*
         * At this point, calculate the day and month
         * values in day_ret and month_ret respectively.
         */
        *day_p = day_ret;
        *month_p = month_ret;
}
```

(Example 5.2)

Notice carefully the advance declaration of date showing that it takes two arguments of type 'pointer to int'. It returns void, because the values are passed back via the pointers, not the usual return value. The main function passes pointers as arguments to date, which first uses the internal variables day_ret and month_ret for its calculations, then takes those values and assigns them to the places pointed to by its arguments.

When date is called, the situation looks like Figure 5.5.

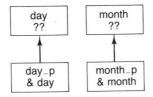

**Figure 5.5**  Just as date is called.

The arguments have been passed to date, but in main, day and month are uninitialized. When date reaches the return statement, the situation is as shown in Figure 5.6 (assuming that the values for day and month are 12 and 5 respectively).

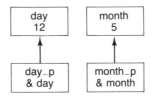

**Figure 5.6**  Just as date is about to return.

One of the great benefits introduced by the new Standard is that it allows the types of the arguments to date to be declared in advance. A great favourite (and disastrous) mistake in C is to forget that a function expects pointers as its arguments, and to pass something else instead. Imagine what would have happened if the call of date above had read

```
date(day, month);
```

and no previous declaration of date had been visible. The compiler would not have known that date expects pointers as arguments, so it would pass the int values of day and month as the arguments. On a large number of computers, pointers and integers can be passed in the same way, so the function would execute, then pass back its return values by putting them into wherever day and month would point if their contents were pointers. This is very unlikely to give any sensible results, and in general causes unexpected corruption of data elsewhere in the computer's store. It can be extremely hard to track down!

Fortunately, by declaring date in advance, the compiler has enough information to warn that a mistake has almost certainly been made.

Perhaps surprisingly, it isn't all that common to see pointers used to give this call-by-reference functionality. In the majority of cases, call-by-value and a single return value are adequate. What is *much* more common is to use pointers to 'walk' along arrays.

### 5.3.2 Arrays and pointers

Array elements are just like other variables: they have addresses.

```
int ar[20], *ip;

ip = &ar[5];
*ip = 0;          /* equivalent to ar[5] = 0; */
```

The address of ar[5] is put into ip, then the place pointed to has zero assigned to it. By itself, this isn't particularly exciting. What *is* interesting is the way that pointer arithmetic works. Although it's simple, it's one of the cornerstones of C.

Adding an integral value to a pointer results in another pointer of the same type. Adding *n* gives a pointer which points *n* elements further along an array than the original pointer did. (Since *n* can be negative, subtraction is obviously possible too.) In the example above, a statement of the form

```
*(ip + 1) = 0;
```

would set ar[6] to zero, and so on. Again, this is not obviously any improvement on 'ordinary' ways of accessing an array, but the following is.

```
int ar[20], *ip;

for(ip = &ar[0]; ip < &ar[20]; ip++)
        *ip = 0;
```

That example is a classic fragment of C. A pointer is set to point to the start of an array, then, while it still points inside the array, array elements are accessed one by one, the pointer incrementing between each one. The Standard endorses existing practice by guaranteeing that it's permissible to use the *address* of ar[20] even though no such element exists. This allows you to use it for checks in loops like the one above. The guarantee only extends to one element beyond the end of an array and no further.

Why is the example better than indexing? Well, most arrays are accessed sequentially. Very few programming examples actually make use of the 'random access' feature of arrays. If you do just want sequential access, using a pointer can give a worthwhile improvement in speed. In terms of the underlying address arithmetic, on most architectures it takes one multiplication and one addition to access a one-dimensional array through a subscript. Pointers require no arithmetic at all – they nearly always hold the store address of the object that they refer to. In the example above, the only arithmetic that has to be done is in the for loop, where one comparison and one addition are done each time round the loop. The equivalent, using indices, would be this:

```
int ar[20], i;

for(i = 0; i < 20; i++)
        ar[i] = 0;
```

The same amount of arithmetic occurs in the loop statement, but an extra address calculation has to be performed for every array access.

Efficiency is not normally an important issue, but here it can be. Loops often get traversed a substantial number of times, and every microsecond saved in a big loop can matter. It isn't always easy for even a smart compiler to recognize that this is the sort of code that could be 'pointerized' behind the scenes, and to convert from indexing (what the programmer wrote) to actually use a pointer in the generated code.

If you have found things easy so far, read on. If not, it's a good idea to skip to Section 5.3.3. What follows, while interesting, isn't essential. It has been known to frighten even experienced C programmers.

To be honest, C doesn't really 'understand' array indexing, except in declarations. As far as the compiler is concerned, an expression like x[n] is translated into *(x + n) and use made of the fact that an array name is converted into a pointer to the array's first element whenever the name occurs in an expression. That's why, amongst other things, array elements count from zero: if x is an array name, then in an expression, x is equivalent to &x[0], that is, a pointer to the first element of the array. So, since *(&x[0]) uses the pointer to get to x[0], *(&x[0] + 5) is the same as *(x + 5) which is the same as x[5]. A curiosity springs out of all this. If x[5] is translated into *(x + 5), and the expression x + 5 gives the same result as 5 + x (it does), then 5[x] should give the identical result to x[5]! If you don't believe that, here is a program that compiles and runs successfully:

```
#include ⟨stdio.h⟩
#include ⟨stdlib.h⟩

#define ARSZ 20

main(){
        int ar[ARSZ], i;

        for(i = 0; i < ARSZ; i++){
                ar[i] = i;
                i[ar]++;
                printf("ar[%d] now = %d\n", i, ar[i]);
        }
        printf("15[ar] = %d\n", 15[ar]);
        exit(EXIT_SUCCESS);
}
```

(Example 5.3)

☐  **SUMMARY**

○  Arrays always index from zero – end of story.

○  There are no multidimensional arrays; you use arrays of arrays instead.

○  Pointers point to things; pointers to different types are themselves different types. They have nothing in common with each other or any other types in C; there are no automatic conversions between pointers and other types.

○  Pointers can be used to simulate 'call by reference' to functions, but it takes a little work to do it.

○  Incrementing or adding something to a pointer can be used to step along arrays.

○  To facilitate array access by incrementing pointers, the Standard guarantees that in an $n$-element array, although element $n$ does not exist, use of its address is not an error – the valid range of addresses for an array declared as int ar[N] is &ar[0] through to &ar[N]. You must not try to access this last pseudo-element.

### 5.3.3 Qualified types

If you are confident that you have got a good grasp of the basic declaration and use of pointers we can continue. If not, it's important to go back over the previous material and make sure that there is nothing in it that you still find obscure; although what comes next looks more complicated than it really is, there's no need to make it worse by starting unprepared.

The Standard introduces two things called **type qualifiers**, neither of which were in Old C. They can be applied to any declared type to modify its behaviour – hence the term 'qualifier' – and although one of them can be ignored for the moment (the one named volatile), the other, const, cannot.

If a declaration is prefixed with the keyword const, then the thing that is declared is announced to the world as being constant. You must not attempt to modify (change the value of) const objects, or you get undefined behaviour. Unless you have used some very dirty tricks, the compiler will know that the thing you are trying to modify is constant, so it can warn you.

There are two benefits in being able to declare things to be const.

(1)  It documents the fact that the thing is unmodifiable and the compiler helps to check. This is especially reassuring in the case of functions which take pointers as arguments. If the declaration of a function shows that the arguments are pointers to constant objects, then you know that the function is not allowed to change them through the pointers.

(2)  If the compiler knows that things are constant, it can often do increased amounts of optimization or generate better code.

Of course, constants are not much use unless you can assign an initial value to them. We won't go into the rules about initialization here (they are in Chapter 6), but for the moment just note that any declaration can also assign the value of a constant expression to the thing being declared. Here are some example declarations involving const:

```
const int x = 1;        /* x is constant */
const float f = 3.5;    /* f is constant */
const char y[10];       /* y is an array of 10 const ints */
                        /* don't think about initializing it yet! */
```

What is more interesting is that pointers can have this qualifier applied in two ways: either to the thing that it points to (pointer to const), or to the pointer itself (constant pointer). Here are examples of *that*:

```
int i;                  /* i is an ordinary int */
const int ci = 1;       /* ci is a constant int */
int *pi;                /* pi is a pointer to an int */
const int *pci;         /* pc is a pointer to a constant int */
          /* and now the more complicated stuff */

/* cpi is a constant pointer to an int */
int *const cpi = &i;

/* cpci is a constant pointer to a constant int */
const int *const cpci = &ci;
```

The first declaration (of i) is unsurprising. Next, the declaration of ci shows that it is a constant integer, and therefore may not be modified. If we didn't initialize it, it would be pretty well useless.

It isn't hard to understand what a pointer to an integer and a pointer to a constant integer do – but note that they are different types of pointer now and can't be freely intermixed. You can change the values of both pi and pci (so that they point to other things); you can change the value of the thing that pi points to (it's not a constant integer), but you are only allowed to inspect the value of the thing that pci points to because that *is* a constant.

The last two declarations are the most complicated. If the pointers themselves are constant, then you are not allowed to make them point somewhere else – so they need to be initialized, just like ci. Independent of the const or other status of the pointer itself, naturally the thing that it points to can also be const or non-const, with the appropriate constraints on what you can do with it.

A final piece of clarification: what constitutes a qualified type? In the example, ci was clearly of a qualified type, but pci was not, since the pointer was not qualified, only the thing that it points to. The only things that had qualified type in that list were: ci, cpi and cpci.

Although the declarations do take some mental gymnastics to understand, it just takes a little time to get used to seeing them, after which you will find that they seem quite natural. The complications come later when we have to explain whether or not you are allowed to (say) compare an ordinary pointer with a constant pointer, and if so, what does it mean? Most of those rules are 'obvious' but they do have to be stated.

Type qualifiers are given a further airing in Chapter 8.


### 5.3.4 Pointer arithmetic

Although a more rigorous description of pointer arithmetic is given later, we'll start with an approximate version that will do for the moment.

Not only can you add an integral value to a pointer, but you can also compare or subtract two pointers of the same type. They must both point into the same array, or the result is undefined. The difference between two pointers is defined to be the number of array elements separating them; the type of this difference is implementation defined and will be one of short, int, or long. This next example shows how the difference can be calculated and used, but before you read it, you need to know an important point.

*In an expression the name of an array is converted to a pointer to the first element of the array.* The only places where that is not true are when an array name is used in conjunction with sizeof, when a string is used to initialize an array or when the array name is the subject of the address-of operator (unary &). We haven't seen any of those cases yet, they will be discussed later. Here's the example:

```
#include ⟨stdio.h⟩
#include ⟨stdlib.h⟩

#define ARSZ 10

main(){
        float fa[ARSZ], *fp1, *fp2;

        fp1 = fp2 = fa; /* address of first element */
        while(fp2 != &fa[ARSZ]){
                printf("Difference: %d\n", (int)(fp2 - fp1));
                fp2++;
        }
        exit(EXIT_SUCCESS);
}
```
                                                                    **(Example 5.4)**

The pointer fp2 is stepped along the array, and the difference between its current and original values is printed. To make sure that printf isn't handed the wrong type of argument, the difference between the two pointers is forced to be of type int by using the cast (int). That allows for machines where the difference between two pointers is specified to be long.

Unfortunately, if the difference does happen to be long and the array is enormous, the last example may give the wrong answers. This is a safe version, using a cast to force a long value to be passed:

```
#include (stdio.h)
#define ARSZ 10

main(){
        float fa[ARSZ], *fp1, *fp2;

        fp1 = fp2 = fa; /* address of first element */
        while(fp2 != &fa[ARSZ]){
                printf("Difference: %ld\n", (long)(fp2 - fp1));
                fp2++;
        }
        return(0);
}
```

(**Example** 5.5)

### 5.3.5 Void, **null and dubious pointers**

C is careful to keep track of the type of each pointer and will not in general allow you to use pointers of different types in the same expression. A pointer to char is a different type of pointer from a pointer to int (say) and you cannot assign one to the other, compare them, substitute one for the other as an argument to a function ... in fact they may even be stored differently in memory and even be of different lengths.

*Pointers of different types are not the same. There are no implicit conversions from one to the other (unlike the arithmetic types).*

There are a few occasions when you *do* want to be able to sidestep some of those restrictions, so what can you do?

The solution is to use the special type, introduced for this purpose, of 'pointer to void'. This is one of the Standard's invented features: before, it was tacitly assumed that 'pointer to char' was adequate for the task. This has been a reasonably successful assumption, but was a rather untidy thing to do; the new solution is both safer and less misleading. There isn't any other use for a pointer of that type – void * can't actually point to anything – so it improves readability. A pointer of type void * can have the value of any other pointer assigned to and can, conversely, be assigned to any other pointer. This must be used with *great* care, because you can end up in some heinous situations. We'll see it being used safely later with the malloc library function.

You may also on occasion want a pointer that is guaranteed not to point to any object – the so-called **null pointer**. It's common practice in C to write routines that return pointers. If, for some reason, they can't return a valid pointer (perhaps in case of an error), then they will indicate failure by returning a null pointer instead. An example could be a table lookup routine, which returns a pointer to the object searched for if it is in the table, or a null pointer if it is not.

How do you write a null pointer? There are two ways of doing it and both of them are equivalent: either an integral constant with the value of 0 or that value converted to type void * by using a cast. Both versions are called the **null pointer constant**. If you assign a null pointer constant to any other pointer, or compare it for equality with any other pointer, then it is first converted the type of that other pointer (neatly solving any problems about type compatibility) and will not appear to have a value that is equal to a pointer to any object in the program.

The only values that can be assigned to pointers apart from 0 are the values of other pointers of the same type. However, one of the things that makes C a useful replacement for assembly language is that it allows you to do the sort of things that most other languages prevent. Try this:

```
int *ip;
ip = (int *)6;
*ip = 0xFF;
```

What does that do? The pointer has been initialized to the value of 6 (notice the cast to turn an integer 6 into a pointer). This is a highly machine-specific operation, and the bit pattern that ends up in the pointer is quite possibly nothing like the machine representation of 6. After the initialization, hexadecimal FF is written into wherever the pointer is pointing. The int at location 6 has had 0xFF written into it – subject to whatever 'location 6' means on this particular machine.

It may or may not make sense to do that sort of thing; C gives you the power to express it, it's up to you to get it right. As always, it's possible to do things like this by accident, too, and to be *very* surprised by the results.

## 5.4 Character handling

C is widely used for character and string handling applications. This is odd, in some ways, because the language doesn't really have any built-in string handling features. If you're used to languages that know about string handling, you will almost certainly find C tedious to begin with.

The standard library contains lots of functions to help with string processing but the fact remains that it still feels like hard work. To compare two strings you have to call a function instead of using an equality operator. There is a bright side to this, though. It means that the language isn't burdened by having to support string processing directly, which helps to keep it small and less cluttered. What's more, once you get your string handling programs working in C, they do tend to run very quickly.

Character handling in C is done by declaring arrays (or allocating them dynamically) and moving characters in and out of them 'by hand'. Here is an example of a program which reads text a line at a time from its standard input. If the line consists of the string of characters stop, it stops; otherwise it prints the length of the line. It uses a technique which is invariably used in C programs; it reads the characters into an array and indicates the end of them with an extra character whose value is explicitly 0 (zero). It uses the library strcmp function to compare two strings.

```
#include <stdio.h>
#include <stdlib.h>
#include <string.h>
```

```
#define LINELNG 100      /* max. length of input line */


main(){
        char in_line[LINELNG];
        char *cp;
        int c;

        cp = in_line;
        while((c = getc(stdin)) != EOF){
                if(cp == &in_line[LINELNG-1] || c == '\n'){
                        /*
                         * Insert end-of-line marker
                         */
                        *cp = 0;
                        if(strcmp(in_line, "stop") == 0 )
                                exit(EXIT_SUCCESS);
                        else
                                printf("line was %d characters long\n",
                                        (int)cp-in_line);
                        cp = in_line;
                }
                else
                        *cp++ = c;
        }
        exit(EXIT_SUCCESS);
}
```
                                                    **(Example 5.6)**

Once more, the example illustrates some interesting methods used widely in C programs. By far the most important is the way that strings are represented and manipulated.

Here is a possible implementation of strcmp, which compares two strings for equality and returns zero if they are the same. The library function actually does a bit more than that, but the added complication can be ignored for the moment. Notice the use of const in the argument declarations. This shows that the function will not modify the contents of the strings, but just inspects them. The definitions of the standard library functions make extensive use of this technique.

```
/*
 * Compare two strings for equality.
 * Return ''false'' if they are.
 */
int
str_eq(const char *s1, const char *s2){
        while(*s1 == *s2){
                /*
                 * At end of string return 0.
                 */
```

```
                    if(*s1 == 0)
                            return(0);
                    s1++; s2++;
            }
            /* Difference detected! */
            return(1);
    }
```

(Example 5.7)

### 5.4.1 Strings

Every C programmer 'knows' what a string is. It is an array of char variables, with the last character in the string followed by a null. 'But I thought a string was something in double quote marks', you cry. You are right, too. In C, a sequence like this

```
    "a string"
```

is really a character array. It's the only example in C where you can declare something at the point of its use.

*Be warned:* in Old C, strings were stored just like any other character array, and were modifiable. Now, the Standard states that although they are arrays of char, (not const char), attempting to modify them results in undefined behaviour.

Whenever a string in quotes is seen, it has two effects: it provides a declaration and a substitute for a name. It makes a hidden declaration of a char array, whose contents are initialized to the character values in the string, followed by a character whose integer value is zero. The array has no name. So, apart from the name being present, we have a situation like this:

```
    char secret[9];
    secret[0] = 'a';
    secret[1] = ' ';
    secret[2] = 's';
    secret[3] = 't';
    secret[4] = 'r';
    secret[5] = 'i';
    secret[6] = 'n';
    secret[7] = 'g';
    secret[8] = 0;
```

an array of characters, terminated by zero, with character values in it. But when it's declared using the string notation, it hasn't got a name. How can we use it?

Whenever C sees a quoted string, the presence of the string itself serves as the name of the hidden array – not only is the string an implicit sort of declaration, it is as if an array name had been given. Now, we all remember that the name of an array is equivalent to giving the address of its first element, so what is the type of this?

```
    "a string"
```

It's a pointer of course: a pointer to the first element of the hidden unnamed array, which is of type char, so the pointer is of type 'pointer to char'. The situation is shown in Figure 5.7.

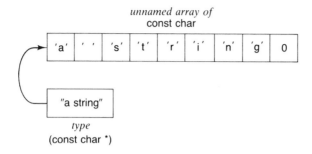

Figure 5.7 Effect of using a string.

For proof of that, look at the following program:

```
#include (stdio.h)
#include (stdlib.h)

main(){
        int i;
        char *cp;

        cp = "a string";
        while(*cp != 0){
                putchar(*cp);
                cp++;
        }
        putchar('\n');

        for(i = 0; i < 8; i++)
                putchar("a string"[i]);
        putchar('\n');
        exit(EXIT_SUCCESS);
}
```
(Example 5.8)

The first loop sets a pointer to the start of the array, then walks along until it finds the zero at the end. The second one 'knows' about the length of the string and is less useful as a result. Notice how the first one is independent of the length – that is a most important point to remember. It's the way that strings are handled in C almost without exception; it's certainly the format that all of the library string manipulation functions expect. The zero at the end allows string processing routines to find out that they have reached the end of the string – look back now to the example function str_eq. The function takes two character pointers as arguments (so a string would be acceptable as one or both arguments). It compares them for equality by checking that the strings are character-for-character the same. If they are the same at any point, then it checks to make sure it hasn't reached the end of them both with if(*s1 == 0): if it has, then it returns 0 to show that they were equal. The test could just as easily have been on *s2, it wouldn't have made any difference. Otherwise a difference has been detected, so it returns 1 to indicate failure.

In the example, strcmp is called with two arguments which look quite different. One is a character array, the other is a string. In fact they're the same thing – a character array terminated by zero (the program is careful to put a zero in the first 'empty' element of in_line), and a string in quotes – which is a character array terminated by a zero. Their use as arguments to strcmp results in character pointers being passed, for the reasons explained to the point of tedium above.

### 5.4.2 Pointers and increment operators

We said that we'd eventually revisit expressions like

```
(*p)++;
```

and now it's time. Pointers are used so often to walk down arrays that it just seems natural to use the ++ and -- operators on them. Here we write zeros into an array:

```
#define ARLEN 10

int ar[ARLEN], *ip;

ip = ar;
while(ip < &ar[ARLEN])
        *(ip++) = 0;
```
                                                                      (Example 5.9)

The pointer ip is set to the start of the array. While it remains inside the array, the place that it points to has zero written into it, then the increment takes effect and the pointer is stepped one element along the array. The postfix form of ++ is particularly useful here.

This is very common stuff indeed. In most programs you'll find pointers and increment operators used together like that, not just once or twice, but on almost every line (or so it seems while you find them difficult). What is happening, and what combinations can we get? Well, the * means indirection, and ++ or -- mean increment; either pre- or post-increment. The combinations can be pre- or post-increment of either the pointer or the thing it points to, depending on where the brackets are put. Table 5.1 gives a list. Read it carefully; make sure that you understand the combinations.

The expressions in Table 5.1 can usually be understood after a bit of head-scratching. Now, given that the precedence of *, ++ and -- is the same in all three cases and that they associate *right to left*, can you work out what happens if the brackets are removed? Nasty, isn't it? Table 5.2 shows that there's only one case where the brackets have to be there.

**Table 5.1**   Pointer notation.

| | |
|---|---|
| ++(*p) | pre-increment thing pointed to |
| (*p)++ | post-increment thing pointed to |
| *(p++) | access via pointer, post-increment pointer |
| *(++p) | access via pointer which has already been incremented |

**Table 5.2**   More pointer notation.

| With parentheses | Without, if possible |
|---|---|
| ++(*p) | ++*p |
| (*p)++ | (*p)++ |
| *(p++) | *p++ |
| *(++p) | *++p |

The usual reaction to that horrible sight is to decide that you don't care that the parentheses can be removed; you will *always* use them in your code. That's all very well but the problem is that most C programmers have learnt the important precedence rules (or at least learnt the table above) and *they* very rarely put the parentheses in. Like them, we don't – so if you want to be able to read the rest of the examples, you had better learn to read those expressions with or without parentheses. It'll be worth the effort in the end.

### 5.4.3 Untyped pointers

In certain cases it's essential to be able to convert pointers from one type to another. This is always done with the aid of casts, in expressions like the one below:

(*type* *) *expression*

The *expression* is converted into 'pointer to *type*', regardless of the expression's previous type. This is only supposed to be done if you're sure that you know what you're trying to do. It is not a good idea to do much of it until you have got plenty of experience. Furthermore, do *not* assume that the cast simply suppresses diagnostics of the 'mismatched pointer' sort from your compiler. On several architectures it is necessary to calculate new values when pointer types are changed.

There are also some occasions when you will want to use a 'generic' pointer. The most common example is the malloc library function, which is used to allocate storage for objects that haven't been declared. It is used by telling it how much storage is wanted – enough for a float, or an array of int, or whatever. It passes back a pointer to enough storage, which it allocates in its own mysterious way from a pool of free storage (the way that it does this is its own business). That pointer is then cast into the right type – for example if a `float` needs four bytes of free store, this is the flavour of what you would write:

```
float *fp;

fp = (float *)malloc(4);
```

`Malloc` finds four bytes of store, then the address of that piece of storage is cast into pointer-to-float and assigned to the pointer.

What type should `malloc` be declared to have? The type must be able to represent every known value of every type of pointer; there is no guarantee that *any* of the basic types in C can hold such a value.

The solution is to use the `void *` type that we've already talked about. Here is the last example with a declaration of `malloc`:

```
void *malloc();
float *fp;

fp = (float *)malloc(4);
```

The rules for assignment of pointers show that there is no need to use a cast on the return value from `malloc`, but it is often done in practice.

Obviously there needs to be a way to find out what value the argument to `malloc` should be: it will be different on different machines, so you can't just use a constant like `4`. That is what the `sizeof` operator is for.

## 5.5 `Sizeof` and storage allocation

The `sizeof` operator returns the size in bytes of its operand. Whether the result of `sizeof` is `unsigned int` or `unsigned long` is implementation defined – which is why the declaration of `malloc` above ducked the issue by omitting any parameter information; normally you would use the `stdlib.h` header file to declare `malloc` correctly. Here is the last example done portably:

```
#include <stdlib.h>      /* declares malloc() */
float *fp;

fp = (float *)malloc(sizeof(float));
```

The operand of `sizeof` only has to be parenthesized if it's a type name, as it was in the example. If you are using the name of a data object instead, then the parentheses can be omitted, but they rarely are.

```
#include <stdlib.h>
```

```
int *ip, ar[100];
ip = (int *)malloc(sizeof ar);
```

In the last example, the array ar is an array of 100 ints; after the call to malloc (assuming that it was successful), ip will point to a region of store that can also be treated as an array of 100 ints.

The fundamental unit of storage in C is the char, and by definition

```
sizeof(char)
```

is equal to 1, so you could allocate space for an array of ten chars with

```
malloc(10)
```

while to allocate room for an array of ten ints, you would have to use

```
malloc(sizeof(int[10]))
```

If malloc can't find enough free space to satisfy a request it returns a null pointer to indicate failure. For historical reasons, the stdio.h header file contains a defined constant called NULL which is traditionally used to check the return value from malloc and some other library functions. An explicit 0 or (void *)0 could equally well be used.

As a first illustration of the use of malloc, here's a program which reads up to MAXSTRING strings from its input and sorts them into alphabetical order using the library strcmp routine. The strings are terminated by a '\n' character. The sort is done by keeping an array of pointers to the strings and simply exchanging the pointers until the order is correct. This saves having to copy the strings themselves, which improves the efficiency somewhat.

The example is done first using fixed size arrays, then another version uses malloc and allocates space for the strings at run time. Unfortunately, the array of pointers is still fixed in size: a better solution would use a linked list or similar data structure to store the pointers and would have no fixed arrays at all. At the moment, we haven't seen how to do that.

The overall structure is this:

```
while(number of strings read < MAXSTRING && input still remains){
                read next string;
}
sort array of pointers;
print array of pointers;
exit;
```

A number of functions are used to implement this program:

```
char *next_string(char *destination)
```
Read a line of characters terminated by '\n' from the program's input. The first MAXLEN-1 characters are written into the array pointed to by destination.

If the first character read is EOF, return a null pointer, otherwise return the address of the start of the string (destination). On return, destination always points to a null-terminated string.

```
void sort_arr(const char *p_array[])
```
P_array[] is an array of pointers to characters. The array can be arbitrarily long; its end is indicated by the first element containing a null pointer.

Sort_arr sorts the pointers so that the pointers point to strings which are in alphabetical order when the array is traversed in index order.

```
void print_arr(const char *p_array[])
```
Like sort_arr, but prints the strings in index order.

It will help to understand the examples if you remember that in an expression, an array's name is converted to the address of its first element. Similarly, for a two-dimensional array (such as strings below), then the expression strings[1][2] has type char, but strings[1] has type 'array of char' which is therefore converted to the address of the first element: it is equivalent to &strings[1][0].

```
        #include ⟨stdio.h⟩
        #include ⟨stdlib.h⟩
        #include ⟨string.h⟩

        #define MAXSTRING     50     /* max no. of strings */
        #define MAXLEN        80     /* max length. of strings */

        void print_arr(const char *p_array[]);
        void sort_arr(const char *p_array[]);
        char *next_string(char *destination);

        main(){
                /* leave room for null at end */
                char *p_array[MAXSTRING + 1];

                /* storage for strings */
                char strings[MAXSTRING][MAXLEN];

                /* count of strings read */
                int nstrings;

                nstrings = 0;
                while(nstrings < MAXSTRING &&
                        next_string(strings[nstrings]) != 0){
```

```
                p_array[nstrings] = strings[nstrings];
                nstrings++;
        }
        /* terminate p_array */
        p_array[nstrings] = 0;

        sort_arr(p_array);
        print_arr(p_array);
        exit(EXIT_SUCCESS);
}

void
print_arr(const char *p_array[]){
        int index;

        for(index = 0; p_array[index] != 0; index++)
                printf("%s\n", p_array[index]);
}

void
sort_arr(const char *p_array[]){
        int comp_val, low_index, hi_index;
        const char *tmp;

        for(low_index = 0;
                p_array[low_index] != 0 &&
                                p_array[low_index+1] != 0;
                        low_index++){

                for(hi_index = low_index + 1;
                        p_array[hi_index] != 0;
                                hi_index++){

                        comp_val = strcmp(p_array[hi_index],
                                p_array[low_index]);
                        if(comp_val >= 0)
                                continue;
                        /* swap strings */
                        tmp = p_array[hi_index];
                        p_array[hi_index] = p_array[low_index];
                        p_array[low_index] = tmp;
                }
        }
}

char
*next_string(char *destination){
        char *cp;
        int c;
```

```
        cp = destination;
        while((c = getchar()) != '\n' && c != EOF){
                if(cp - destination < MAXLEN - 1)
                        *cp++ = c;
        }
        *cp = 0;
        if(c == EOF && cp == destination)
                return(0);
        return(destination);
}
```

**(Example 5.10)**

It is no accident that next_string returns a pointer. We can now dispense with the strings array by getting next_string to allocate its own storage.

```
#include ⟨stdio.h⟩
#include ⟨stdlib.h⟩
#include ⟨string.h⟩

#define MAXSTRING    50      /* max no. of strings */
#define MAXLEN       80      /* max length. of strings */

void print_arr(const char *p_array[]);
void sort_arr(const char *p_array[]);
char *next_string(void);

main(){
        char *p_array[MAXSTRING + 1];
        int nstrings;

        nstrings = 0;
        while(nstrings < MAXSTRING &&
                (p_array[nstrings] = next_string()) != 0){

                nstrings++;
        }
        /* terminate p_array */
        p_array[nstrings] = 0;

        sort_arr(p_array);
        print_arr(p_array);
        exit(EXIT_SUCCESS);
}


void
print_arr(const char *p_array[]){
        int index;
```

```
                for(index = 0; p_array[index] != 0; index++)
                        printf("%s\n", p_array[index]);
}


void
sort_arr(const char *p_array[]){
        int comp_val, low_index, hi_index;
        const char *tmp;

        for(low_index = 0;
                p_array[low_index] != 0 &&
                        p_array[low_index + 1] != 0;
                        low_index++){

                for(hi_index = low_index + 1;
                        p_array[hi_index] != 0;
                                hi_index++){

                        comp_val = strcmp(p_array[hi_index],
                                p_array[low_index]);
                        if(comp_val >= 0)
                                continue;
                        /* swap strings */
                        tmp = p_array[hi_index];
                        p_array[hi_index] = p_array[low_index];
                        p_array[low_index] = tmp;
                }
        }
}


char
*next_string(void){
        char *cp, *destination;
        int c;

        destination = (char *)malloc(MAXLEN);
        if(destination != 0){
                cp = destination;
                while((c = getchar()) != '\n' && c != EOF){
                        if(cp - destination < MAXLEN - 1)
                                *cp++ = c;
                }
                *cp = 0;
                if(c == EOF && cp == destination)
                        return(0);
        }
        return(destination);
}
```

**(Example 5.11)**

Finally, for the extremely brave, here is the whole thing with even p_array allocated using malloc. Further, most of the array indexing is rewritten to use pointer notation. If you are feeling queasy, skip this example. It is hard. One word of explanation: char **p means a pointer to a pointer to a character. Many C programmers find this hard to deal with.

```c
#include <stdio.h>
#include <stdlib.h>
#include <string.h>

#define MAXSTRING      50     /* max no. of strings */
#define MAXLEN         80     /* max length. of strings */

void print_arr(const char **p_array);
void sort_arr(const char **p_array);
char *next_string(void);

main(){
        char **p_array;
        int nstrings;   /* count of strings read */

        p_array = (char **)malloc(
                        sizeof(char *[MAXSTRING + 1]));
        if(p_array == 0){
                printf("No memory\n");
                exit(EXIT_FAILURE);
        }

        nstrings = 0;
        while(nstrings < MAXSTRING &&
                (p_array[nstrings] = next_string()) != 0){

                nstrings++;
        }
        /* terminate p_array */
        p_array[nstrings] = 0;

        sort_arr(p_array);
        print_arr(p_array);
        exit(EXIT_SUCCESS);
}

void print_arr(const char **p_array){
        while(*p_array)
                printf("%s\n", *p_array++);
}

void
sort_arr(const char **p_array){
        const char **lo_p, **hi_p, *tmp;
```

```
        for(lo_p = p_array;
                *lo_p != 0 && *(lo_p + 1) != 0;
                                        lo_p++){
                for(hi_p = lo_p + 1; *hi_p != 0; hi_p++){

                        if(strcmp(*hi_p, *lo_p) >= 0)
                                continue;
                        /* swap strings */
                        tmp = *hi_p;
                        *hi_p = *lo_p;
                        *lo_p = tmp;
                }
        }
}


char
*next_string(void){
        char *cp, *destination;
        int c;

        destination = (char *)malloc(MAXLEN);
        if(destination != 0){
                cp = destination;
                while((c = getchar()) != '\n' && c != EOF){
                        if(cp - destination < MAXLEN - 1)
                                *cp++ = c;
                }
                *cp = 0;
                if(c == EOF && cp == destination)
                        return(0);
        }
        return(destination);
}
```
(Example 5.12)

To further illustrate the use of malloc, another example program follows which can cope with arbitrarily long strings. It simply reads strings from its standard input, looking for a newline character to mark the end of the string, then prints the string on its standard output. It stops when it detects end-of-file. The characters are put into an array, the end of the string being indicated (as always) by a zero. The newline is not stored, but used to detect when a full line of input should be printed on the output. The program doesn't know how long the string will be, so it starts by allocating ten characters – enough for a short string.

If the string is more than ten characters long, malloc is called to allocate room for the current string plus ten more characters. The current characters are copied into the new space, the old storage previously allocated is released and the program continues using the new storage.

To release storage allocated by malloc, the library function free is used. If you don't release storage when it isn't needed any more, it just hangs around taking up space. Using free allows it to be 'given away', or at least re-used later.

The program reports errors by using fprintf, a close cousin of printf. The only difference between them is that fprintf takes an additional first argument which indicates where its output should go. There are two constants of the right type for this purpose defined in stdio.h. Using stdout indicates that the program's standard output is to be used; stderr refers to the program's standard error stream. On some systems both may be the same, but other systems do make the distinction.

```c
#include ⟨stdio.h⟩
#include ⟨stdlib.h⟩
#include ⟨string.h⟩


#define GROW_BY 10      /* string grows by 10 chars */


main(){
        char *str_p, *next_p, *tmp_p;
        int ch, need, chars_read;


        if(GROW_BY < 2){
                fprintf(stderr,
                        "Growth constant too small\n");
                exit(EXIT_FAILURE);
        }


        str_p = (char *)malloc(GROW_BY);
        if(str_p == NULL){
                fprintf(stderr,"No initial store\n");
                exit(EXIT_FAILURE);
        }


        next_p = str_p;
        chars_read = 0;
        while((ch = getchar()) != EOF){
                /*
                 * Completely restart at each new line.
                 * There will always be room for the
                 * terminating zero in the string,
                 * because of the check further down,
                 * unless GROW_BY is less than 2,
                 * and that has already been checked.
                 */
```

```
if(ch == '\n'){
        /* indicate end of line */
        *next_p = 0;
        printf("%s\n", str_p);
        free(str_p);
        chars_read = 0;
        str_p = (char *)malloc(GROW_BY);
        if(str_p == NULL){
                fprintf(stderr,"No initial store\n");
                exit(EXIT_FAILURE);
        }
        next_p = str_p;
        continue;
}
/*
 * Have we reached the end of the current
 * allocation ?
 */
if(chars_read == GROW_BY-1){
        *next_p = 0;     /* mark end of string */
        /*
         * use pointer subtraction
         * to find length of
         * current string.
         */
        need = next_p - str_p + 1;
        tmp_p = (char *)malloc(need + GROW_BY);
        if(tmp_p == NULL){
                fprintf(stderr,"No more store\n");
                exit(EXIT_FAILURE);
        }
        /*
         * Copy the string using library.
         */
        strcpy(tmp_p, str_p);
        free(str_p);
        str_p = tmp_p;
        /*
         * and reset next_p, character count
         */
        next_p = str_p + need - 1;
        chars_read = 0;
}
/*
 * Put character at end of current string.
 */
*next_p++ = ch;
chars_read++;
}
```

```
/*
 * EOF — but do unprinted characters exist?
 */
if(str_p — next_p){
        *next_p = 0;
        fprintf(stderr,"Incomplete last line\n");
        printf("%s\n", str_p);
}
exit(EXIT_SUCCESS);
}
```

(Example 5.13)

That may not be a particularly realistic example of how to handle arbitrarily long strings – for one thing, the maximum storage demand is *twice* the amount needed for the longest string – but it does actually work. It also costs rather a lot in terms of copying around. Both problems could be reduced by using the library realloc function instead.

A more sophisticated method might use a linked list, implemented with the use of **structures**, as described in the next chapter. That would have its drawbacks too though, because then the standard library routines wouldn't work for a different method of storing strings.

### 5.5.1 What sizeof can't do

One common mistake made by beginners is shown below:

```
#include (stdio.h)
#include (stdlib.h)

const char arr[] = "hello";
const char *cp = arr;

main(){
        printf("Size of arr %lu\n", (unsigned long)
                        sizeof(arr));
        printf("Size of *cp %lu\n", (unsigned long)
                        sizeof(*cp));
        exit(EXIT_SUCCESS);
}
```

(Example 5.14)

The numbers printed will *not* be the same. The first will, correctly, identify the size of arr as 6; five characters followed by a null. The second one will always, on every system, print 1. That's because the type of *cp is const char, which can only have a size of 1, whereas the type of arr is different: array of const char. The confusion arises because this is the one place that the use of an array is *not* converted into a pointer first. It is never possible, using sizeof, to find out how long an array a pointer points to; you *must* have a genuine array name instead.

### 5.5.2 **The type of** sizeof

Now comes the question of just what this does:

sizeof ( sizeof (*anything legal*) )

That is to say, what type does the result of sizeof have? The answer is that it is implementation defined, and will be either unsigned long or unsigned int, depending on your implementation. There are two safe things to do: either always cast the return value to unsigned long, as the examples have done, or to use the defined type size_t provided in the ⟨stddef.h⟩ header file. For example:

```
#include ⟨stddef.h⟩
#include ⟨stdio.h⟩
#include ⟨stdlib.h⟩

main(){
        size_t sz;
        sz = sizeof(sz);
        printf("size of sizeof is %lu\n",
                (unsigned long)sz);
        exit(EXIT_SUCCESS);
}
```
                                                        (**Example 5.15**)

## 5.6 **Pointers to functions**

A useful technique is the ability to have pointers to functions. Their declaration is easy: write the declaration as it would be for the function, say

```
int func(int a, float b);
```

and simply put brackets around the name and a * in front of it: that declares the pointer. Because of precedence, if you don't parenthesize the name, you declare a function returning a pointer:

```
/* function returning pointer to int */
int *func(int a, float b);

/* pointer to function returning int */
int (*func)(int a, float b);
```

Once you've got the pointer, you can assign the address of the right sort of function just by using its name: like an array, a function name is turned into an address when it's used in an expression. You can call the function using one of two forms:

```
(*func)(1,2);
/* or */
func(1,2);
```

The second form has been newly blessed by the Standard. Here's a simple example.

```
#include ⟨stdio.h⟩
#include ⟨stdlib.h⟩

void func(int);

main(){
        void (*fp)(int);

        fp = func;
        (*fp)(1);
        fp(2);
        exit(EXIT_SUCCESS);
}

void
func(int arg){
        printf("%d\n", arg);
}
```
(Example 5.16)

If you like writing finite state machines, you might like to know that you can have an array of pointers to functions, with declaration and use like this:

```
void (*fparr[])(int, float) = {
                        /* initializers */
            };
/* then call one */

fparr[5](1, 3.4);
```
(Example 5.17)

But we'll draw a veil over it at this point!

## 5.7 Expressions involving pointers

Because of the introduction of qualified types and of the notion of incomplete types, together with the use of void *, there are now some complicated rules about how you can mix pointers and what arithmetic with pointers really permits you to do. Most people will survive quite well without ever learning this explicitly, because a lot of it is 'obvious', but we will include it here in case you do want to know. For the final word in accuracy, obviously you will want to see what the Standard says. What follows is our interpretation in (we hope) plainer English.

You don't yet know the Standard means when it talks about **objects** or **incomplete types**. So far we have tended to use the term loosely, but properly speaking an object is a piece of data storage whose contents is to be interpreted as a value. A function is not an object. An incomplete type is one whose name and type are mostly known, but whose size hasn't yet been determined. You can get these in two ways:

(1) By declaring an array but omitting information about its size: `int x[];`. In that case, there must be additional information given later in a definition for the array. The type remains incomplete until the later definition.

(2) By declaring a **structure** or **union** but not defining its contents. The contents must be defined in a later declaration. The type remains incomplete until the later declaration.

There will be some more discussion of incomplete types in later chapters.

Now for what you are allowed to do with pointers. Note that wherever we talk about qualified types they can be qualified with `const`, `volatile`, or both; the examples are illustrated with `const` only.

### 5.7.1 Conversions

Pointers to `void` can be freely converted backwards and forwards with pointers to any object or incomplete type. Converting a pointer to an object or an incomplete type to `void *` and then back gives a value which is equal to the original one:

```
int i;
int *ip;
void *vp;

ip = &i;
vp = ip;
ip = vp;
if(ip != &i)
        printf("Compiler error\n");
```

An unqualified pointer type may be converted to a qualified pointer type, but the reverse is not true. The two values will be equal:

```
int i;
int *pi, *const cpi;

ip = &i;
cpi = ip;        /* permitted */
if(cpi != ip)
        printf("Compiler error\n");
ip = cpi;        /* not permitted */
```

A null pointer constant (see earlier) will not be equal to a pointer to any object or function.


### 5.7.2 Arithmetic

Expressions can add (or subtract, which is equivalent to adding negative values) integral values to the value of a pointer to any object type. The result has the type of the pointer and if $n$ is added, then the result points $n$ array elements away from the pointer. The most common use is repeatedly to add 1 to a pointer to step it from the start to the end of an array, but addition or subtraction of values other than one is possible.

If the pointer resulting from the addition points in front of the array or past the non-existent element just after the last element of the array, then you have had overflow or underflow and the result is undefined.

The last-plus-one element of an array has always been assumed to be a valid address for a pointer and the Standard confirms this. You mustn't actually access that element, but the address is guaranteed to exist rather than being an overflow condition.

We've been careful to use the term 'expression' rather than saying that you actually add something to the pointer itself. You can do that, but only if the pointer is not qualified with const (of course). The increment and decrement operators are equivalent to adding or subtracting 1.

Two pointers to **compatible types** whether or not qualified may be subtracted. The result has the type ptrdiff_t, which is defined in the header file ⟨stddef.h⟩. Both pointers must point into the same array, or one past the end of the array, otherwise the behaviour is undefined. The value of the result is the number of array elements that separate the two pointers. For example:

```
int x[100];
int *pi, *cpi = &x[99]; /* cpi points to the last element of x */

pi = x;
if((cpi - pi) != 99)
        printf("Error\n");
pi = cpi;
pi++;                    /* increment past end of x */
if((pi - cpi) != 1)
        printf("Error\n");
```


### 5.7.3 Relational expressions

These allow us to compare pointers with each other. You can only compare

- Pointers to compatible object types with each other
- Pointers to compatible incomplete types with each other.

It does not matter if the types that are pointed to are qualified or unqualified.

If two pointers compare equal to each other then they point to the same thing, whether it is an object or the non-existent element off the end of an array (see arithmetic, above). If two pointers point to the same thing, then they compare equal to each other. The relational operators >, <= and so on all give the result that you would expect if the pointers point into the same array: if one pointer compares less than another, then it points nearer to the front of the array.

A null pointer constant can be assigned to a pointer; that pointer will then compare equal to the null pointer constant (which is pretty obvious). A null pointer constant or a null pointer will not compare equal to a pointer that points to anything which actually exists.

### 5.7.4 Assignment

You can use pointers with the assignment operators if the following conditions are met:

- The left-hand operand is a pointer and the right-hand operand is a null pointer constant.
- One operand is a pointer to an object or incomplete type; the other is a pointer to void (whether qualified or not).
- Both of the operands are pointers to compatible types (whether qualified or not).

In the last two cases, the type pointed to by the left-hand side must have at least the same qualifiers as the type pointed to by the right-hand side (possibly more).

So, you can assign a pointer to int to a pointer to const int (more qualifiers on the left than the right) but you cannot assign a pointer to const int to a pointer to int. If you think about it, it makes sense.

The += and -= operators can involve pointers as long as the left-hand side is a pointer to an object and the right-hand side is an integral expression. The arithmetic rules above describe what happens.

### 5.7.5 Conditional operator

The description of the behaviour of this operator when it is used with pointers has already been given in Chapter 3.

## 5.8 Arrays, the & operator and function declarations

We have already emphasized that in most cases the name of an array is converted into the address of its first element; one notable exception being when it is the operand of sizeof, which is essential if the stuff to do with malloc is to work. Another case is when an array name is the operand of the & address-of operator. Here, it is converted into the *address of the whole array*. What's the difference? Even if you think that addresses would be in some way 'the same', the critical difference is that they have different types. For an array of *n* elements of type *T*, then the address of the first element has type 'pointer to *T*'; the address of the whole array has type 'pointer to array of *n* elements of type *T*'; clearly very different. Here's an example of it:

```
int ar[10];
int *ip;
int (*ar10i)[10];      /* pointer to array of 10 ints */

ip = ar;               /* address of first element */
ip = &ar[0];           /* address of first element */
ar10i = &ar;           /* address of whole array */
```

Where do pointers to arrays matter? Not often, in truth, although of course we know that declarations that look like multidimensional arrays are really arrays of arrays. Here is an example which uses that fact, but you'll have to work out what it does for yourself. It is *not* common to do this sort of thing in practice:

```
int ar2d[5][4];
int (*ar4i)[4]; /* pointer to array of 4 ints */

for(ar4i= ar2d; ar4i < &(ar2d[5]); ar4i++)
        (*ar4i)[2] = 0; /* ar2d[n][2] = 0 */
```

More important than addresses of arrays is what happens when you declare a function that takes an array as an argument. Because of the 'conversion to the address of its first element' rule, even if you do try to pass an array to a function by giving its name as an argument, you actually end up passing a pointer to its first element. The usual rule really does apply in this case! But what if you declare that the function *does* have an argument whose type is 'array of something' – like this:

```
void f(int ar[10]);
```

What happens? The answer may surprise you slightly. The compiler looks at that and says to itself 'Ho ho. That's going to be a pointer when the function is called' and then rewrites the parameter type to be a pointer. As a result, all three of these declarations are identical:

```
void f(int ar[10]);
void f(int *ar);
void f(int ar[]);      /* since the size of the array is irrelevant! */
```

Having seen that, your reaction might be to look for a solid object to bang your head against for a while, but we don't recommend it. Take a grip on yourself instead and put in the effort to work out:

- Why that isn't really such a shock
- Why, given a function declaration like that, then within the function, expressions of the form ar[5] and so on work as expected anyhow.

Give that last one some thought. When you get to the bottom of it, you really *will* have grasped what arrays and pointers are about.

## ■ 5.9 SUMMARY

You have been introduced to arrays, pointers and the storage allocater. The last of the topics will prove to be more useful in the next chapter, but the other two are central to the language.

You *cannot* use C properly without understanding the use of pointers. Arrays are simple and unsurprising, except for the fact that when it's used in an expression, an array name usually converts into a pointer to its first element; that often takes time to sink in.

The C approach to support for strings often causes raised eyebrows. The null-terminated array of character model is both powerful and flexible. The fact that string manipulation is not built in to the language at first glance seems to rule C out of serious contention for character-oriented work, yet that is exactly where the language scores well compared with the alternatives, at least when speed is important. All the same, it's hard work for the programmer.

Pointer arithmetic is easy and extremely convenient. It's harder for ex-assembler programmers to learn, because of the tendency to try to translate it into what they 'know' the machine is doing. However, much harder for people with very low-level experience is the idea of the non-equivalence of pointers of different types. Try hard to throw away the idea that pointers contain addresses (in the hardware sense) and it will repay the effort.

The facility to obtain arbitrary pieces of storage using malloc and the associated stuff is extremely important. You might wish to defer it for a while, but don't leave it for too long. An obvious feature of C programs written by inexperienced users is their dependence on fixed size arrays. Malloc gives you considerably more flexibility and is worth the effort to learn about.

The examples of the use of sizeof should help to eliminate a few common misconceptions about what it does. You may not use it all that often, but when you do need it, there's no substitute.

## EXERCISES

5.1  What is the valid range of indices for an array of ten objects?

5.2  What happens if you take the address of the 11th member of that array?

5.3  When is it valid to compare the values of two pointers?

**5.4**   What is the use of a pointer to void?

**5.5**   Write functions which:

(a) Compare two strings for equality. If they are equal, zero is returned, otherwise the difference in value between the first two non-matching characters.

(b) Find the first occurrence of a specific character in a given string. Return a pointer to the occurrence in the string, or zero if it is not found.

(c) Take two strings as arguments. If the first exists in the second as a substring, return a pointer to the first occurrence, otherwise zero.

**5.6**   Explain the examples using malloc to somebody else.

# CHAPTER 6

# Structured Data Types

## 6.1 History

The development of the early computer languages went either one way or the other. COBOL concentrated on the structure of data but not on arithmetic or algorithms, FORTRAN and ALGOL leant the other way. Scientific users wanted to do numeric work on relatively unstructured data (although arrays were soon found to be indispensable) and commercial users needed only basic arithmetic but knew that the key issue was the structure of the data.

The ideas that have influenced C are a mixture of the two schools; it has the structured control of flow expected in a language of its age, and has also made a start on data structures. So far we have concentrated on the algorithmic aspects of the language and haven't thought hard about data storage. Whilst it's true that arrays fall into the general category of data structuring, they are so simple, and so commonly in use, that they don't deserve a chapter to themselves. Until now we have been looking at a kind of block-structured FORTRAN.

The trend in the late 1980s and early '90s seems to be towards integrating both the data and the algorithms; it's then called Object-Oriented programming. There is no specific support for that in C. C++ is a language based on C that does offer support for Object-Oriented techniques, but it is out of our scope to discuss it further.

For a large class of problems in computing, it is the data and not the algorithms that is the most interesting. If the initial design gets its data structures right, the rest of the effort in putting a program together is often quite small. However, you need

145

help from the language. If there is no support for structured data types other than arrays, writing programs becomes both less convenient and also more prone to errors. It is the job of a good language to do more than just *allow* you to do something; it must actively *help* as well.

C offers arrays, structures and unions as its contribution to data structuring. They have proved to be entirely adequate for most users' needs over the years and remain essentially unchanged by the Standard.

## 6.2 Structures

Arrays allow for a named collection of identical objects. This is suitable for a number of tasks, but isn't really very flexible. Most real data objects are complicated things with an inherent structure that does not fit well on to array style storage. Let's use a concrete example.

Imagine that the job is something to do with a typesetting package. In this system, the individual characters have not only their character values but also some additional attributes like font and point size. The font doesn't affect the character as such, but only the way that it is displayed: this is the normal font, *this is in italics* and **this is in bold font**. Point size is similar. It describes the size of the characters when they are printed. For example, the point size of this text increases by two now. It goes back again now. If our characters have three independent attributes, how can they be represented in a single object?

With C it's easy. First work out how to represent the individual attributes in the basic types. Let's assume that we can still store the character itself in a char, that the font can be encoded into a short (1 for regular, 2 italic, 3 bold and so on) and that the point size will also fit a short. These are all quite reasonable assumptions. Most systems only support a few tens of fonts even if they are very sophisticated, and point sizes are normally in the range six to the small hundreds. Below six is almost invisible, above 50 is bigger than the biggest newspaper banner headlines. So we have a char and two shorts that are to be treated as a single entity. Here's how to declare it in C.

```
struct wp_char{
        char wp_cval;
        short wp_font;
        short wp_psize;
};
```

That effectively declares a new type of object which can be used in your program. The whole thing is introduced by the struct keyword, which is followed by an optional identifier known as the tag, wp_char in this case. The tag only serves the purpose of giving a name to this type of structure and allows us to refer to the type later on. After a declaration like the one just seen, the tag can be used like this:

```
struct wp_char x, y;
```

That defines two variables called x and y just as it would have done if the definition had been

```
int x, y;
```

but of course in the first example the variables are of type struct wp_char, and in the second their type is int. The tag is a name for the new type that we have introduced.

It's worth remembering that structure tags can safely be used as ordinary identifiers as well. They only mean something special when they are preceded by the keyword struct. It is quite common to see a structured object being defined with the same name as its structure tag.

```
struct wp_char wp_char;
```

That defines a variable called wp_char of type struct wp_char. This is described by saying that structure tags have their own 'name space' and cannot collide with other names. We'll investigate tags some more in the discussion of 'incomplete types'.

Variables can also be defined immediately following a structure declaration.

```
struct wp_char{
        char wp_cval;
        short wp_font;
        short wp_psize;
}v1;

struct wp_char v2;
```

We now have two variables, v1 and v2. If all the necessary objects are defined at the end of the structure declaration, the way that v1 was, then the tag becomes unnecessary (except if it is needed later for use with sizeof and in casts) and is often not present.

The two variables are structured objects, each containing three separate *members* called wp_cval, wp_font and wp_psize. To access the individual members of the structures, the 'dot' operator is used:

```
v1.wp_cval = 'x';
v1.wp_font = 1;
v1.wp_psize = 10;

v2 = v1;
```

The individual members of v1 are initialized to suitable values, then the whole of v1 is copied into v2 in an assignment.

In fact the only operation permitted on whole structures is assignment: they can be assigned to each other, passed as arguments to functions and returned by functions. However, it is not a very efficient operation to copy structures and most programs avoid structure copying by manipulating pointers to structures instead. It is generally quicker to copy pointers around than structures. A surprising omission from the language is the facility to compare structures for equality, but there is a good reason for this which will be mentioned shortly.

Here is an example using an array of structures like the one before. A function is used to read characters from the program's standard input and return an appropriately initialized structure. When a newline has been read or the array is full, the structures are sorted into order depending on the character value, and then printed out.

```
#include <stdio.h>
#include <stdlib.h>

#define ARSIZE 10

struct wp_char{
        char wp_cval;
        short wp_font;
        short wp_psize;
}ar[ARSIZE];

/*
 * type of the input function -
 * could equally have been declared above;
 * it returns a structure and takes no arguments.
 */
struct wp_char infun(void);

main(){
        int icount, lo_indx, hi_indx;

        for(icount = 0; icount < ARSIZE; icount++){
                ar[icount] = infun();
                if(ar[icount].wp_cval == '\n'){
                        /*
                         * Leave the loop.
                         * not incrementing icount means that the
                         * '\n' is ignored in the sort
                         */
                        break;
                }
        }

        /* now a simple exchange sort */

        for(lo_indx = 0; lo_indx <= icount - 2; lo_indx++)
                for(hi_indx = lo_indx + 1; hi_indx <= icount - 1; hi_indx++){
                        if(ar[lo_indx].wp_cval > ar[hi_indx].wp_cval){
                                /*
                                 * Swap the two structures.
                                 */
```

```
                         struct wp_char wp_tmp = ar[lo_indx];
                         ar[lo_indx] = ar[hi_indx];
                         ar[hi_indx] = wp_tmp;
              }
      }


      /* now print */
      for(lo_indx = 0; lo_indx < icount; lo_indx++){
              printf("%c %d %d\n", ar[lo_indx].wp_cval,
                              ar[lo_indx].wp_font,
                              ar[lo_indx].wp_psize);
      }
      exit(EXIT_SUCCESS);
}


struct wp_char
infun(void){
      struct wp_char wp_char;

      wp_char.wp_cval = getchar();
      wp_char.wp_font = 2;
      wp_char.wp_psize = 10;
      return(wp_char);
}
```
                                                    **(Example 6.1)**

Once it is possible to declare structures it seems pretty natural to declare arrays of them, use them as members of other structures and so on. In fact the only restriction is that a structure cannot contain an example of itself as a member – in which case its size would be an interesting concept for philosophers to debate, but hardly useful to a C programmer.


## 6.2.1 Pointers and structures

If what the last section says is true – that it is more common to use pointers to structures than to use the structures directly – we need to know how to do it. Declaring pointers is easy of course:

```
struct wp_char *wp_p;
```

gives us one straight away. But how do we access the members of the structure? One way might be to look through the pointer to get the whole structure, then select the member:

```
/* get the structure, then select a member */
(*wp_p).wp_cval
```

that would certainly work (the parentheses are there because . has a higher precedence than *). It's not an easy notation to work with though, so C introduces a new
operator to clean things up; it is usually known as the 'pointing-to' operator. Here it is
being used:

```
/* the wp_cval in the structure wp_p points to */
wp_p->wp_cval = 'x';
```

and although it might not look a lot easier than its alternative, it pays off when the
structure contains pointers, as in a linked list. The pointing-to syntax is much easier if
you want to follow two or three stages down the links of a linked list. If you haven't
come across linked lists before, you're going to learn a lot more than just the use of
structures before this chapter finishes!

  If the thing on the left of the . or -> operator is qualified (with const or volatile)
then the result also has those qualifiers associated with it. Here it is, illustrated with
pointers; when the pointer points to a qualified type the result that you get is also
qualified:

```
#include ⟨stdio.h⟩
#include ⟨stdlib.h⟩

struct somestruct{
        int i;
};

main(){
        struct somestruct *ssp, s_item;
        const struct somestruct *cssp;

        s_item.i = 1;    /* fine */
        ssp = &s_item;
        ssp->i += 2;     /* fine */
        cssp = &s_item;
        cssp->i = 0;     /* not permitted — cssp points to const objects */
        exit(EXIT_SUCCESS);
}
```

Not all compiler writers seem to have noticed that requirement – the compiler that we
used to test the last example failed to warn that the final assignment violated a
constraint.

  Here is Example 6.1 rewritten using pointers, and with the input function
infun changed to accept a pointer to a structure rather than returning one. This is
much more likely to be what would be seen in practice.

  (It is fair to say that, for a really efficient implementation, even the copying of
structures would probably be dropped, especially if they were large. Instead, an array
of pointers would be used, and the pointers exchanged until the sorted data could be

found by traversing the pointer array in index order. That would complicate things too much for a simple example.)

```c
#include (stdio.h)
#include (stdlib.h)

#define ARSIZE 10

struct wp_char{
        char wp_cval;
        short wp_font;
        short wp_psize;
}ar[ARSIZE];

void infun(struct wp_char *);

main(){
        struct wp_char wp_tmp, *lo_indx, *hi_indx, *in_p;

        for(in_p = ar; in_p < &ar[ARSIZE]; in_p++){
                infun(in_p);
                if(in_p->wp_cval == '\n'){
                        /*
                         * Leave the loop.
                         * not incrementing in_p means that the
                         * '\n' is ignored in the sort
                         */
                        break;
                }
        }

        /*
         * Now a simple exchange sort.
         * We must be careful to avoid the danger of pointer underflow,
         * so check that there are at least two entries to sort.
         */

        if(in_p-ar > 1) for(lo_indx = ar; lo_indx <= in_p - 2; lo_indx++){
                for(hi_indx = lo_indx + 1; hi_indx <= in_p - 1; hi_indx++){
                        if(lo_indx->wp_cval > hi_indx->wp_cval){
                                /*
                                 * Swap the structures.
                                 */
                                struct wp_char wp_tmp = *lo_indx;
                                *lo_indx = *hi_indx;
                                *hi_indx = wp_tmp;
                        }
                }
        }
}
```

```
            /* now print */
            for(lo_indx = ar; lo_indx < in_p; lo_indx++){
                    printf("%c %d %d\n", lo_indx->wp_cval,
                                         lo_indx->wp_font,
                                         lo_indx->wp_psize);
            }
            exit(EXIT_SUCCESS);
    }


    void
    infun( struct wp_char *inp){
            inp->wp_cval = getchar();
            inp->wp_font = 2;
            inp->wp_psize = 10;

            return;
    }
```
                                                            **(Example 6.2)**

The next issue is to consider what a structure looks like in terms of storage layout. It's best not to worry about this too much, but it is sometimes useful if you have to use C to access record-structured data written by other programs. The wp_char structure will be allocated storage as shown in Figure 6.1.

struct wp_char

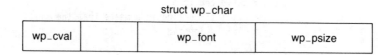

**Figure 6.1**   Storage layout of a structure.

The diagram assumes a number of things: that a char takes one byte of storage; that a short needs two bytes; and that shorts must be aligned on even byte addresses in this architecture. As a result the structure contains an unnamed 1-byte member inserted by the compiler for architectural reasons. Such addressing restrictions are quite common and can often result in structures containing 'holes'.

The Standard makes some guarantees about the layout of structures and unions:

- Members of a structure are allocated within the structure in the order of their appearance in the declaration and have ascending addresses.
- There must not be any padding in front of the first member.
- The address of a structure is the same as the address of its first member, provided that the appropriate cast is used. Given the previous declaration of struct wp_char, if item is of type struct wp_char, then (char *)item == &item.wp_cval.
- Bit fields (see Section 6.4) don't actually have addresses, but are conceptually packed into **units** which obey the rules above.

### 6.2.2 Linked lists and other structures

The combination of structures and pointers opens up a lot of interesting possibilities. This is not a textbook on complex linked data structures, but it will go on to describe two very common examples of the breed: linked lists and trees. Both have a feature in common: they consist of structures containing pointers to other structures, all the structures typically being of the same type. Figure 6.2 shows a picture of a linked list.

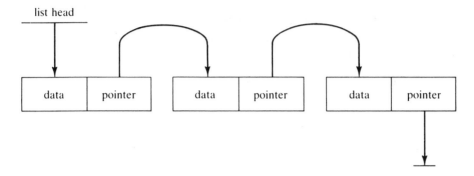

**Figure 6.2**   List linked by pointers.

The sort of declaration needed for that is this:

```
struct list_ele{
        int data;        /* or whatever you like here */
        struct list_ele *ele_p;
};
```

Now, at first glance, it seems to contain itself – which is forbidden – but in fact it only contains a *pointer* to itself. How come the pointer declaration is allowed? Well, by the time the compiler reaches the pointer declaration it already knows that there is such a thing as a struct list_ele so the declaration is permitted. In fact, it is possible to make an incomplete declaration of a structure by saying

```
struct list_ele;
```

at some point before the full declaration. A declaration like that declares an **incomplete type**. This will allow the declaration of pointers before the full declaration is seen. It is also important in the case of cross-referencing structures where each must contain a pointer to the other, as shown in the following example.

```
struct s_1;      /* incomplete type */

struct s_2{
        int something;
        struct s_1 *sp;
};
```

```
struct s_1{      /* now the full declaration */
        float something;
        struct s_2 *sp;
};
```
                                                            **(Example 6.3)**

This illustrates the need for incomplete types. It also illustrates an important thing about the names of structure members: they inhabit a name-space per structure, so element names can be the same in different structures without causing any problems.

Incomplete types may only be used where the size of the structure isn't needed yet. A full declaration must have been given by the time that the size is used. The later full declaration mustn't be in an inner block because then it becomes a new declaration of a different structure.

```
struct x;       /* incomplete type */

/* valid uses of the tag */
struct x *p, func(void);

void f1(void){
        struct x{int i;};       /* redeclaration! */
}

/* full declaration now */
struct x{
        float f;
}s_x;

void
f2(void){
        /* valid statements */
        p = &s_x;
        *p = func();
        s_x = func();
}

struct x
func(void){
        struct x tmp;
        tmp.f = 0;
        return (tmp);
}
```
                                                            **(Example 6.4)**

There's one thing to watch out for: you get an incomplete type of a structure *simply by mentioning its name!* That means that this works:

```
struct abc{ struct xyz *p;};
        /* the incomplete type 'struct xyz' now declared */
struct xyz{ struct abc *p;};
        /* the incomplete type is now completed */
```

There's a horrible danger in the last example, though, as this shows:

```
struct xyz{float x;} var1;

main(){
        struct abc{ struct xyz *p;} var2;

        /* AAAGH — struct xyz REDECLARED */
        struct xyz{ struct abc *p;} var3;
}
```

The result is that var2.p can hold the address of var1, but emphatically not the address of var3 which is of a different type! It can be fixed (assuming that it's not what you wanted) like this:

```
struct xyz{float x;} var1;

main(){
        struct xyz;      /* new incomplete type 'struct xyz' */
        struct abc{ struct xyz *p;} var2;
        struct xyz{ struct abc *p;} var3;
}
```

The type of a structure or union is completed when the closing } of its declaration is seen; it must contain at least one member or the behaviour is undefined.

The other principal way to get incomplete types is to declare arrays without specifying their size – their type is incomplete until a later declaration provides the missing information:

```
int ar[];      /* incomplete type */
int ar[5];     /* completes the type */
```

If you try that out, it will only work if the declarations are outside any blocks (external declarations), but that's for other reasons.

Back to the linked list. There were three elements linked into the list, which could have been built like this:

```
struct list_ele{
        int data;
        struct list_ele *pointer;
}ar[3];

main(){
        ar[0].data = 5;
        ar[0].pointer = &ar[1];
        ar[1].data = 99;
        ar[1].pointer = &ar[2];
        ar[2].data = -7;
        ar[2].pointer = 0;      /* mark end of list */
        return(0);
}
```
(Example 6.5)

and the contents of the list can be printed in two ways. The array can be traversed in order of index, or the pointers can be used as in the following example.

```
#include (stdio.h)
#include (stdlib.h)

struct list_ele{
        int data;
        struct list_ele *pointer;
}ar[3];

main(){
        struct list_ele *lp;

        ar[0].data = 5;
        ar[0].pointer = &ar[1];
        ar[1].data = 99;
        ar[1].pointer = &ar[2];
        ar[2].data = -7;
        ar[2].pointer = 0;      /* mark end of list */

        /* follow pointers */
        lp = ar;
        while(lp){
                printf("contents %d\n", lp->data);
                lp = lp->pointer;
        }
        exit(EXIT_SUCCESS);
}
```

                                                                    (Example 6.6)

It's the way that the pointers are followed which makes the example interesting. Notice how the pointer in each element is used to refer to the next one, until the pointer whose value is 0 is found. That value causes the while loop to stop. Of course the pointers can be arranged in any order at all, which is what makes the list such a flexible structure. Here is a function which could be included as part of the last program to sort the linked list into numeric order of its data fields. It rearranges the pointers so that the list, when traversed in pointer sequence, is found to be in order. It is important to note that the data itself is not copied. The function must return a pointer to the head of the list, because that is not necessarily at ar[0] any more.

```
struct list_ele *
sortfun( struct list_ele *list )
{
        int exchange;
        struct list_ele *nextp, *thisp, dummy;
```

```
/*
 * Algorithm is this:
 * Repeatedly scan list.
 * If two list items are out of order,
 * link them in the other way round.
 * Stop if a full pass is made and no
 * exchanges are required.
 * The whole business is confused by
 * working one element behind the
 * first one of interest.
 * This is because of the simple mechanics of
 * linking and unlinking elements.
 */

    dummy.pointer = list;
    do{
            exchange = 0;
            thisp = &dummy;
            while( (nextp = thisp->pointer)
                    && nextp->pointer){
                    if(nextp->data < nextp->pointer->data){
                            /* exchange */
                            exchange = 1;
                            thisp->pointer = nextp->pointer;
                            nextp->pointer =
                                    thisp->pointer->pointer;
                            thisp->pointer->pointer = nextp;
                    }
                    thisp = thisp->pointer;
            }
    }while(exchange);
    return(dummy.pointer);
}
```
                                                                **(Example 6.7)**

Expressions such as thisp->pointer->pointer are commonplace in list processing.
It's worth making sure that you understand it; the notation emphasizes the way that
links are followed.


## 6.2.3 Trees

Another very popular data structure is the tree. It's actually a linked list with
branches; a common type is the *binary tree* which has elements (nodes) looking like
this:

```
struct tree_node{
        int data;
        struct tree_node *left_p, *right_p;
};
```

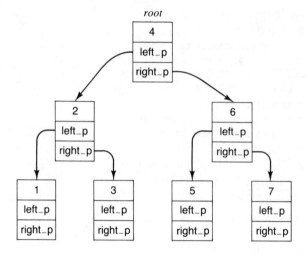

**Figure 6.3** A tree.

For historical and essentially irrelevant reasons, trees in computer science work upside down. They have their *root* node at the top and their *branches* spread out downwards. In Figure 6.3, the 'data' members of the nodes are replaced by values which will be used in the discussion that follows.

Trees may not seem very exciting if your main interest lies in routine character handling and processing, but they are extremely important to the designers of databases, compilers and other complex tools.

The advantage of a tree is that, if it is properly arranged, the layout of the data can support binary searching very simply. It is always possible to add new nodes to a tree at the appropriate place and a tree is basically a flexible and useful data structure.

Look at Figure 6.3. The tree is carefully constructed so that it can be searched to find whether a given value can be found in the data portions of the nodes. Let's say we want to find if a value x is already present in the tree. The algorithm is this:

> Start at the root of the tree:
> if the tree is empty (no nodes)
> then return 'failure'.
> else if the data in the current node is equal to the value being searched for
> then return 'success'
> else if the data in the current node is greater than the value being searched for
> then search the tree indicated by the left pointer
> else search the tree indicated by the right pointer.

Here it is in C:

```
#include <stdio.h>
#include <stdlib.h>
```

```
struct tree_node{
        int data;
        struct tree_node *left_p, *right_p;
}tree[7];
/*
 * Tree search algorithm.
 * Searches for value ''v'' in tree,
 * returns pointer to first node found containing
 * the value otherwise 0.
 */
struct tree_node *
t_search(struct tree_node *root, int v){
        while(root){
                if(root->data == v)
                        return(root);
                if(root->data > v)
                        root = root->left_p;
                else
                        root = root->right_p;
        }
        /* value not found, no tree left */
        return(0);
}
main(){
        /* construct tree by hand */
        struct tree_node *tp, *root_p;
        int i;
        for(i = 0; i < 7; i++){
                int j;
                j = i + 1;
                tree[i].data = j;
                if(j == 2 || j == 6){
                        tree[i].left_p = &tree[i - 1];
                        tree[i].right_p = &tree[i + 1];
                }
        }
        /* root */
        root_p = &tree[3];
        root_p->left_p = &tree[1];
        root_p->right_p = &tree[5];
        /* try the search */
        tp = t_search(root_p, 9);
        if(tp)
                printf("found at position %d\n", tp-tree);
        else
                printf("value not found\n");
        exit(EXIT_SUCCESS);
}
```

(Example 6.8)

So that works fine. It is also interesting to note that, given a value, it can always be inserted at the appropriate point in the tree. The same search algorithm is used, but, instead of giving up when it finds that the value is not already in the tree, a new node is allocated by malloc, and is hung on the tree at the very place where the first null pointer was found. This is a mite more complicated to do because of the problem of handling the root pointer itself, and so a pointer to a pointer is used. Read the example carefully; it is not likely that you ever find anything more complicated than this in practice. If you can understand it, there is not much that should worry you about the vast majority of C language programs.

```
#include (stdio.h)
#include (stdlib.h)


struct tree_node{
        int data;
        struct tree_node *left_p, *right_p;
};


/*
 * Tree search algorithm.
 * Searches for value ''v'' in tree,
 * returns pointer to first node found containing
 * the value otherwise 0.
 */
struct tree_node *
t_search(struct tree_node *root, int v){

        while(root){
                printf("looking for %d, looking at %d\n",
                        v, root->data);
                if(root->data == v)
                        return(root);
                if(root->data > v)
                        root = root->left_p;
                else
                        root = root->right_p;
        }
        /* value not found, no tree left */
        return(0);
}
/*
 * Insert node into tree.
 * Return 0 for success,
 * 1 for value already in tree,
 * 2 for malloc error
 */
```

```
int
t_insert(struct tree_node **root, int v){
        while(*root){
                if((*root)->data == v)
                        return(1);
                if((*root)->data > v)
                        root = &((*root)->left_p);
                else
                        root = &((*root)->right_p);
        }
        /* value not found, no tree left */
        if((*root = (struct tree_node *)
                malloc(sizeof (struct tree_node)))
                        == 0)
                return(2);
        (*root)->data = v;
        (*root)->left_p = 0;
        (*root)->right_p = 0;
        return(0);
}

main(){
        /* construct tree by hand */
        struct tree_node *tp, *root_p = 0;
        int i;

        /* we ingore the return value of t_insert */
        t_insert(&root_p, 4);
        t_insert(&root_p, 2);
        t_insert(&root_p, 6);
        t_insert(&root_p, 1);
        t_insert(&root_p, 3);
        t_insert(&root_p, 5);
        t_insert(&root_p, 7);

        /* try the search */
        for(i = 1; i < 9; i++){
                tp = t_search(root_p, i);
                if(tp)
                        printf("%d found\n", i);
                else
                        printf("%d not found\n", i);
        }
        exit(EXIT_SUCCESS);
}
```
                                                        (Example 6.9)

Finally, the algorithm that allows you to walk along the tree visiting all the nodes in order is beautiful. It is the cleanest example of recursion that you are likely to see. Look at it and work out what it does.

```
void
t_walk(struct tree_node *root_p){

        if(root_p == 0)
                return;
        t_walk(root_p->left_p);
        printf("%d\n", root_p->data);
        t_walk(root_p->right_p);
}
```

(Example 6.10)

## 6.3 Unions

Unions don't take long to explain. They are the same as structures, except that, where you would have written struct before, now you write union. Everything works the same way, but with one big exception. In a structure, the members are allocated separate consecutive chunks of storage. In a union, every member is allocated the *same* piece of storage. What would you use them for? Well, sometimes you want a structure to contain different values of different types at different times but to conserve space as much as possible. Using a union, it's up to you to keep track of whatever type you put into it and make sure that you retrieve the right type at the right time. Here's an example:

```
#include ⟨stdio.h⟩
#include ⟨stdlib.h⟩

main(){
        union {
                float u_f;
                int u_i;
        }var;

        var.u_f = 23.5;
        printf("value is %f\n", var.u_f);
        var.u_i = 5;
        printf("value is %d\n", var.u_i);
        exit(EXIT_SUCCESS);
}
```

(Example 6.11)

If the example had, say, put a float into the union and then extracted it as an int, a strange value would have resulted. The two types are almost certainly not only stored differently, but of different lengths. The int retrieved would probably be the low-order bits of the machine representation of a float, and might easily be made up of part of the mantissa of the float plus a piece of the exponent. The Standard says that if you do this, the behaviour is implementation defined (not undefined). The behaviour is defined by the Standard in one case: if some of the members of a union are structures with a 'common initial sequence' (the first members of each structure have compatible type and in the case of **bitfields** are the same length), and the union currently contains one of them, then the common initial part of each can be used interchangeably. Oh good.

The C compiler does no more than work out what the biggest member in a union can be and allocates enough storage (appropriately aligned if necessary). In particular, no checking is done to make sure that the right sort of use is made of the members. That is your task, and you'll soon find out if you get it wrong. The members of a union all start at the same address – there is guaranteed to be no padding in front of any of them.

The most common way of remembering what is in a union is to embed it in a structure, with another member of the structure used to indicate the type of thing currently in the union. Here is how it might be used:

```c
#include (stdio.h)
#include (stdlib.h)

/* code for types in union */
#define FLOAT_TYPE      1
#define CHAR_TYPE       2
#define INT_TYPE        3

struct var_type{
        int type_in_union;
        union{
                float   un_float;
                char    un_char;
                int     un_int;
        }vt_un;
}var_type;

void
print_vt(void){

        switch(var_type.type_in_union){
                default:
                        printf("Unknown type in union\n");
                        break;
                case FLOAT_TYPE:
                        printf("%f\n", var_type.vt_un.un_float);
                        break;
                case CHAR_TYPE:
                        printf("%c\n", var_type.vt_un.un_char);
                        break;
                case INT_TYPE:
                        printf("%d\n", var_type.vt_un.un_int);
                        break;
        }
}
```

```
    main(){

            var_type.type_in_union = FLOAT_TYPE;
            var_type.vt_un.un_float = 3.5;

            print_vt();

            var_type.type_in_union = CHAR_TYPE;
            var_type.vt_un.un_char = 'a';

            print_vt();
            exit(EXIT_SUCCESS);
    }
```
                                                                    **(Example 6.12)**

That also demonstrates how the dot notation is used to access structures or unions inside other structures or unions. Some current C compilers allow you to miss bits out of the names of embedded objects provided that they are not ambiguous. In the example, such an unambiguous name would be var_type.un_int and the compiler would work out what you meant. None the less this is not permitted by the Standard.

It is because of unions that structures cannot be compared for equality. The possibility that a structure might contain a union makes it hard to compare such structures; the compiler can't tell what the union currently contains and so wouldn't know how to compare the structures. This sounds a bit hard to swallow and isn't 100% true – most structures don't contain unions – but there is also a philosophical issue at stake about just what is meant by 'equality' when applied to structures. Anyhow, the union business gives the Standard a good excuse to avoid the issue by not supporting structure comparison.


## 6.4 Bitfields

While we're on the subject of structures, we might as well look at bitfields. They can only be declared inside a structure or a union, and allow you to specify some very small objects of a given number of bits in length. Their usefulness is limited and they aren't seen in many programs, but we'll deal with them anyway. This example should help to make things clear:

```
    struct {
            /* field 4 bits wide */
            unsigned field1 :4;
            /*
             * unnamed 3 bit field
             * unnamed fields allow for padding
             */
            unsigned        :3;
```

```
/*
 * one-bit field
 * can only be 0 or -1 in two's complement!
 */
signed field2   :1;
/* align next field on a storage unit */
unsigned        :0;
unsigned field3 :6;
}full_of_fields;                                    (Example 6.13)
```

Each field is accessed and manipulated as if it were an ordinary member of a structure. The keywords signed and unsigned mean what you would expect, except that it is interesting to note that a 1-bit signed field on a two's complement machine can only take the values 0 or -1. The declarations are permitted to include the const and volatile qualifiers.

The main use of bitfields is either to allow tight packing of data or to be able to specify the fields within some externally produced data files. C gives no guarantee of the ordering of fields within machine words, so if you do use them for the latter reason, your program will not only be non-portable, it will be compiler-dependent too. The Standard says that fields are packed into 'storage units', which are typically machine words. The packing order, and whether or not a bitfield may cross a storage unit boundary, are implementation defined. To force alignment to a storage unit boundary, a zero width field is used before the one that you want to have aligned.

Be careful using them. It can require a surprising amount of run-time code to manipulate these things and you can end up using more space than they save.

Bit fields do not have addresses – you can't have pointers to them or arrays of them.

## 6.5 Enums

These fall into the category of 'half baked'. They aren't proper enumerated types, as in Pascal, and only really serve to help you reduce the number of #define statements in your program. They look like this:

```
enum e_tag{
      a, b, c, d = 20, e, f, g = 20, h
}var;
```

Just as with structures and unions, the e_tag is the tag, and var is the definition of a variable.

The names declared inside the enumeration are constants with int type. Their values are these:

```
a == 0
b == 1
c == 2
d == 20
e == 21
f == 22
g == 20
h == 21
```

so you can see that, in the absence of anything to the contrary, the values assigned start at zero and increase. A specific value can be given if you want, when the increase will continue one at a time afterwards; the specific value must be an **integral constant** (see later) that is representable in an int. It is possible for more than one of the names to have the same value.

The only use for these things is to give a better-scoped version of this:

```
#define a 0
#define b 1
/* and so on */
```

It's better scoped because the declaration of enumerations follows the standard scope rules for C, whereas #define statements have file scope.

Not that you are likely to care, but the Standard states that enumeration types are of a type that is compatible with an implementation-defined one of the integral types. So what? For interest's sake here is an illustration:

```
enum ee{a,b,c}e_var, *ep;
```

The names a, b, and c all behave as if they were int constants when you use them; e_var has type enum ee and ep is a pointer to enum ee. The compatibility requirement means that (amongst other implications) there will be an integral type whose address can be assigned to ep without violating the type-compatibility requirements for pointers.

## 6.6 Qualifiers and derived types

Arrays, structures and unions are 'derived from' (contain) other types; none of them may be derived from incomplete types. This means that a structure or union cannot contain an example of itself, because its own type is incomplete until the declaration is complete. Since a pointer to an incomplete type is not itself an incomplete type, it *can* be used in the derivation of arrays, structures and unions.

If any of the types that these things are derived from are qualified with const or volatile, they do *not* inherit that qualification. This means that if a structure contains a const object, the structure itself is not qualified with const and any non-const members can still be modified. This is what you would expect. However, the

Standard does say that if any derived type contains a type that is qualified with const (or recursively any inner type does) then it is not modifiable – so a structure that contains a const cannot be on the left-hand side of an assignment operator.

## 6.7 Initialization

Now that we have seen all of the data types supported by C, we can look at the subject of initialization. C allows ordinary variables, structures, unions and arrays to be given initial values in their definitions. Old C had some strange rules about this, reflecting an unwillingness by compiler writers to work too hard. The Standard has rationalized this, and now it is possible to initialize things as and when you want.

There are basically two sorts of initialization: at compile time, and at run time. Which one you get depends on the **storage duration** of the thing being initialized.

Objects with **static duration** are declared either outside functions, or inside them with the keyword extern or static as part of the declaration. These can *only* be initialized at compile time.

Any other object has **automatic duration**, and can only be initialized at run time. The two categories are mutually exclusive.

Although they are related, storage duration and **linkage** (see Chapter 4) are different and should not be confused.

Compile-time initialization can only be done using **constant expressions**; run-time initialization can be done using *any* expression at all. The Old C restriction, that only simple variables (not arrays, structures or unions) could be initialized at run time, has been lifted.

### 6.7.1 Constant expressions

There are a number of places where constant expressions must be used. The definition of what constitutes a constant expression is relatively simple.

A **constant expression** is evaluated by the compiler, not at run time. It may be used anywhere that a constant may be used. Unless it is part of the operand of sizeof, it may not contain any assignment, increment or decrement operations, function calls or comma operators; that may seem odd, but it's because sizeof only needs to evaluate the type of an expression, not its value.

If real numbers are evaluated at compile time, then the Standard insists that they are evaluated with at least as much precision and range as will be used at run time.

A more restricted form, called the **integral constant expression** exists. This has integral type and only involves operands that are integer constants, enumeration constants, character constants, sizeof expressions and real constants that are the immediate operands of casts. Any cast operators are only allowed to convert arithmetic types to integral types. As with the previous note on sizeof expressions, since they don't have to be evaluated, just their type determined, no restrictions apply to their contents.

The **arithmetic constant expression** is like the integral constant expression, but allows real constants to be used and restricts the use of casts to converting one arithmetic type to another.

The **address constant** is a pointer to an object that has static storage duration or a pointer to a function. You can get these by using the & operator or through the usual conversions of array and function names into pointers when they are used in expressions. The operators [], ., ->, & (address of) and * (pointer dereference) as well as casts of pointers can all be used in the expression as long as they don't involve accessing the value of any object.

### 6.7.2 More initialization

The various types of constants are permitted in various places; integral constant expressions are particularly important because they are the only type of expression that may be used to specify the size of arrays and the values in case statement prefixes. The types of constants that are permitted in initializer expressions are less restricted; you are allowed to use: arithmetic constant expressions; null pointer or address constants; an address constant for an object plus or minus an integral constant expression. Of course it depends on the type of thing being initialized whether or not a particular type of constant expression is appropriate.

Here is an example using several initialized variables:

```
#include <stdio.h>
#include <stdlib.h>

#define NMONTHS 12

int month = 0;

short month_days[] =
        {31,28,31,30,31,30,31,31,30,31,30,31};

char *mnames[] ={
        "January", "February",
        "March", "April",
        "May", "June",
        "July", "August",
        "September", "October",
        "November", "December"
};

main(){
        int day_count = month;
```

```
for(day_count = month; day_count < NMONTHS;
        day_count++){
        printf("%d days in %s\n",
                month_days[day_count],
                mnames[day_count]);
}
exit(EXIT_SUCCESS);
}
```
(Example 6.14)

Initializing ordinary variables is easy: put = expression after the variable name in a declaration, and the variable is initialized to the value of the expression. As with all objects, whether you can use any expression, or just a constant expression, depends on its storage duration.

Initializing arrays is easy for one-dimensional arrays. Just put a list of the values you want, separated by commas, inside curly brackets. The example shows how to do it. If you don't give a size for the array, then the number of initializers will determine the size. If you do give a size, then there must be at most that many initializers in the list. Too many is an error, too few will just initialize the first elements of the array.

You could build up a string like this:

```
char str[] = {'h', 'e', 'l', 'l', 'o', 0};
```

but because it is so often necessary to do that, it is also permitted to use a quoted string literal to initialize an array of chars:

```
char str[] = "hello";
```

In that case, the null at the end of the string will also be included if there is room, or if no size was specified. Here are examples:

```
/* no room for the null */
char str[5] = "hello";

/* room for the null */
char str[6] = "hello";
```

The example program used string literals for a different purpose: *there* they were being used to initialize an array of character pointers; a very different prospect.

For structures that have automatic duration, an expression of the right type can be used to initialize them, or else a bracketed list of constant expressions must be used:

```
#include <stdio.h>
#include <stdlib.h>
```

```
struct s{
        int a;
        char b;
        char *cp;
}ex_s = {
        1, 'a', "hello"
        };


main(){
        struct s first = ex_s;
        struct s second = {
                2, 'b', "byebye"
                };


        exit(EXIT_SUCCESS);
}
```

(Example 6.15)

Only the first member of a union can be initialized.

If a structure or union contains unnamed members, whether unnamed bitfields or padding for alignment, they are ignored in the initialization process; they don't have to be counted when you provide the initializers for the real members of the structure.

For objects that contain sub-objects within them, there are two ways of writing the initializer. It can be written out with an initializer for each member:

```
struct s{
        int a;
        struct ss{
                int c;
                char d;
        }e;
}x[] = {
        1, 2, 'a',
        3, 4, 'b'
        };
```

(Example 6.16)

which will assign 1 to x[0].a, 2 to x[0].e.c, a to x[0].e.d and 3 to x[1].a and so on.

It is *much* safer to use internal braces to show what you mean, or one missed value will cause havoc.

```
struct s{
        int a;
        struct ss{
                int c;
                char d;
        }e;
```

```
}x[] = {
        {1, {2, 'a'}},
        {3, {4, 'b'}}
        };
```
                                                                    (Example 6.17)

*Always* fully bracket initializers – that is much the safest thing to do.
It is the same for arrays as for structures:

```
float y[4][3] = {
        {1, 3, 5},     /* y[0][0], y[0][1], y[0][2] */
        {2, 4, 6},     /* y[1][0], y[1][1], y[1][2] */
        {3, 5, 7}      /* y[2][0], y[2][1], y[2][2] */
        };
```
                                                                    (Example 6.18)

That gives full initialization to the first three rows of y. The fourth row, y[3], is
uninitialized.

Unless they have an explicit initializer, all objects with static duration are given
implicit initializers – the effect is as if the constant 0 had been assigned to their
components. This is in fact widely used – it is an assumption made by most C
programs that external objects and internal static objects start with the value zero.

Initialization of objects with automatic duration is only guaranteed if their
compound statement is entered 'at the top'. Jumping into the middle of one may
result in the initialization not happening – this is often undesirable and should be
avoided. It is explicitly noted by the Standard with regard to switch statements, where
providing initializers in declarations *cannot* be of any use; this is because a declaration
is not linguistically a 'statement' and only statements may be labelled. As a result it is
not possible for initializers in switch statements ever to be executed, because the entry
to the block containing them *must* be below the declarations!

A declaration inside a function (block scope) can, using various techniques
outlined in Chapters 4 and 8, be made to refer to an object that has either **external** or
**internal linkage**. If you've managed to do that, and it's not likely to happen by
accident, then you can't initialize the object as part of that declaration. Here is one
way of trying it:

```
int x;                  /* external linkage */
main(){
        extern int x = 5;   /* forbidden */
}
```

Our test compiler didn't notice that one, either.


■   **6.8 SUMMARY**

You now understand structures and unions. Bitfields and enumeration types
really are not very important and you could manage quite well without them.

It is hard to emphasize how important is the use of structures, pointers and malloc in serious programs. If you aren't familiar with the use of structured data in the form of lists, trees and so on, get a good book now. Better still, try to enrol on a good course. Except in very specialized applications, it is usually the ability to structure data well, not the ability to write complicated algorithms, that makes it possible to construct clean, small and maintainable programs. Experienced software designers often say that once the right structure of the data has been determined, the rest is 'simple'.

Undoubtedly, one of the reasons for the popularity of C among experienced software specialists is the freedom that it gives in the structuring of data, without sacrificing speed.

Initialization should not be overlooked. Although simple in concept, it is surprising how inconvenient many other languages make this. The ludicrous extreme is to insist on the use of assignment statements; C has a practical and convenient approach. If the concept of 'fully bracketed initializers' seems a bit unpleasant, don't worry. It is rare that you have to do it in practice; all that you need is to know how to do simple initialization and to know a book that describes the more complex initialization. To get the full low-down read the Standard, which is uncharacteristically penetrable when it discusses the matter, verging at times on lucidity.

## EXERCISES

**6.1**   What is the declaration of an untagged structure containing two ints called a and b?

**6.2**   Why is such a declaration of limited use?

**6.3**   What would the structure look like with a tag of int_struc and two variables called x and y of the structure type being defined?

**6.4**   How would you declare a third variable later, with the the same type as x and y but called z?

**6.5**   Assuming that p is the right type of pointer, how would you make it point to z and then set z.a to zero, using the pointer?

**6.6**   What are the two ways of declaring a structure with incomplete type?

**6.7**   What is unusual about a string "like this" when it's used to initialize a character array?

**6.8**   What if it initializes a char *?

**6.9**   Find out what a doubly linked list is. Reimplement the linked list example using one. Is it any easier to insert and delete elements in a doubly linked list?

# CHAPTER 7

# The Preprocessor

7.1 Effect of the Standard
7.2 How the preprocessor works
7.3 Directives
7.4 Summary

## 7.1 Effect of the Standard

There's a neither-fish-nor-fowl feel to the preprocessor. It leads an uncomfortable existence bolted on to the side of C without the benefit of either integrating properly with the rest of the language or, given one's natural reaction of revulsion at its ugly nature, being something that you could choose to do without. Back in the pre-history of C it actually was optional and people did write C without it; it's more or less an accident that it's come to be seen as being part of the bag and baggage of the C programming environment. It was used to make up for a couple of modest deficiencies in the language – the definition of constants and the inclusion of standard definitions – and slipped in through the back door as a result.

There has never been a widely accepted formal standard for a lot of what the preprocessor does and differing versions of it have been implemented in different systems. As a result, programs using anything other than the very basic features have proved to be a problem: it's hard to port them.

The primary job of the Standard was to define the behaviour of the preprocessor in line with common practice; this has been done and will not surprise anyone who was familiar with Old C. The Standard has gone further, amid an element of controversy, and specifies a number of additional features that were pioneered in some of the preprocessor's more popular dialects. The controversy results from the fact that although these features may be useful, there has never been much agreement on how to implement them. On the grounds that programs using these techniques were clearly non-portable already, the Standard has not worried too much about backwards compatibility in these areas. The fact that there *is* now a standard for these advanced features should improve the overall portability of C programs in the future.

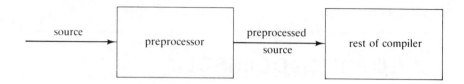

**Figure 7.1**   The preprocessor.

At the simplest level the preprocessor is easy to use and can help a lot to make programs easy to read and maintain. Using the advanced features is best left to experts. In our experience, only the very simplest use of #define and the conditional compilation #if family are suitable for beginners. If this is your first encounter with C, read the chapter once to see what you can pick up and use the exercises to test your basic understanding. Otherwise, we would suggest that at least six months experience is the minimum prerequisite for a full attack. Because of that, we don't try too hard to give an easy introduction in this chapter, but concentrate on getting down to detail.

## 7.2  How the preprocessor works

Although the preprocessor (Figure 7.1) is probably going to be implemented as an integral part of a Standard C compiler, it can equally well be thought of as a separate program which transforms C source code containing preprocessor directives into source code with the directives removed.

It's important to remember that the preprocessor is not working to the same rules as the rest of C. It works on a line-by-line basis, so the end of a line means something special to it. The rest of C thinks that end-of-line is little different from a space or tab character.

The preprocessor doesn't know about the scope rules of C. Preprocessor directives like #define take effect as soon as they are seen and remain in effect until the end of the file that contains them; the program's block structure is irrelevant. This is one of the reasons why it's a good idea to make sparing use of these directives. The less you have in your program that doesn't obey the 'normal' scope rules, the less likely you are to make mistakes. This is mainly what gives rise to our comments about the poor level of integration between the preprocessor and the rest of C.

The Standard gives some complicated rules for the syntax of the preprocessor, especially with respect to **tokens**. To understand the operation of the preprocessor you need to know a little about them. The text that is being processed is not considered to be a uniform stream of characters, but is separated into tokens *then* processed piecemeal.

For a full definition of the process, it is best to refer to the Standard, but an informal description follows. Each of the terms used to head the list below is used later in descriptions of the rules.

(1) *header-name*

- '<' *almost any character* '>'

(2) *preprocessing-token*

- a *header-name* as above but only when the subject of # include,
- or an *identifier* which is any C identifier or keyword,
- or a *constant* which is any integral or floating constant,
- or a *string-literal* which is a normal C string,
- or an *operator* which is one of the C operators,
- or one of *[] () { }* * , : = ; ... # (punctuators),
- or any non-white-space character not covered by the list above.

The '*almost any character*' above means any character except '>' or newline.


## 7.3 Directives

Directives are always introduced by a line that starts with a # character, optionally preceded by white space characters (although it isn't common practice to indent the #). Table 7.1 is a list of the directives defined in the Standard. The meanings and use of these features are described in the following sections. Make a note that the # and the following keyword, if any, are individual items. They may be separated by white space.

**Table 7.1** Preprocessor directives.

| Directive | Meaning |
|-----------|---------|
| # include | include a source file |
| # define | define a macro |
| # undef | undefine a macro |
| # if | conditional compilation |
| # ifdef | conditional compilation |
| # ifndef | conditional compilation |
| # elif | conditional compilation |
| # else | conditional compilation |
| # endif | conditional compilation |
| # line | control error reporting |
| # error | force an error message |
| # pragma | used for implementation-dependent control |
| # | null directive; no effect |


### 7.3.1 The null directive

This is simple: a plain # on a line by itself does nothing!

### 7.3.2 #define

There are two ways of defining **macros**, one of which looks like a function and one which does not. Here is an example of each:

```
#define FMAC(a, b) a here, then b

#define NONFMAC some text here
```

Both definitions define a macro and some *replacement text*, which will be used to replace later occurrences of the macro name in the rest of the program. After those definitions, they can be used as follows, with the effect of the macro replacement shown in comments:

```
NONFMAC
/* some text here */

FMAC(first text, some more)
/* first text here, then some more */
```

For the non-function macro, its name is simply replaced by its replacement text. The function macro is also replaced by its replacement text; wherever the replacement text contains an identifier which is the name of one of the macro's 'formal parameters', the actual text given as the argument is used in place of the identifier in the replacement text. The scope of the names of the formal parameters is limited to the body of the #define directive.

For both forms of macro, leading or trailing white space around the replacement text is discarded.

A curious ambiguity arises with macros: how do you define a non-function macro whose replacement text happens to start with the opening parenthesis character (? The answer is simple. If the definition of the macro has a space in front of the (, then it isn't the definition of a function macro, but a simple replacement macro instead. When you *use* function-like macros, there's no equivalent restriction.

The Standard allows either type of macro to be redefined at any time, using another # define, provided that there isn't any attempt to change the type of the macro and that the tokens making up both the original definition and the redefinition are identical in number, ordering, spelling and use of white space. In this context all white space is considered equal, so this would be correct:

```
# define XXX abc/*comment*/def hij
# define XXX abc def hij
```

because comment is a form of white space. The token sequence for both cases (*w-s* stands for a white-space token) is:

```
# w-s define w-s XXX w-s abc w-s def w-s hij w-s
```

### *Macro substitution*

Where will occurrences of the macro name cause the replacement text to be substituted in its place? Practically anywhere in a program that the identifier is recognized as a separate token, except as the identifier following the # of a preprocessor directive. You can't do this:

```
#define define XXX

#define YYY ZZZ
```

and expect the second #define to be replaced by #XXX, causing an error.

When the identifier associated with a non-function macro is seen, it is replaced by the macro replacement tokens, then **rescanned** (see later) for further replacements to make.

Function macros can be used like real functions; white space around the macro name, the argument list and so on, may include the newline character:

```
#define FMAC(a, b) printf("%s %s\n", a, b)

FMAC ("hello",
        "sailor"
        );
/* results in */
printf("%s %s\n", "hello", "sailor")
```

The 'arguments' of a function macro can be almost any arbitrary token sequence. Commas are used to separate the arguments from each other but can be hidden by enclosing them within parentheses, ( and ). Matched pairs of ( and ) inside the argument list balance each other out, so a ) only ends the invocation of the macro if the corresponding ( is the one that started the macro invocation.

```
#define CALL(a, b) a b

CALL(printf, ("%d %d %s\n",1, 24, "urgh"));
/* results in */
printf ("%d %d %s\n",1, 24, "urgh");
```

Note very carefully that the parentheses around the second argument to CALL were preserved in the replacement: they were not stripped from the text.

If you want to use macros like printf, taking a variable number of arguments, the Standard is no help to you. They are not supported.

If any argument contains no preprocessor tokens then the behaviour is undefined. The same is true if the sequence of preprocessor tokens that forms the argument would otherwise have been another preprocessor directive:

```
#define CALL(a, b) a b
```

```
/* undefined behaviour in each case.... */
CALL(,hello)
CALL(xyz,
#define abc def)
```

In our opinion, the second of the erroneous uses of CALL *should* result in defined behaviour – anyone capable of writing that would clearly benefit from the attentions of a champion weightlifter wielding a heavy leather bullwhip.

When a function macro is being processed, the steps are as follows:

(1) All of its arguments are identified.

(2) Except in the cases listed in item 3 below, if any of the tokens in an argument are themselves candidates for macro replacement, the replacement is done until no further replacement is possible. If this introduces commas into the argument list, there is no danger of the macro suddenly seeming to have a different number of arguments; the arguments are *only* determined in the step above.

(3) In the macro replacement text, identifiers naming one of the macro formal arguments are replaced by the (by now expanded) token sequence supplied as the actual argument. The replacement is suppressed only if the identifier is preceded by one of # or ##, or followed by ##.

### Stringizing

There is special treatment for places in the macro replacement text where one of the macro formal parameters is found preceded by #. The token list for the actual argument has any leading or trailing white space discarded, then the # and the token list are turned into a single string literal. Spaces between the tokens are treated as space characters in the string. To prevent 'unexpected' results, any " or \ characters within the new string literal are preceded by \.

This example demonstrates the feature:

```
#define MESSAGE(x) printf("Message: %s\n", #x)

MESSAGE (Text with "quotes");
/*
 * Result is
 * printf("Message: %s\n", "Text with \"quotes\"");
 */
```

### Token pasting

A ## operator may occur anywhere in the replacement text for a macro except at the beginning or end. If a parameter name of a function macro occurs in the replacement text preceded or followed by one of these operators, the actual token sequence for the corresponding macro argument is used to replace it. Then, for both function and non-function macros, the tokens surrounding the ## operator are joined together. If they don't form a valid token, the behaviour is undefined. Then rescanning occurs.

As an example of token pasting, here is a multi-stage operation, involving rescanning (which is described next).

```
#define REPLACE some replacement text
#define JOIN(a, b) a ## b

JOIN(REP, LACE)
```
*becomes, after token pasting,*
```
REPLACE
```
*becomes, after rescanning,*
```
some replacement text
```

## Rescanning

Once the processing described above has occurred, the replacement text plus the following tokens of the source file is rescanned, looking for more macro names to replace. The one exception is that, within a macro's replacement text, the name of the macro itself is not expanded. Because macro replacement can be nested, it is possible for several macros to be in the process of being replaced at any one point: none of their names is a candidate for further replacement in the 'inner' levels of this process. This allows redefinition of existing functions as macros:

```
#define exit(x) exit((x) + 1)
```

These macro names which were not replaced now become tokens which are immune from future replacement, even if later processing might have meant that they had become available for replacement. This prevents the danger of infinite recursion occurring in the preprocessor. The suppression of replacement is only if the macro name results directly from *replacement* text, not the other source text of the program. Here is what we mean:

```
#define m(x) m((x) + 1)
/* so */
m(abc);
/* expands to */
m((abc) + 1);
/*
 * even though the m((abc) + 1) above looks like a macro,
 * the rules say it is not to be re-replaced
 */

m(m(abc));
/*
 * the outer m( starts a macro invocation,
 * but the inner one is replaced first (as above)
 * with m((abc) + 1), which becomes the argument to the outer call,
 * giving us effectively
 */
```

```
m(m((abc + 1));
/*
 * which expands to
 */
m((m((abc + 1)) + 1);
```

If that doesn't make your brain hurt, then go and read what the Standard says about it, which will.

### Notes

There is a subtle problem when using arguments to function macros.

```
/* warning — subtle problem in this example */
#define SQR(x)  ( x * x )
/*
 * Wherever the formal parameters occur in
 * the replacement text, they are replaced
 * by the actual parameters to the macro.
 */
printf("sqr of %d is %d\n", 2, SQR(2));
```

The formal parameter of SQR is x; the actual argument is 2. The replacement text results in

```
printf("sqr of %d is %d\n", 2, ( 2 * 2 ));
```

The use of the parentheses should be noticed. The following example is likely to give trouble:

```
/* bad example */
#define DOUBLE(y) y + y

printf("twice %d is %d\n", 2, DOUBLE(2));
printf("six times %d is %d\n", 2, 3 * DOUBLE(2));
```

The problem is that the last expression in the second printf is replaced by

```
3 * 2 + 2
```

which results in 8, not 12! The rule is that when using macros to build expressions, careful parenthesizing is necessary. Here's another example:

```
SQR(3 + 4)

/* expands to */

( 3 + 4 * 3 + 4 )
/* oh dear, still wrong! */
```

so, when formal parameters occur in the replacement text, you should look carefully at them too. Correct versions of SQR and DOUBLE are these:

```
#define SQR(x) ((x) * (x))
#define DOUBLE(x) ((x) + (x))
```

Macros have a last little trick to surprise you with, as this shows:

```
#include ⟨stdio.h⟩
#include ⟨stdlib.h⟩

#define DOUBLE(x) ((x) + (x))

main(){
        int a[20], *ip;

        ip = a;
        a[0] = 1;
        a[1] = 2;
        printf("%d\n", DOUBLE(*ip++));
        exit(EXIT_SUCCESS);
}
```
                                                                    **(Example 7.1)**

Why is this going to cause problems? Because the replacement text of the macro refers to *ip++ twice, so ip gets incremented twice. Macros should never be used with expressions that involve side effects, unless you check very carefully that they are safe.

Despite these warnings, they provide a very useful feature, and one which will be used a lot from now on.


### 7.3.3 # undef

The name of any #defined identifier can be forcibly forgotten by saying

```
#undef  NAME
```

It isn't an error to #undef a name which isn't currently defined.

This occasionally comes in handy. Chapter 9 points out that some library functions may actually be macros, not functions, but by undefing their names you are guaranteed access to a real function.


### 7.3.4 # include

This comes in two flavours:

```
#include ⟨filename⟩
#include "filename"
```

both of which cause a new file to be read at the point where they occur. It's as if the single line containing the directive is replaced by the contents of the specified file. If that file contains erroneous statements, you can reasonably expect that the errors will be reported with a correct file name and line number. It's the compiler writer's job to get that right. The Standard specifies that at least eight nested levels of # include must be supported.

The effect of using brackets ⟨⟩ or quotes " " around the filename is to change the places searched to find the specified file. The brackets cause a search of a number of implementation defined places, the quotes cause a search of somewhere associated with the original source file. Your implementation notes must tell you the specific details of what is meant by 'place'. If the form using quotes can't find the file, it tries again as if you had used brackets.

In general, brackets are used when you specify standard library header files, quotes are used for private header files – often specific to one program only.

Although the Standard doesn't define what constitutes a valid file name, it does specify that there must be an implementation-defined unique way of translating file names of the form xxx.x (where x represents a 'letter'), into source file names. Distinctions of upper and lower case may be ignored and the implementation may choose only to use six significant characters before the '.' character.

You can also write this:

```
# define NAME ⟨stdio.h⟩
# include NAME
```

to get the same effect as

```
# include ⟨stdio.h⟩
```

but it's a rather roundabout way of doing it, and unfortunately it's subject to implementation defined rules about how the text between ⟨ and ⟩ is treated.

It's simpler if the replacement text for NAME comes out to be a string, for example

```
#define NAME "stdio.h"

#include NAME
```

There is no problem with implementation defined behaviour here, but the paths searched are different, as explained above.

For the first case, what happens is that the token sequence which replaces NAME is (by the rules already given)

```
⟨
stdio
.
h
⟩
```

and for the second case

```
"stdio.h"
```

The second case is easy, since it's just a *string-literal* which is a legal token for a
# include directive. It is implementation defined how the first case is treated, and
whether or not the sequence of tokens forms a legal *header-name*.
   Finally, the last character of a file which is being included must be a plain
newline. Failure to include a file successfully is treated as an error.


## 7.3.5 Predefined names

The following names are predefined within the preprocessor:

\_\_LINE\_\_
   The current source file line number, a decimal integer constant.
\_\_FILE\_\_
   The 'name' of the current source code file, a string literal.
\_\_DATE\_\_
   The current date, a string literal. The form is

```
Apr 21 1990
```

   where the month name is as defined in the library function asctime and the first
   digit of the date is a space if the date is less than 10.
\_\_TIME\_\_
   The time of the translation; again a string literal in the form produced by
   asctime, which has the form "hh:mm:ss".
\_\_STDC\_\_
   The integer constant 1. This is used to test if the compiler is Standard-
   conforming, the intention being that it will have different values for different
   releases of the Standard.

   A common way of using these predefined names is the following:

```
#define TEST(x) if(!(x))\
        printf("test failed, line %d file %s\n",\
            __LINE__, __FILE__)
/**/

TEST(a != 23);

/**/                                                      (Example 7.2)
```

If the argument to TEST gives a false result, the message is printed, including the
filename and line number in the message.

There's only one minor caveat: the use of the if statement can cause confusion in a case like this:

```
if(expression)
        TEST(expr2);
else
        statement_n;
```

The else will get associated with the hidden if generated by expanding the TEST macro. This is most unlikely to happen in practice, but will be a thorough pain to track down if it ever does sneak up on you. It's good style to make the bodies of every control of flow statement compound anyway; then the problem goes away.

None of the names __LINE__, __FILE__, __DATE__, __TIME__, __STDC__ or defined may be used in #define or #undef directives.

The Standard specifies that any other reserved names will either start with an underscore followed by an upper case letter or another underscore, so you know that you are free to use any other names for your own purposes (but watch out for additional names reserved in Library header files that you may have included).

## 7.3.6 #line

This is used to set the value of the built in names __LINE__ and __FILE__. Why do this? Because a lot of tools nowadays actually generate C as their output. This directive allows them to control the current line number. It is of very limited interest to the 'ordinary' C programmer.

Its form is

# line *number optional-string-literal newline*

The number sets the value of __LINE__, the string literal, if present, sets the value of __FILE__.

In fact, the sequence of tokens following #line will be macro expanded. After expansion, they are expected to provide a valid directive of the right form.

## 7.3.7 Conditional compilation

A number of the directives control conditional compilation, which allows certain portions of a program to be selectively compiled or ignored depending upon specified conditions. The directives concerned are: #if, #ifdef, #ifndef, #elif, #else, #endif together with the preprocessor unary operator defined.

The way that they are used is like this:

```
#ifdef  NAME
/* compile these lines if NAME is defined */
#endif
```

```
#ifndef NAME
/* compile these lines if NAME is not defined */
#else
/* compile these lines if NAME is defined */
#endif
```

So, #ifdef and #endif can be used to test the definition or otherwise of a given macro name. Of course the #else can be used with #ifdef (and #if or #elif) too. There is no ambiguity about what a given #else binds to, because the use of #endif to delimit the scope of these directives eliminates any possible ambiguity. The Standard specifies that at least eight levels of nesting of conditional directives must be supported, but in practice there is not likely to be any real limit.

These directives are most commonly used to select small fragments of C that are machine specific (when it is not possible to make the whole program completely machine independent), or sometimes to select different algorithms depending on the need to make trade-offs.

The #if and #elif constructs take a single integral constant expression as their arguments. Preprocessor integral constant expressions are the same as other integral constant expressions except that they must not contain cast operators. The token sequence that makes up the constant expression undergoes macro replacement, except that names prefixed by defined are not expanded. In this context, the expression defined NAME or defined ( NAME ) evaluates to 1 if NAME is currently defined, 0 if it is not. Any other identifiers in the expression *including those that are C keywords* are replaced with the value 0. Then the expression is evaluated. The replacement even of keywords means that sizeof can't be used in these expressions to get the result that you would normally expect.

As with the other conditional statements in C, a resulting value of zero is used to represent 'false', anything else is 'true'.

The preprocessor always must use arithmetic with at least the ranges defined in the ⟨limits.h⟩ file and treats int expressions as long int and unsigned int as unsigned long int. Character constants do not necessarily have the same values as they do at execution time, so for highly portable programs, it's best to avoid using them in preprocessor expressions. Overall, the rules mean that it is possible to get arithmetic results from the preprocessor which are different from the results at run time; although presumably only if the translation and execution are done on different machines. Here's an example:

```
#include ⟨limits.h⟩

#if ULONG_MAX + 1 != 0
        printf("Preprocessor: ULONG_MAX + 1 != 0\n");
#endif

        if(ULONG_MAX + 1 !=.0)
                printf("Runtime: ULONG_MAX + 1 != 0\n");          (Example 7.3)
```

It is conceivable that the preprocessor might perform arithmetic with a greater range than that used in the target environment. In that case, the preprocessor expression ULONG_MAX + 1 might not 'overflow' to give the result of 0, whereas in the execution environment, it *must*.

The following skeleton example illustrates the use of such constants and also the 'conditional else', #elif.

```
#define NAME    100

#if     ((NAME > 50) && (defined __STDC__))
/* do something */
#elif   NAME > 25
/* do something else*/
#elif   NAME > 10
/* do something else */
#else
/* last possibility */
#endif
```

A word of warning. These conditional compilation directives do not obey the same scope rules as the rest of C. They should be used sparingly, unless your program is rapidly to become unreadable. It is impossible to read C when it is laced with these things every few lines. The urge to maim the author of a piece of code becomes very strong when you suddenly come across

```
#else
        }
#endif
```

with no #if or whatever immediately visible above. They should be treated like chilli sauce; essential at times, but more than a tiny sprinkle is too much.

### 7.3.8 #pragma

This was the Standard Committee's way of 'opening the back door'. It allows implementation-defined things to take place. If the implementation was not expecting what you wrote (that is, doesn't recognize it), it is ignored. Here is a possible example:

```
#pragma byte_align
```

which could be used to tell the implementation that all structure members should be aligned on byte addresses – some processor architectures are able to cope with word-sized structure members aligned on byte addresses, but with a penalty in access speed being incurred.

It could, of course, mean anything else that the implementation chooses it to mean.

If your implementation doesn't have any special meaning for this, then it will have no effect. It will *not* count as an error.

It will be interesting to see the sort of things that this gets used for.

### 7.3.9 #error

This directive is followed by one or more tokens at the end of the line. A diagnostic message is produced by the compiler, which includes those tokens, but no further detail is given in the Standard. It might be used like this to abort a compilation on unsuitable hardware:

```
#include ⟨limits.h⟩
#if CHAR_MIN > -128
#error character range smaller than required
#endif
```

which would be expected to produce some sort of meaningful compilation error and message.

## ■ 7.4 SUMMARY

To be honest, although many of the facilities provided by the preprocessor undoubtedly provide extra power and flexibility, it really is rather overcomplicated.

There are only a very few aspects that are really important.

The ability to define macros and function macros is very important, being widely used in almost every C program except the most trivial.

The conditional compilation has two important uses; one is the ability to compile with or without debugging statements included in a program, the other is to be able to select machine or application dependent statements.

Obviously, file inclusion is fundamentally important.

Having said the above, most of the rest of the features described in this chapter can be forgotten with very little loss of functionality. Perhaps each programming team should have just one preprocessor specialist who has the job of designing project-dependent macros using the arcane features such as stringizing and token pasting. Most users of C would benefit much more by putting that learning effort into other parts of the language, or, when they fully understand C, techniques of software quality control. The world would be a better place.

## EXERCISES

These exercises are intended to test only a basic understanding of the pre-processor, suitable for a beginner. Many users will never need a more detailed understanding.

**7.1**   How would you arrange that the identifier MAXLEN is replaced by the value 100 throughout a program?

**7.2**   What is likely to cause problems in a definition of the form #define VALUE 100 + MAXLEN?

**7.3**   Write a macro called REM which takes two integer arguments and 'returns' the remainder when the first is divided by the second.

**7.4**   Repeat the last example, but use casts so that any arithmetic type of argument may be used, assuming that there are no overflow problems.

**7.5**   What do the <> brackets around a filename in a #include directive signify?

**7.6**   What would "" mean in place of the <>?

**7.7**   How would you use the preprocessor to select implementation-specific fragments of a program?

**7.8**   What sort of arithmetic does the preprocessor use?

# CHAPTER 8

# Specialized Areas of C

## 8.1 Government Health Warning

The previous chapters have introduced the fundamentals of the language and have covered nearly all of the language that the Standard defines. There are a number of murky and convoluted backwaters left unexplored on grounds of sympathy and compassion for the sufferer, and some without any better home. This chapter gathers them together – it's the toxic waste dump for the nasty bits of C.

Pull on your rubber gloves, read the following sections and make notes where you think the material is important to you; reread them from time to time as well. What seemed uninteresting and painful the first time round may change as your experience grows, or your natural immunity improves.

What we cover here is *not* an exhumation of all the pathogenic elements – we leave that for another book – but it does serve to round up most of the commonly encountered difficult or extraordinary material.

## 8.2 Declarations, definitions and accessibility

Chapter 4 introduced the concepts of **scope** and **linkage**, showing how they can be combined to control the accessibility of things throughout a program. We deliberately gave a vague description of exactly what constitutes a **definition** on the grounds that it would give you more pain than gain at that stage. Eventually it has to be spelled out in detail, which we do in this chapter. Just to make things interesting, we need to throw in **storage class** too.

You'll probably find the interactions between these various elements to be both complex and confusing: that's because they are! We try to eliminate some of the confusion and give some useful rules of thumb in Section 8.2.5 below – but to understand them, you still need to read the stuff in between at least once.

For a full understanding, you need a good grasp of three distinct but related concepts. The Standard calls them:

- duration
- scope
- linkage

and describes what they mean in a fairly readable way (for a standard). Scope and linkage have already been described in Chapter 4, although we do present a review of them below.

### 8.2.1 Storage class specifiers

There are five keywords under the category of **storage class specifiers**, although one of them, typedef, is there more out of convenience than utility; it has its own section later since it doesn't really belong here. The ones remaining are auto, extern, register, and static.

Storage class specifiers help you to specify the type of storage used for data objects. Only one storage class specifier is permitted in a declaration – this makes sense, as there is only one way of storing things – and if you omit the storage class specifier in a declaration, a default is chosen. The default depends on whether the declaration is made outside a function (external declarations) or inside a function (internal declarations). For external declarations the default storage class specifier will be extern and for internal declarations it will be auto. The only exception to this rule is the declaration of functions, whose *default* storage class specifier is always extern.

The positioning of a declaration, the storage class specifiers used (or their defaults) and, in some cases, preceding declarations of the same name, can all affect the linkage of a name, although fortunately not its scope or duration. We will investigate the easier items first.

*Duration*

The **duration** of an object describes whether its storage is allocated once only, at program start-up, or is more transient in its nature, being allocated and freed as necessary.

There are only two types of duration of objects: **static duration** and **automatic duration**. Static duration means that the object has its storage allocated permanently, automatic means that the storage is allocated and freed as necessary. It's easy to tell which is which: you only get automatic duration if

- the declaration is inside a function
- *and* the declaration does not contain the static or extern keywords
- *and* the declaration is not the declaration of a function.

(If you work through the rules, you'll find that the formal parameters of a function always meet all three requirements – they are always 'automatic'.)

Although the presence of static in a declaration unambiguously ensures that it has static duration, it's interesting to see that it is by no means the only way. This is a notorious source of confusion, but we just have to accept it.

Data objects declared inside functions are given the default storage class specifier of auto unless some other storage class specifier is used. In the vast majority of cases, you don't want these objects to be accessible from outside the function, so you want them to have *no linkage*. Either the default, auto, or the explicit register storage class specifier results in an object with no linkage and **automatic duration**. Neither auto nor register can be applied to a declaration that occurs outside a function.

The register storage class is quite interesting, although it is tending to fall into disuse nowadays. It suggests to the compiler that it would be a good idea to store the object in one or more hardware registers in the interests of speed. The compiler does not have to take any notice of this, but to make things easy for it, register variables do not have an address (the & address-of operator is forbidden) because some computers don't support the idea of addressable registers. Declaring too many register objects may slow the program down, rather than speed it up, because the compiler may either have to save more registers on entrance to a function, often a slow process, or there won't be enough registers remaining to be used for intermediate calculations. Determining when to use registers will be a machine-specific choice and should only be taken when detailed measurements show that a particular function needs to be speeded up. Then you will have to experiment. In our opinion, you should never declare register variables during program development. Get the program working first, then measure it, then, maybe, judicious use of registers will give a useful increase in performance. But that work will have to be repeated for every type of processor you move the program to; even within one family of processors the characteristics are often different.

A final note on register variables: this is the only storage class specifier that may be used in a function prototype or function definition. In a function prototype, the storage class specifier is simply ignored, in a function definition it is a hint that the actual parameter should be stored in a register if possible. This example shows how it might be used:

```
#include (stdio.h)
#include (stdlib.h)


void func(register int arg1, double arg2);
```

```
main(){
        func(5, 2);
        exit(EXIT_SUCCESS);
}


/*
 * Function illustrating that formal parameters
 * may be declared to have register storage class.
 */
void
func(register int arg1, double arg2){

        /*
         * Illustrative only — nobody would do this
         * in this context.
         * Cannot take address of arg1, even if you want to
         */
        double *fp = &arg2;

        while(arg1){
                printf("res = %f\n", arg1 * (*fp));
                arg1--;
        }

}
```
                                                                    **(Example 8.1)**

So the duration of an object depends on the storage class specifier used, whether it's a
data object or function, and the position (block or file scope) of the declaration
concerned. The linkage is also dependent on the storage class specifier, what kind of
object it is and the scope of the declaration. Tables 8.1 and 8.2 show the resulting
storage duration and apparent linkage for the various combinations of storage class
specifiers and location of the declaration. The actual linkage of objects with static
duration is a bit more complicated, so use these tables only as a guide to the simple
cases and take a look at what we say later about definitions. Table 8.1 omits the
register and auto storage class specifiers because they are not permitted in file-scope
(external) declarations. Internal static variables retain their values between calls of
the function that contains them, which is useful in certain circumstances (see
Chapter 4).

**Table 8.1**    External declarations (outside a function).

| Storage class specifier | Function or data object | Linkage | Duration |
|---|---|---|---|
| static | either | internal | static |
| extern | either | probably external | static |
| none | function | probably external | static |
| none | data object | external | static |

**Table 8.2**   Internal declarations.

| Storage class specifier | Function or data object | Linkage | Duration |
|---|---|---|---|
| register | data object only | none | automatic |
| auto | data object only | none | automatic |
| static | data object only | none | static |
| extern | either | probably external | static |
| none | data object | none | automatic |
| none | function | probably external | static |

## 8.2.2 Scope

Now we must look again at the **scope** of the names of objects, which defines when and where a given name has a particular meaning. The different types of scope are the following:

- function scope
- file scope
- block scope
- function prototype scope.

The easiest is **function scope**. This only applies to labels, whose names are visible throughout the function where they are declared, irrespective of the block structure. No two labels in the same function may have the same name, but because the name only has function scope, the same name can be used for labels in every function. Labels are *not* objects – they have no storage associated with them and the concepts of linkage and duration have no meaning for them.

Any name declared outside a function has **file scope**, which means that the name is usable at any point from the declaration on to the end of the source code file containing the declaration. Of course it is possible for these names to be temporarily hidden by declarations within compound statements. As we know, function definitions *must* be outside other functions, so the name introduced by any function definition will always have file scope.

A name declared inside a compound statement, or as a formal parameter to a function, has **block scope** and is usable up to the end of the associated } which closes the compound statement. Any declaration of a name within a compound statement hides any outer declaration of the same name until the end of the compound statement.

A special and rather trivial example of scope is **function prototype scope** where a declaration of a name extends only to the end of the function prototype. That means simply that this is wrong (same name used twice):

```
void func(int i, int i);
```

and this is all right:

```
void func(int i, int j);
```

The names declared inside the parentheses disappear outside them.

The scope of a name is completely independent of any storage class specifier that may be used in its declaration.

### 8.2.3 Linkage

We will briefly review the subject of **linkage** here, too. **Linkage** is used to determine what makes the same name declared in different scopes refer to the same thing. An object only ever has one name, but in many cases we would like to be able to refer to the same object from different scopes. A typical example is the wish to be able to call printf from several different places in a program, even if those places are not all in the same source file.

The Standard warns that declarations which refer to the same thing must all have **compatible type,** or the behaviour of the program will be undefined. A full description of compatible type is given later; for the moment you can take it to mean that, except for the use of the storage class specifier, the declarations must be identical. It's the responsibility of the programmer to get this right, though there will probably be tools available to help you check this out.

The three different types of linkage are:

- external linkage
- internal linkage
- no linkage.

In an entire program, built up perhaps from a number of source files and libraries, if a name has **external linkage**, then every instance of that name refers to the same object throughout the program.

For something which has **internal linkage**, it is only within a given source code file that instances of the same name will refer to the same thing.

Finally, names with **no linkage** refer to separate things.

### 8.2.4 Linkage and definitions

Every data object or function that is actually used in a program (except as the operand of a sizeof operator) *must have one and only one* corresponding **definition**. This is actually very important, although we haven't really come across it yet because most of our examples have used only data objects with automatic duration, whose declarations are axiomatically definitions, or functions which we have defined by providing their bodies.

This 'exactly one' rule means that for objects with external linkage there must be exactly one definition in the whole program; for things with internal linkage (confined to one source code file) there must be exactly one definition in the file where it is declared; for things with no linkage, whose declaration is always a definition, there is exactly one definition as well.

Now we try to draw everything together. The real questions are

(1)  How do I get the sort of linkage that I want?

(2)  What actually constitutes a definition?

We need to look into linkage first, then definitions.

How do you get the appropriate linkage for a particular name? The rules are a little complicated.

(1)  A declaration outside a function (file scope) which contains the static storage class specifier results in **internal linkage** for that name. (The Standard requires that function declarations which contain static *must* be at file scope, outside any block.)

(2)  If a declaration contains the extern storage class specifier, or is the declaration of a function with no storage class specifier (or both), then:
    – If there is already a visible declaration of that identifier with file scope, the resulting linkage is the same as that of the visible declaration;
    – otherwise the result is **external linkage**.

(3)  If a file scope declaration is neither the declaration of a function nor contains an explicit storage class specifier, then the result is **external linkage**.

(4)  Any other form of declaration results in **no linkage**.

(5)  In any one source code file, if a given identifer has both internal and external linkage then the result is undefined.

These rules were used to derive the 'linkage' columns of Tables 8.1 and 8.2, without the full application of rule 2 – hence the use of the 'probably external' term. Rule 2 allows you to determine the precise linkage in those cases.

What makes a declaration into a definition?

• Declarations that result in no linkage are also definitions.

• Declarations that include an initializer are always definitions; this includes the 'initialization' of functions by providing their body. Declarations with block scope may only have initializers if they also have no linkage.

• Otherwise, the declaration of a name with file scope and with either no storage class specifier or with the static storage class specifier is a **tentative definition**. If a source code file contains one or more tentative definitions for an object, then if that file contains no actual definitions, a default definition is provided for that object as if it had an initializer of 0. (Structures and arrays have all their elements initialized to 0). Functions do not have tentative definitions.

A consequence of the foregoing is that unless you also provide an initializer, declarations that explicitly include the extern storage class specifier do *not* result in a definition.

### 8.2.5 Realistic use of linkage and definitions

The rules that determine the linkage and definition associated with declarations look quite complicated. The combinations used in practice are nothing like as bad; so let's investigate the usual cases.

The three types of accessibility that you will want of data objects or functions are:

- throughout the entire program,
- restricted to one source file,
- restricted to one function (or perhaps a single compound statement).

For the three cases above, you will want external linkage, internal linkage, and no linkage respectively. The recommended practice for the first two cases is to declare all of the names in each of the relevant source files *before* you define any functions. The recommended layout of a source file would be as shown in Figure 8.1.

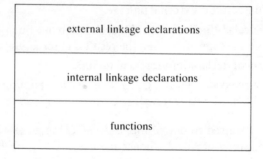

**Figure 8.1** Layout of a source file.

The external linkage declarations would be prefixed with extern, the internal linkage declarations with static. Here's an example:

```
/* example of a single source file layout */
#include (stdio.h)

/* Things with external linkage:
 * accessible throughout program.
 * These are declarations, not definitions, so
 * we assume their definition is somewhere else.
 */
```

```
extern int important_variable;
extern int library_func(double, int);

/*
 * Definitions with external linkage.
 */
extern int ext_int_def = 0;      /* explicit definition */
int tent_ext_int_def;            /* tentative definition */

/*
 * Things with internal linkage:
 * only accessible inside this file.
 * The use of static means that they are also
 * tentative definitions.
 */

static int less_important_variable;
static struct{
        int member_1;
        int member_2;
}local_struct;

/*
 * Also with internal linkage, but not a tentative
 * definition because this is a function.
 */
static void lf(void);

/*
 * Definition with internal linkage.
 */
static float int_link_f_def = 5.3;

/*
 * Finally definitions of functions within this file
 */

/*
 * This function has external linkage and can be called
 * from anywhere in the program.
 */
void f1(int a){}

/*
 * These two functions can only be invoked by name from
 * within this file.
 */
static int
local_function(int a1, int a2){
        return(a1 * a2);
}
```

```
        static void
        lf(void){
                /*
                 * A static variable with no linkage,
                 * so usable only within this function.
                 * Also a definition (because of no linkage)
                 */
                static int count;
                /*
                 * Automatic variable with no linkage but
                 * an initializer
                 */
                int i = 1;

                printf("lf called for time no %d\n", ++count);
        }
        /*
         * Actual definitions are implicitly provided for
         * all remaining tentative definitions at the end of
         * the file
         */
```
                                                    **(Example 8.2)**

We suggest that you reread the preceding sections to see how the rules have been applied in Example 8.2.


## 8.3 Typedef

Although typedef is thought of as being a storage class, it isn't really. It allows you to introduce synonyms for types which could have been declared some other way. The new name becomes equivalent to the type that you wanted, as this example shows:

```
        typedef int aaa, bbb, ccc;
        typedef int ar[15], arr[9][6];
        typedef char c, *cp, carr[100];

        /* now declare some objects */

        /* all ints */
        aaa     int1;
        bbb     int2;
        ccc     int3;

        ar      yyy;    /* array of 15 ints */
        arr     xxx;    /* 9*6 array of int */

        c       ch;     /* a char */
        cp      pnt;    /* pointer to char */
        carr    chry;   /* array of 100 char */
```

The general rule with the use of typedef is to write out a declaration as if you were declaring variables of the types that you want. Where a declaration would have introduced names with particular types, prefixing the whole thing with typedef means that, instead of getting variables declared, you declare new type names instead. Those new type names can then be used as the prefix to the declaration of variables of the new type.

The use of typedef isn't a particularly common sight in most programs; it's typically found only in header files and is rarely the province of day-to-day coding.

It is sometimes found in applications requiring very high portability: there, new types will be defined for the basic variables of the program and appropriate typedefs used to tailor the program to the target machine. This can lead to code which C programmers from other environments will find difficult to interpret if it's used to excess. The flavour of it is shown below:

```
/* file 'mytype.h' */
typedef short    SMALLINT      /* range ±30000 */
typedef int      BIGINT        /* range ± 2E9 */


/* program */
#include "mytype.h"

SMALLINT         i;
BIGINT           loop_count;
```

On some machines, the range of an int would not be adequate for a BIGINT which would have to be re-typedef'd to be long.

To reuse a name already declared as a typedef, its declaration must include at least one type specifier, which removes any ambiguity:

```
typedef int new_thing;
func(new_thing x){
        float new_thing;
        new_thing = x;
}
```

As a word of warning, typedef can only be used to declare the type of return value from a function, not the overall type of the function. The overall type includes information about the function's parameters as well as the type of its return value.

```
/*
 * Using typedef, declare 'func' to have type
 * 'function taking two int arguments, returning int'
 */
typedef int func(int, int);
```

```
/* ERROR */
func func_name{ /*....*/ }

/* Correct. Returns pointer to a type 'func' */
func *func_name(){ /*....*/ }

/*
 * Correct if functions could return functions,
 * but C can't.
 */
func func_name(){ /*....*/ }
```

If a typedef of a particular identifier is in scope, that identifier may not be used as the formal parameter of a function. This is because something like the following declaration causes a problem:

```
typedef int i1_t, i2_t, i3_t, i4_t;

int f(i1_t, i2_t, i3_t, i4_t)/* THIS IS POINT 'X' */
```

A compiler reading the function declaration reaches point 'X' and still doesn't know whether it is looking at a function declaration, essentially similar to

```
int f(int, int, int, int) /* prototype */
```

or

```
int f(a, b, c, d) /* not a prototype */
```

– the problem is only resolvable (in the worst case) by looking at what follows point 'X'; if it is a semicolon, then that was a declaration, if it is a { then that was a definition. The rule forbidding typedef names to be formal parameters means that a compiler can always tell whether it is processing a declaration or a definition by looking at the first identifier following the function name.

The use of typedef is also valuable when you want to declare things whose declaration syntax is painfully impenetrable, like 'array of ten pointers to array of five integers', which tends to cause panic even amongst the hardy. Hiding it in a typedef means you only have to read it once and can also help to break it up into manageable pieces:

```
typedef int (*a10ptoa5i[10])[5];
/* or */
typedef int a5i[5];
typedef a5i *atenptoa5i[10];
```

Try it out!

## 8.4 Const **and** volatile

These are new in Standard C, although the idea of const has been borrowed from C++. Let us get one thing straight: the concepts of const and volatile are *completely independent*. A common misconception is to imagine that somehow const is the opposite of volatile and vice versa. They are unrelated and you should remember the fact.

Since const declarations are the simpler, we'll look at them first, but only after we have seen where both of these **type qualifiers** may be used. The complete list of relevant keywords is

```
char      long      float    volatile
short     signed    double   void
int       unsigned  const
```

In that list, const and volatile are type qualifiers, the rest are **type specifiers**. Various combinations of type specifiers are permitted:

```
char, signed char, unsigned char
int, signed int, unsigned int
short int, signed short int, unsigned short int
long int, signed long int, unsigned long int
float
double
long double
```

A few points should be noted. All declarations to do with an int will be signed anyway, so signed is redundant in that context. If *any* other type specifier or qualifier is present, then the int part may be dropped, as that is the default.

The keywords const and volatile can be applied to any declaration, including those of structures, unions, enumerated types or typedef names. Applying them to a declaration is called **qualifying** the declaration – that's why const and volatile are called type qualifiers, rather than type specifiers. Here are a few representative examples:

```
volatile i;
volatile int j;
const long q;
const volatile unsigned long int rt_clk;
struct{
        const long int li;
        signed char sc;
}volatile vs;
```

Don't be put off; some of them are deliberately complicated: what they mean will be explained later. Remember that they could also be further complicated by introducing storage class specifications as well! In fact, the truly spectacular

```
extern const volatile unsigned long int rt_clk;
```

is a strong possibility in some real-time operating system kernels.

### 8.4.1 Const

Let's look at what is meant when const is used. It's really quite simple: const means that something is not modifiable, so a data object that is declared with const as a part of its type specification must not be assigned to in any way during the run of a program. It is very likely that the definition of the object will contain an initializer (otherwise, since you can't assign to it, how would it ever get a value?), but this is not always the case. For example, if you were accessing a hardware port at a fixed memory address and promised only to read from it, then it would be declared to be const but not initialized.

Taking the address of a data object of a type which isn't const and putting it into a pointer to the const-qualified version of the same type is both safe and explicitly permitted; you will be able to use the pointer to inspect the object, but not modify it. Putting the address of a const type into a pointer to the unqualified type is much more dangerous and consequently prohibited (although you can get around this by using a cast). Here is an example:

```
#include ⟨stdio.h⟩
#include ⟨stdlib.h⟩

main(){
        int i;
        const int ci = 123;

        /* declare a pointer to a const.. */
        const int *cpi;

        /* ordinary pointer to a non-const */
        int *ncpi;

        cpi = &ci;
        ncpi = &i;

        /*
         * this is allowed
         */
        cpi = ncpi;
```

```
/*
 * this needs a cast
 * because it is usually a big mistake,
 * see what it permits below.
 */
ncpi = (int *)cpi;

/*
 * now to get undefined behaviour...
 * modify a const through a pointer
 */
*ncpi = 0;

exit(EXIT_SUCCESS);
}
```
(Example 8.3)

As the example shows, it is possible to take the address of a constant object, generate a pointer to a non-constant, then use the new pointer. This is *an error* in your program and results in undefined behaviour.

The main intention of introducing const objects was to allow them to be put into read-only store, and to permit compilers to do extra consistency checking in a program. Unless you defeat the intent by doing naughty things with pointers, a compiler is able to check that const objects are not modified explicitly by the user.

An interesting extra feature pops up now. What does this mean?

```
char c;
char *const cp = &c;
```

It's simple really; cp is a pointer to a char, which is exactly what it would be if the const weren't there. The const means that cp is not to be modified, although whatever it points to can be – the pointer is constant, not the thing that it points to. The other way round is

```
const char *cp;
```

which means that now cp is an ordinary, modifiable pointer, but the thing that it points to must not be modified. So, depending on what you choose to do, both the pointer and the thing it points to may be modifiable or not; just choose the appropriate declaration.

## 8.4.2 Volatile

After const, we treat volatile. The reason for having this type qualifier is mainly to do with the problems that are encountered in real-time or embedded systems programming using C. Imagine that you are writing code that controls a hardware device by placing appropriate values in hardware registers at known absolute addresses.

Let's imagine that the device has two registers, each 16 bits long, at ascending memory addresses; the first one is the control and status register (csr) and the second is a data port. The traditional way of accessing such a device is like this:

```c
/* Standard C example but without const or volatile */
/*
 * Declare the device registers
 * Whether to use int or short
 * is implementation dependent
 */

struct devregs{
        unsigned short  csr;     /* control & status */
        unsigned short  data;    /* data port */
};

/* bit patterns in the csr */
#define ERROR    0x1
#define READY    0x2
#define RESET    0x4

/* absolute address of the device */
#define DEVADDR ((struct devregs *)0xffff0004)

/* number of such devices in system */
#define NDEVS    4

/*
 * Busy-wait function to read a byte from device n.
 * check range of device number.
 * Wait until READY or ERROR
 * if no error, read byte, return it
 * otherwise reset error, return 0xffff
 */
unsigned int
read_dev(unsigned devno){
        struct devregs *dvp = DEVADDR + devno;

        if(devno >= NDEVS)
                return(0xffff);

        while((dvp->csr & (READY | ERROR)) == 0)
                ; /* NULL — wait till done */

        if(dvp->csr & ERROR){
                dvp->csr = RESET;
                return(0xffff);
        }
        return((dvp->data) & 0xff);
}
```

(Example 8.4)

The technique of using a structure declaration to describe the device register layout and names is very common practice. Notice that there aren't actually any objects of that type defined, so the declaration simply indicates the structure without using up any store.

To access the device registers, an appropriately cast constant is used as if it were pointing to such a structure, but of course it points to memory addresses instead.

However, a major problem with previous C compilers would be in the while loop which tests the status register and waits for the ERROR or READY bit to come on. Any self-respecting optimizing compiler would notice that the loop tests the same memory address over and over again. It would almost certainly arrange to reference memory once only, and copy the value into a hardware register, thus speeding up the loop. This is, of course, exactly what we don't want; this is one of the few places where we *must* look at the place where the pointer points, every time around the loop.

Because of this problem, most C compilers have been unable to make that sort of optimization in the past. To remove the problem (and other similar ones to do with when to write to where a pointer points), the keyword volatile was introduced. It tells the compiler that the object is subject to sudden change for reasons which cannot be predicted from a study of the program itself, and forces every reference to such an object to be a genuine reference.

Here is how you would rewrite the example, making use of const and volatile to get what you want:

```
/*
 * Declare the device registers
 * Whether to use int or short
 * is implementation dependent
 */


struct devregs{
        unsigned short volatile csr;
        unsigned short const volatile data;
};


/* bit patterns in the csr */
#define ERROR    0x1
#define READY    0x2
#define RESET    0x4


/* absolute address of the device */
#define DEVADDR ((struct devregs *)0xffff0004)


/* number of such devices in system */
#define NDEVS    4
```

```
/*
 * Busy-wait function to read a byte from device n.
 * check range of device number.
 * Wait until READY or ERROR
 * if no error, read byte, return it
 * otherwise reset error, return 0xffff
 */
unsigned int
read_dev(unsigned devno){
        struct devregs * const dvp = DEVADDR + devno;

        if(devno >= NDEVS)
                return(0xffff);

        while((dvp->csr & (READY | ERROR)) == 0)
                ; /* NULL — wait till done */

        if(dvp->csr & ERROR){
                dvp->csr = RESET;
                return(0xffff);
        }
        return((dvp->data) & 0xff);
}
```

**(Example 8.5)**

The rules about mixing volatile and regular types resemble those for const. A pointer to a volatile object can be assigned the address of a regular object with safety, but it is dangerous (and needs a cast) to take the address of a volatile object and put it into a pointer to a regular object. Using such a derived pointer results in undefined behaviour.

If an array, union or structure is declared with const or volatile attributes, then all of the members take on that attribute too. This makes sense when you think about it – how could a member of a const structure be modifiable?

That means that an alternative rewrite of the last example would be possible. Instead of declaring the device registers to be volatile in the structure, the pointer could have been declared to point to a volatile structure instead, like this:

```
struct devregs{
        unsigned short  csr;    /* control & status */
        unsigned short  data;   /* data port */
};

volatile struct devregs *const dvp = DEVADDR + devno;
```

Since dvp points to a volatile object, it is not permitted to optimize references through the pointer. Our feeling is that, although this would work, it is bad style. The volatile declaration belongs in the structure: it is the device registers which are volatile and that is where the information should be kept; it reinforces the fact for a human reader.

So for any object likely to be subject to modification either by hardware or asynchronous interrupt service routines, the volatile type qualifier is important.

Now, just when you thought that you understood all that, here comes the final twist. A declaration like this:

```
volatile struct devregs{
        /* stuff */
}v_decl;
```

declares the type struct devregs and also a volatile-qualified object of that type, called v_decl. A later declaration like this

```
struct devregs nv_decl;
```

declares nv_decl which is *not* qualified with volatile! The qualification is *not* part of the type of struct devregs but applies only to the declaration of v_decl. Look at it this way round, which perhaps makes the situation more clear (the two declarations are the same in their effect):

```
struct devregs{
        /* stuff */
}volatile v_decl;
```

If you do want to get a shorthand way of attaching a qualifier to another type, you can use typedef to do it:

```
struct x{
        int a;
};
typedef const struct x csx;

csx const_sx;
struct x non_const_sx = {1};

const_sx = non_const_sx;        /* error - attempt to modify a const */
```

### Indivisible operations

Those of you who are familiar with techniques that involve hardware interrupts and other 'real time' aspects of programming will recognise the need for volatile types. Related to this area is the need to ensure that accesses to data objects are 'atomic', or uninterruptable. To discuss this in any depth would take us beyond the scope of this book, but we can at least outline some of the issues.

Be careful not to assume that any operations written in C are uninterruptable. For example,

```
extern const volatile unsigned long realtimeclock;
```

could be a counter which is updated by a clock interrupt routine. It is essential to make it volatile because of the asynchronous updates to it, and it is marked const because it should not be changed by anything other than the interrupt routine. If the program accesses it like this:

```
unsigned long int time_of_day;

time_of_day = real_time_clock;
```

there may be a problem. What if, to copy one long into another, it takes several machine instructions to copy the two words making up real_time_clock and time_of_day? It is possible that an interrupt will occur in the middle of the assignment and that in the worst case, when the low-order word of real_time_clock is 0xffff and the high-order word is 0x0000, then the low-order word of time_of_day will receive 0xffff. The interrupt arrives and increments the low-order word of real_time_clock to 0x0 and then the high-order word to 0x1, then returns. The rest of the assignment then completes, with time_of_day ending up containing 0x0001ffff and real_time_clock containing the correct value, 0x00010000.

This whole class of problem is what is known as a **critical region**, and is well understood by those who regularly work in asynchronous environments. It should be understood that Standard C takes no special precautions to avoid these problems, and that the usual techniques should be employed.

The header ⟨signal.h⟩ declares a type called sig_atomic_t which is guaranteed to be modifiable safely in the presence of asynchronous events. This means only that it can be modified by assigning a value to it; incrementing or decrementing it, or anything else which produces a new value depending on its previous value, is not safe.

## 8.5  Sequence points

Associated with, but distinct from, the problems of real-time programming are **sequence points**. These are the Standard's attempt to define when certain sorts of optimization may and may not be permitted to be in effect. For example, look at this program:

```
#include ⟨stdio.h⟩
#include ⟨stdlib.h⟩

int i_var;
void func(void);

main(){
        while(i_var != 10000){
                func();
                i_var++;
        }
        exit(EXIT_SUCCESS);
}
```

```
void
func(void){
        printf("in func, i_var is %d\n", i_var);
}
```
(Example 8.6)

The compiler might want to optimize the loop so that i_var can be stored in a machine register for speed. However, the function needs to have access to the correct value of i_var so that it can print the right value. This means that the register must be stored back into i_var at each function call (at least). When and where these conditions must occur are described by the Standard. At each sequence point, the side effects of all previous expressions will be completed. This is why you cannot rely on expressions such as:

```
a[i] = i++;
```

because there is no sequence point specified for the assignment, increment or index operators, you don't know when the effect of the increment on i occurs.

The sequence points laid down in the Standard are the following:

- The point of calling a function, after evaluating its arguments.
- The end of the first operand of the && operator.
- The end of the first operand of the || operator.
- The end of the first operand of the ?: conditional operator.
- The end of the each operand of the comma operator.
- Completing the evaluation of a full expression. They are the following:
  - Evaluating the initializer of an auto object.
  - The expression in an 'ordinary' statement – an expression followed by semicolon.
  - The controlling expressions in do, while, if, switch or for statements.
  - The other two expressions in a for statement.
  - The expression in a return statement.

## ■ 8.6 SUMMARY

This is a chapter describing specialized areas of the language.

Undoubtedly, the issues of scope, linkage and duration are important. If you find the whole topic too much to digest, just learn the simple rules. The problem is that the Standard tries to be complete and unambiguous, so it has to lay down lots of rules. It's much easier if you just stick to the easy way of doing things and don't try to get too clever. Use Example 8.2 as a model if in doubt.

The use of typedef depends on your level of experience. Its most common use is to help avoid some of the more unpleasant aspects of complicated type declarations.

The use of const will be widespread in many programs. The idea of a pointer to something which is not modifiable is well and truly emphasized in the library function prototypes.

Only specialized applications will use volatile. If you work in the field of real-time programming, or embedded systems, this will matter to you. Otherwise it probably won't. The same goes for sequence points. How well the early compilers will support these last two features will be a very interesting question.

# CHAPTER 9

---

# Libraries

---

---

## 9.1 Introduction

There is no doubt that the Standard Committee's decision to define a set of library routines will prove to be a huge benefit to users of C. Previously there were *no* standard, accepted definitions of library routines to provide support for the language. As a result, portability suffered seriously.

The library routines do not have to be present; they will only be present in a **hosted environment** – typically the case for applications programmers. Writers of embedded systems and the writers of the hosted environment libraries will not have the libraries present. They are using 'raw' C, in a **freestanding environment**, and this chapter will not be of much interest to them.

The descriptions (except for this introduction) are not meant to be read as a whole chapter, but as individual pieces. The material included here is meant more for information and convenient reference than as a full tutorial introduction. It would take a full book by itself to do real justice to the libraries.

### 9.1.1 Headers and standard types

A number of types and macros are used widely by the library functions. Where necessary, they are defined in the appropriate #include file for that function. The header will also declare appropriate types and prototypes for the library functions. Some important points should be noted here:

- All external identifiers and macro names declared in any of the library headers are reserved. They must not be used, or redefined, for any other purpose. In some cases they may be 'magic' – their names may be known to the compiler and cause it to use special methods to implement them.

- All identifiers that begin with an underscore are reserved.

- Headers may be included in any order, and more than once, but must be included outside of any external declaration or definition and before any use of the functions or macros defined inside them.

- Giving a 'bad value' to a function – say a null pointer, or a value outside the range of values expected by the function – results in undefined behaviour unless otherwise stated.

The Standard isn't quite as restrictive about identifiers as the list above is, but it's a brave move to make use of the loopholes. Play safe instead.

The Standard headers are:

```
⟨assert.h⟩   ⟨locale.h⟩   ⟨stddef.h⟩
⟨ctype.h⟩    ⟨math.h⟩     ⟨stdio.h⟩
⟨errno.h⟩    ⟨setjmp.h⟩   ⟨stdlib.h⟩
⟨float.h⟩    ⟨signal.h⟩   ⟨string.h⟩
⟨limits.h⟩   ⟨stdarg.h⟩   ⟨time.h⟩
```

A last general point is that many of the library routines may be implemented as macros, provided that there will be no problems to do with side-effects (as Chapter 7 describes). The Standard guarantees that, if a function *is* normally implemented as a macro, there will also be a true function provided to do the same job. To use the real function, either undefine the macro name with #undef, or enclose its name in parentheses, which ensures that it won't be treated as a macro:

```
somefunction("Might be a macro\n");
(somefunction)("Can't be a macro\n");
```

### 9.1.2 Character set and cultural dependencies

The Committee has introduced features that attempt to cater for the use of C in environments which are not based on the character set of US ASCII and where there are cultural dependencies such as the use of comma or full stop to indicate the decimal point. Facilities have been provided (see Section 9.4) for setting a program's idea of its **locale**, which is used to control the behaviour of the library functions.

Providing full support for different native languages and customs is a difficult and poorly understood task; the facilities provided by the C library are only a first step on the road to a full solution.

In several places the 'C locale' is referred to. This is the only locale defined by the Standard and effectively provides support for the way that Old C worked. Other locale settings may provide different behaviour in implementation-defined ways.

### 9.1.3 The ⟨stddef.h⟩ header

There are a small number of types and macros, found in ⟨stddef.h⟩, which are widely used in other headers. They are described in the following paragraphs.

Subtracting one pointer from another gives a result whose type differs between different implementations. To allow safe use of the difference, the type is defined in ⟨stddef.h⟩ to be ptrdiff_t. Similarly, you can use size_t to store the result of sizeof.

For reasons which still escape us, there is an 'implementation defined null pointer constant' defined in ⟨stddef.h⟩ called NULL. Since the language explicitly defines the integer constant 0 to be the value which can be assigned to, and compared with, a null pointer, this would seem to be unnecessary. However, it is *very* common practice among experienced C programmers to write this sort of thing:

```
#include ⟨stdio.h⟩
#include ⟨stddef.h⟩

FILE *fp;

if((fp = fopen("somefile", "r")) != NULL){
        /* and so on */
```

There is also a macro called offsetof which can be used to find the offset, in bytes, of a structure member. The offset is the distance between the member and the start of the structure. It would be used like this:

```
#include ⟨stdio.h⟩
#include ⟨stdlib.h⟩
#include ⟨stddef.h⟩
```

```
main(){
        size_t distance;
        struct x{
                int a, b, c;
        }s_tr;

        distance = offsetof(s_tr, c);
        printf("Offset of x.c is %lu bytes\n",
                (unsigned long)distance);
        exit(EXIT_SUCCESS);
}
```

**(Example 9.1)**

The expression s_tr.c must be capable of evaluation as an address constant (see Chapter 6). If the member whose offset you want is a bitfield, then you're out of luck; offsetof has undefined behaviour in that case.

Note carefully the way that a size_t has to be cast to the longest possible unsigned type to ensure that not only is the argument to printf of the type that it expects (%lu is the format string for unsigned long), but also no precision is lost. This is all because the type of size_t is not known to the programmer.

The last item declared in ⟨stddef.h⟩ is wchar_t, an integral type large enough to hold a wide character from any supported extended character sets.

### 9.1.4 The ⟨errno.h⟩ header

This header defines errno along with the macros EDOM and ERANGE, which expand to non-zero integral constant expressions; their form is additionally guaranteed to be acceptable to #if directives. The latter two are used by the mathematical functions to report which kind of errors they encountered and are more fully described later.

errno is provided to tell you when library functions have detected an error. It is not necessarily, as it used to be, an external variable, but is now a 'modifiable lvalue that has type int'. It is set to zero at program start-up, but from then on never reset unless explicitly assigned to; in particular, the library routines never reset it. If an error occurs in a library routine, errno is set to a particular value to indicate what went wrong, and the routine returns a value (often −1) to indicate that it failed. The usual use is like this:

```
#include ⟨stdio.h⟩
#include ⟨stddef.h⟩
#include ⟨errno.h⟩

errno = 0;
if(some_library_function(arguments) < 0){
        /* error processing code... */
        /* may use value of errno directly */
```

The implementation of errno is not known to the programmer, so don't try to do anything other than reset it or inspect its value. It isn't guaranteed to have an address, for example.

What's more, you should only check errno if the particular library function in use documents its effect on errno. Other library functions are free to set it to arbitrary values after a call unless their description explicitly states what they do with it.

## 9.2 Diagnostics

While you are debugging programs, it is often useful to check that the value of an expression is the one that you expected. The assert function provides such a diagnostic aid.

In order to use assert you must first include the header file ⟨assert.h⟩. The function is defined as

```
#include ⟨assert.h⟩

void assert(int expression)
```

If the expression evaluates to zero (that is, false) then assert will write a message about the failing expression, including the name of the source file, the line at which the assertion was made and the expression itself. After this, the abort function is called, which will halt the program.

```
assert(1 == 2);

/* Might result in */

Assertion failed: 1 == 2, file silly.c, line 15
```

Assert is actually defined as a macro, not as a real function. In order to disable assertions when a program is found to work satisfactorily, defining the name NDEBUG *before* including ⟨assert.h⟩ will disable assertions totally. You should beware of side effects that the expression may have: when assertions are turned off with NDEBUG, the expression is *not* evaluated. Thus the following example will behave unexpectedly when debugging is turned off with the #define NDEBUG.

```
#define NDEBUG
#include ⟨assert.h⟩

void
func(void)
{
        int c;
        assert((c = getchar()) != EOF);
        putchar(c);
}
```
(Example 9.2)

Note that assert returns no value.

## 9.3 Character handling

There are a variety of functions provided for testing and mapping characters. The testing functions, which are described first, allow you to test if a character is of a particular type, such as alphabetic, upper or lower case, numeric, a control character, a punctuation mark, printable or not and so on. The character testing functions return an integer, either zero if the character supplied is not of the category specified, or non-zero if it was. The functions all take an integer argument, which should either be an int, the value of which should be representable as unsigned char, or the integer constant EOF, as returned from functions such as getchar(). The behaviour is undefined if it is not.

These functions depend on the program's locale setting.

A **printing character** is a member of an implementation defined character set. Each printing character occupies one printing position. A **control character** is a member of an implementation defined character set, each of which is not a printing character. If the 7-bit ASCII character set is used, the printing characters are those that lie between space (0x20) and tilde (0x7e), the control characters are those between NUL (0x0) and US (0x1f), and the character DEL (0x7f).

The following is a summary of all the character testing functions. The header ⟨ctype.h⟩ must be included before any of them is used.

isalnum(int c)
> True if c is alphabetic or a digit; specifically (isalpha(c)||isdigit(c)).

isalpha(int c)
> True if (isupper(c)||islower(c)).
>
> Also true for an implementation-defined set of characters which do not return true results from any of iscntrl, isdigit, ispunct or isspace. In the C locale, this extra set of characters is empty.

iscntrl(int c)
> True if c is a control character.

isdigit(int c)
> True if c is a decimal digit.

isgraph(int c)
> True if c is any printing character except space.

islower(int c)
> True if c is a lower case alphabetic letter.
>
> Also true for an implementation defined set of characters which do not return true results from any of iscntrl, isdigit, ispunct or isspace. In the C locale, this extra set of characters is empty.

isprint(int c)
> True if c is a printing character (including space).

ispunct(int c)
> True if c is any printing character that is neither a space nor a character which would return true from isalnum.

`isspace(int c)`

> True if c is either a white space character (one of ' ' '\f' '\n' '\r' '\t' '\v') or, in other than the C locale, characters which would not return true from isalnum.

`isupper(int c)`

> True if c is an upper case alphabetic character.

> Also true for an implementation-defined set of characters which do not return true results from any of iscntrl, isdigit, ispunct or isspace. In the C locale, this extra set of characters is empty.

`isxdigit(int c)`

> True if c is a valid hexadecimal digit.

Two additional functions map characters from one set into another. The function tolower will, if given an upper case character as its argument, return the lower case equivalent. For example,

```
tolower('A') == 'a'
```

If tolower is given any character other than an upper case letter, it will return that character.

The converse function toupper maps lower case alphabetic letters on to their upper case equivalent.

For each, the conversion is only performed if there *is* a corresponding character in the alternate case. In some locales, not all upper case characters have lower case equivalents, and vice versa.

## 9.4 Localization

This is where the program's idea of its current locale can be controlled. The header file ⟨locale.h⟩ declares the setlocale and localeconv functions and a number of macros:

```
LC_ALL
LC_COLLATE
LC_CTYPE
LC_MONETARY
LC_NUMERIC
LC_TIME
```

all of which expand to integral constant expressions and are used as values of the category argument to setlocale (other names may also be defined: they will all start with LC_X where X is an upper case letter), and the type

```
struct lconv
```

which is used for storing information about the formatting of numeric values. For members of type char, CHAR_MAX is used to indicate that the value is not available in the current locale.

lconv contains at least the following members:

char *decimal_point

The character used for the decimal point in formatted non-monetary values. "." in the C locale.

char *thousands_sep

The character used for separating groups of digits to the left of the decimal point in formatted non-monetary values. "" in the C locale.

char *grouping

Defines the number of digits in each group when formatting non-monetary values. The elements are interpreted as follows: A value of CHAR_MAX indicates that no further grouping is to be performed; 0 indicates that the previous element should be repeated for the remaining digits; if any other character is used, its integer value represents the number of digits that comprise the current group (the next character in the sequence is interpreted before grouping). "" in the C locale. As an example, "\3" specifies that digits should be grouped in threes; the terminating null in the string signifies that the \3 repeats.

char *int_curr_symbol

The first three characters are used to hold the alphabetic international currency symbol for the current locale, the fourth character is used to separate the international currency symbol from the monetary quantity. "" in the C locale.

char *currency_symbol

The currency symbol for the current locale. "" in the C locale.

char *mon_decimal_point

The character used as the decimal point when formatting monetary values. "" in the C locale.

char *mon_thousands_sep

The digit group separator for formatted monetary values. "" in the C locale.

char *mon_grouping

Defines the number of digits in each group when formatting monetary values. Its elements are interpreted as those for grouping. "" in the C locale.

char *positive_sign

The string used to signify a non-negative monetary value. "" in the C locale.

char *negative_sign

The string used to signify a negative monetary value. "" in the C locale.

char int_frac_digits

The number of digits to be displayed after the decimal point in an internationally formatted monetary value. CHAR_MAX in the C locale.

char frac_digits

The number of digits to be displayed after the decimal point in a non-internationally formatted monetary value. CHAR_MAX in the C locale.

char p_cs_precedes

A value of 1 indicates that the currency_symbol should precede the value when formatting a non-negative monetary quantity; a value of 0 indicates that it should follow. CHAR_MAX in the C locale.

char p_sep_by_space

A value of 1 indicates that the currency symbol is separated by a space from the value when formatting a non-negative monetary quantity; 0 indicates no space. CHAR_MAX in the C locale.

char n_cs_precedes

As p_cs_precedes for negative monetary values. CHAR_MAX in the C locale.

char n_sep_by_space

As p_sep_by_space for negative monetary values. CHAR_MAX in the C locale.

char p_sign_posn

Indicates the position of the positive_sign for a non-negative formatted monetary value according to the following:

0   parentheses surround quantity and currency_symbol
1   the string precedes the quantity and currency_symbol
2   the string follows the quantity and currency_symbol
3   the string precedes the currency_symbol
4   the string follows the currency_symbol

CHARMAX in the C locale.

char n_sign_posn

As p_sign_posn for negative monetary values. CHAR_MAX in the C locale.

### 9.4.1 The setlocale function

```
#include <locale.h>

char *setlocale(int category, const char *locale);
```

This function allows the program's idea of its locale to be set. All or parts of the locale can be set by providing values for category as follows:

LC_ALL

Set entire locale.

LC_COLLATE

Modify behaviour of strcoll and strxfrm.

LC_CTYPE
>    Modify behaviour of character-handling functions.

LC_MONETARY
>    Modify monetary formatting information returned by localeconv.

LC_NUMERIC
>    Modify decimal-point character for formatted I/O and string conversion routines.

LC_TIME
>    Modify behaviour of strftime.

The values for locale can be:

| | |
|---|---|
| "C" | Select the minimal environment for C translation. |
| "" | Select the implementation-defined 'native environment', |
| *implementation defined* | Select other environments. |

When the program starts, it has an environment as if

```
setlocale(LC_ALL, "C");
```

has been executed.

The current string associated with a given category can be queried by passing a null pointer as the value for locale; if the selection can be performed, the string associated with the specified category for the new locale is returned. This string is such that if it is used in a subsequent call to setlocale, along with its associated category, that part of the program's locale will be restored. If the selection cannot be performed, a null pointer is returned and the locale is not changed.

### 9.4.2 The localeconv function

```
#include ⟨locale.h⟩

struct lconv *localeconv(void);
```

The function returns a pointer to a structure of type struct lconv, set according to the current locale, which may be overwritten by subsequent calls to localeconv or setlocale. The structure must not be modified in any other way.

For example, if in the current locale monetary values should be represented as

| | |
|---|---|
| IR£1,234.56 | positive format |
| (IR£1,234.56) | negative format |
| IRP 1,234.56 | international format |

then the monetary members of lconv would have the values:

```
int_curr_symbol        "IRP "
currency_symbol        "IR£"
mon_decimal_point      "."
mon_thousands_sep      ","
mon_grouping           "\3"
positive_sign          ""
negative_sign          ""
int_frac_digits        2
frac_digits            2
p_cs_precedes          1
p_sep_by_space         0
n_cs_precedes          1
n_sep_by_space         0
p_sign_posn            CHAR_MAX
n_sign_posn            0
```

## 9.5 Limits

Two header files ⟨float.h⟩ and ⟨limits.h⟩ define several implementation specific limits.

### 9.5.1 The ⟨limits.h⟩ header

Table 9.1 gives the names declared, the allowable values, and a comment on what they mean. For example, the description of SHRT_MIN shows that in a given implementation

**Table 9.1**  ⟨limits.h⟩.

| Name | Allowable value | Comment |
|------|----------------|---------|
| CHAR_BIT | (≥8) | bits in a char |
| CHAR_MAX | see note | maximum value of a char |
| CHAR_MIN | see note | minimum value of a char |
| INT_MAX | (≥+32767) | maximum value of an int |
| INT_MIN | (≤-32767) | minimum value of an int |
| LONG_MAX | (≥+2 147 483 647) | maximum value of a long |
| LONG_MIN | (≤-2 147 483 647) | minimum value of a long |
| MB_LEN_MAX | (≥1) | maximum number of bytes in a multibyte character |
| SCHAR_MAX | (≥+127) | maximum value of a signed char |
| SCHAR_MIN | (≤-127) | minimum value of a signed char |
| SHRT_MAX | (≥+32767) | maximum value of a short |
| SHRT_MIN | (≤-32767) | minimum value of a short |
| UCHAR_MAX | (≥255U) | maximum value of an unsigned char |
| UINT_MAX | (≥65 535U) | maximum value of an unsigned int |
| ULONG_MAX | (≥4 294 967 295U) | maximum value of an unsigned long |
| USHRT_MAX | (>65 535U) | maximum value of an unsigned short |

Note: if the implementation treats chars as signed, then the values of CHAR_MAX and CHAR_MIN are the same as the equivalent SCHAR versions. If not, then the value of CHAR_MIN is zero and the value of CHAR_MAX is equal to the value of UCHAR_MAX.

the value must be less than or equal to -32767: this means that for maximum portability a program cannot rely on short variables being able to hold values more negative than -32767. Implementations may choose to support values which are more negative but must provide support for at least -32767.

## 9.5.2 The ⟨float.h⟩ header

For floating point numbers, the file ⟨float.h⟩ contains a similar set of allowable values which are described in Table 9.2. (It is assumed that where no minimum value is specified, there is either no minimum, or the value depends on another value.)

Table 9.2   <float.h>.

| Name | Allowable value | Comment |
|------|-----------------|---------|
| FLT_RADIX | (≥2) | the radix of exponent representation |
| DBL_DIG | (≥10) | the number of digits of precision in a double |
| DBL_EPSILON | (≤1E-9) | minimum positive number such that $1.0 + x \neq 1.0$ |
| DBL_MANT_DIG | (-) | the number of base FLT_RADIX digits in the mantissa part of a double |
| DBL_MAX | (≥1E+37) | maximum value of a double |
| DBL_MAX_10_EXP | (≥+37) | maximum value of exponent (base 10) of a double |
| DBL_MAX_EXP | (-) | maximum value of exponent (base FLT_RADIX) of a double |
| DBL_MIN | (≤1E-37) | minimum value of a double |
| DBL_MIN_10_EXP | (≤-37) | minimum value of exponent (base 10) of a double |
| DBL_MIN_EXP | (-) | minimum value of exponent part of a double (base FLT_RADIX) |
| FLTDIG | (≥6) | the number of digits of precision in a float |
| FLT_EPSILON | (≤1E-5) | minimum positive number such that $1.0 + x \neq 1.0$ |
| FLT_MANT_DIG | (-) | the number of base FLT_RADIX digits in the mantissa of a float |
| FLT_MAX | (≥1E+37) | maximum value of a float |
| FLT_MAX_10_EXP | (≥+37) | maximum value (base 10) of exponent part of a float |
| FLT_MAX_EXP | (-) | maximum value (base FLT_RADIX) of exponent part of a float |
| FLT_MIN | (≤1E-37) | minimum value of a float |
| FLT_MIN_10_EXP | (≤-37) | minimum value (base 10) of exponent part of a float |
| FLT_MIN_EXP | (-) | minimum value (base FLT_RADIX) of exponent part of a float |
| FLT_ROUNDS | (0) | affects rounding of floating point addition: |
| | | -1 indeterminate |
| | | 0 towards zero |
| | | 1 to nearest |
| | | 2 towards +infinity |
| | | 3 towards −infinity |
| | | any other value is implementation defined. |
| LDBL_DIG | (≥10) | the number of digits of precision in a long double |
| LDBL_EPSILON | (≤1E-9) | minimum positive number such that $1.0 + x \neq 1.0$ |
| LDBL_MANT_DIG | (-) | the number of base FLT_RADIX digits in the mantissa part of a long double |
| LDBL_MAX | (≥1E+37) | maximum value of a long double |
| LDBL_MAX_10_EXP | (≥+37) | maximum value of exponent (base 10) of a long double |

**Table 9.2**   *cont.*

| Name | Allowable value | Comment |
|------|------|---------|
| LDBL_MAX_EXP | (-) | maximum value of exponent (base FLT_RADIX) of a long double |
| LDBL_MIN | (≤1E-37) | minimum value of a long double |
| LDBL_MIN_10_EXP | (≤-37) | minimum value of exponent part (base 10) of a long double |
| LDBL_MIN_EXP | (-) | minimum value of exponent part of a long double (base FLT_RADIX) |

## 9.6 Mathematical functions

If you are writing mathematical programs, involving floating point calculations and so on, then you will undoubtedly require access to the mathematics library. This set of functions all take double arguments, and return a double result. The functions and associated macros are defined in the include file ⟨math.h⟩.

The macro HUGE_VAL is defined, which expands to a positive double expression, which is not necessarily representable as a float.

For all the functions, a **domain error** occurs if an input argument is outside the domain over which the function is defined. An example might be attempting to take the square root of a negative number. If this occurs, errno is set to the constant EDOM, and the function returns an implementation defined value.

If the result of the function cannot be represented as a double value then a **range error** occurs. If the magnitude of the result is too large, the functions return ±HUGE_VAL (the sign will be correct) and errno is set to ERANGE. If the result is too small, 0.0 is returned and the value of errno is implementation defined.

The following list briefly describes each of the functions available:

double acos(double x);
> Principal value of the arc cosine of x in the range $0 \ldots \pi$ radians.
> Errors: EDOM if x is not in the range -1...1.

double asin(double x);
> Principal value of the arc sine of x in the range $-\pi/2 \ldots +\pi/2$ radians.
> Errors: EDOM if x is not in the range -1...1.

double atan(double x);
> Principal value of the arc tangent of x in the range $-\pi/2 \ldots +\pi/2$ radians.

double atan2(double y, double x);
> Principal value of the arc tangent of y/x in the range $-\pi \ldots +\pi$ radians, using the signs of both arguments to determine the quadrant of the return value.
> Errors: EDOM may occur if both x and y are zero.

double cos(double x);
> Cosine of x (x measured in radians).

double sin(double x);
> Sine of x (x measured in radians).

`double tan(double x);`

>   Tangent of x (x measured in radians). When a range error occurs, the sign of the resulting HUGE_VAL is not guaranteed to be correct.

`double cosh(double x);`

>   Hyperbolic cosine of x.
>   Errors: ERANGE occurs if the magnitude of x is too large.

`double sinh(double x);`

>   Hyperbolic sine of x.
>   Errors: ERANGE occurs if the magnitude of x is too large.

`double tanh(double x);`

>   Hyperbolic tangent of x.

`double exp(double x);`

>   Exponential function of x.
>   Errors: ERANGE occurs if the magnitude of x is too large.

`double frexp(double value, int *exp);`

>   Break a floating point number into a normalized fraction and an integral power of two. This integer is stored in the object pointed to by exp.

`double ldexp(double x, int exp);`

>   Multiply x by 2 to the power exp.
>   Errors: ERANGE may occur.

`double log(double x);`

>   Natural logarithm of x.
>   Errors: EDOM occurs if x is negative. ERANGE may occur if x is zero.

`double log10(double x);`

>   Base-ten logarithm of x.
>   Errors: EDOM occurs if x is negative. ERANGE may occur if x is zero.

`double modf(double value, double *iptr);`

>   Break the argument value into integral and fractional parts, each of which has the same sign as the argument. It stores the integral part as a double in the object pointed to by iptr, and returns the fractional part.

`double pow(double x, double y);`

>   Compute x to the power y.
>   Errors: EDOM occurs if x < 0 and y not integral, or if the result cannot be represented if x is 0, and y is ≤0. ERANGE may also occur.

`double sqrt(double x);`

>   Compute the square root of x.
>   Errors: EDOM occurs if x is negative.

`double ceil(double x);`

>   Smallest integer not less than x.

`double fabs(double x);`

>   Absolute value of x.

```
double floor(double x);
```
> Largest integer not greater than x.

```
double fmod(double x, double y);
```
> Floating point remainder of x/y.
>
> Errors: If y is zero, it is implementation defined whether fmod returns zero or a domain error occurs.

## 9.7 Non-local jumps

Provision is made for you to perform what is, in effect, a goto from one function to another. It isn't possible to do this by means of a goto and a label, since labels have only function scope. However, the macro setjmp and function longjmp provide an alternative, known as a *non-local goto*, or a *non-local jump*.

The file ⟨setjmp.h⟩ declares something called a jmp_buf, which is used by the cooperating macro and function to store the information necessary to make the jump. The declarations are as follows:

```
#include ⟨setjmp.h⟩

int setjmp(jmp_buf env);
void longjmp(jmp_buf env, int val);
```

The setjmp macro is used to initialise the jmp_buf and returns zero on its initial call. The bizarre thing is that it returns *again*, later, with a non-zero value, when the corresponding longjmp call is made! The non-zero value is whatever value was supplied to the call of longjmp. This is best explained by way of an example:

```
#include ⟨stdio.h⟩
#include ⟨stdlib.h⟩
#include ⟨setjmp.h⟩

void func(void);
jmp_buf place;

main(){
        int retval;

        /*
         * First call returns 0,
         * a later longjmp will return non-zero.
         */
        if(setjmp(place)) != 0){
                printf("Returned using longjmp\n");
                exit(EXIT_SUCCESS);
        }
```

```
            /*
             * This call will never return - it
             * ''jumps'' back above.
             */
            func();
            printf("What! func returned!\n");
      }


      void
      func(void){
            /*
             * Return to main.
             * Looks like a second return from setjmp,
             * returning 4!
             */
            longjmp(place, 4);
            printf("What! longjmp returned!\n");
      }
```
                                                                    (Example 9.3)

The val argument to longjmp is the value seen in the second and subsequent 'returns' from setjmp. It should normally be something other than 0; if you attempt to return 0 via longjmp, it will be changed to 1. It is therefore possible to tell whether the setjmp was called directly, or whether it was reached by calling longjmp.

If there has been no call to setjmp before calling longjmp, the effect of longjmp is undefined, almost certainly causing the program to crash. The longjmp function is never expected to return, in the normal sense, to the instructions immediately following the call. All accessible objects on 'return' from setjmp have the values that they had when longjmp was called, except for objects of automatic storage class that do not have volatile type; if they have been changed between the setjmp and longjmp calls, their values are indeterminate.

The longjmp function executes correctly in the contexts of interrupts, signals and any of their associated functions. If longjmp is invoked from a function called as a result of a signal arriving while handling another signal, the behaviour is undefined.

It's a serious error to longjmp to a function which is no longer active (that is, it has already returned or another longjmp call has transferred to a setjmp occurring earlier in a set of nested calls).

The Standard insists that, apart from appearing as the only expression in an expression statement, setjmp may only be used as the entire controlling expression in an if, switch, do, while, or for statement. A slight extension to that rule is that as long as it is the whole controlling expression (as above) the setjmp call may be the subject of the ! operator, or may be directly compared with an integral constant expression using one of the relational or equality operators. No more complex expressions may be employed. Examples are:

```
      setjmp(place);                  /* expression statement */
      if(setjmp(place)) ...           /* whole controlling expression */
```

```
if(!setjmp(place)) ...          /* whole controlling expression */
if(setjmp(place) < 4) ...       /* whole controlling expression */
if(setjmp(place) < 4 && 1 != 2) ...  /* forbidden */
```

## 9.8  Signal handling

Two functions allow for asynchronous event handling to be provided. A **signal** is a condition that may be reported during program execution, and can be ignored, handled specially, or, as is the default, used to terminate the program. One function sends signals, another is used to determine how a signal will be processed. Many of the signals may be generated by the underlying hardware or operating system as well as by means of the signal-sending function raise.

The signals are defined in the include file ⟨signal.h⟩.

SIGABRT

Abnormal termination, such as instigated by the abort function. (Abort.)

SIGFPE

Erroneous arithmetic operation, such as divide by 0 or overflow. (Floating point exception.)

SIGILL

An 'invalid object program' has been detected. This usually means that there is an illegal instruction in the program. (Illegal instruction.)

SIGINT

Interactive attention signal; on interactive systems this is usually generated by typing some 'break-in' key at the terminal. (Interrupt.)

SIGSEGV

Invalid storage access; most frequently caused by attempting to store some value in an object pointed to by a bad pointer. (Segment violation.)

SIGTERM

Termination request made to the program. (Terminate.)

Some implementations may have additional signals available, over and above this standard set. They will be given names that start SIG, and will have unique values, apart from the set above.

The function signal allows you to specify the action taken on receipt of a signal. Associated with each signal condition above, there is a pointer to a function provided to handle this signal. The signal function changes this pointer, and returns the original value. Thus the function is defined as

```
#include ⟨signal.h⟩
void (*signal (int sig, void (*func)(int)))(int);
```

That is to say, signal is a function that returns a pointer to another function. This second function takes a single int argument and returns void. The second argument to signal is similarly a pointer to a function returning void which takes an int argument.

Two special values may be used as the func argument (the signal-handling function), SIG_DFL, the initial, default, signal handler; and SIG_IGN, which is used to ignore a signal. The implementation sets the state of all signals to one or other of these values at the start of the program.

If the call to signal succeeds, the previous value of func for the specified signal is returned. Otherwise, SIG_ERR is returned and errno is set.

When a signal event happens which is not being ignored, if the associated func is a pointer to a function, first the equivalent of signal(sig, SIG_DFL) is executed. This resets the signal handler to the default action, which is to terminate the program. If the signal was SIGILL then this resetting is implementation defined. Implementations may choose to 'block' further instances of the signal instead of doing the resetting.

Next, a call is made to the signal-handling function. If that function returns normally, then under most circumstances the program will resume at the point where the event occurred. However, if the value of sig was SIGFPE (a floating point exception), or any implementation defined computational exception, then the behaviour is undefined. The most usual thing to do in the handler for SIGFPE is to call one of the functions abort, exit, or longjmp.

The following program fragment shows the use of signal to perform a tidy exit to a program on receipt of the interrupt or 'interactive attention' signal.

```c
#include <stdio.h>
#include <stdlib.h>
#include <signal.h>


FILE *temp_file;
void leave(int sig);


main() {
        (void) signal(SIGINT, leave);

        temp_file = fopen("tmp", "w");
        for(;;) {
                /*
                 * Do things...
                 */
                printf("Ready...\n");
                (void)getchar();
        }
        /* can't get here ... */
        exit(EXIT_SUCCESS);
}
```

```
/*
 * on receipt of SIGINT, close tmp file
 * but beware — calling library functions from a
 * signal handler is not guaranteed to work in all
 * implementations...
 * this is not a strictly conforming program
 */

void
leave(int sig) {
        fprintf(temp_file,"\nInterrupted..\n");
        fclose(temp_file);
        exit(sig);
}
```
                                                            (**Example 9.4**)

It is possible for a program to send signals to itself by means of the raise function. This is defined as follows

```
#include ⟨signal.h⟩
int raise (int sig);
```

The signal sig is sent to the program.

Raise returns zero if successful, non-zero otherwise. The abort library function is essentially implementable as follows:

```
#include ⟨signal.h⟩

void
abort(void) {
        raise(SIGABRT);
}
```

If a signal occurs for any reason other than calling abort or raise, the signal-handling function may only call signal or assign a value to a volatile static object of type sig_atomic_t. The type sig_atomic_t is declared in ⟨signal.h⟩. It is the only type of object that can safely be modified as an atomic entity, even in the presence of asynchronous interrupts. This is a very onerous restriction imposed by the Standard, which, for example, invalidates the leave function in the example program above; although the function would work correctly in some environments, it does not follow the strict rules of the Standard.

## 9.9 Variable numbers of arguments

It is often desirable to implement a function where the number of arguments is not known, or is not constant, when the function is written. Such a function is printf, described in Section 9.11. The following example shows the declaration of such a function.

```
int f(int, ... );

int
f(int, ... ) {
        .
        .
        .
}

int
g() {
        f(1, 2, 3);
}
```

(Example 9.5)

In order to access the arguments within the called function, the functions declared in the ⟨stdarg.h⟩ header file must be included. This introduces a new type, called a va_list, and three functions that operate on objects of this type, called va_start, va_arg, and va_end.

Before any attempt can be made to access a variable argument list, va_start *must* be called. It is defined as

```
#include ⟨stdarg.h⟩
void va_start(va_list ap, parmN);
```

The va_start macro initializes ap for subsequent use by the functions va_arg and va_end. The second argument to va_start, *parmN* is the identifier naming the rightmost parameter in the variable parameter list in the function definition (the one just before the , ... ). The identifier *parmN* must not be declared with register storage class or as a function or array type.

Once initialized, the arguments supplied can be accessed sequentially by means of the va_arg macro. This is peculiar because the type returned is determined by an argument to the macro. Note that this is impossible to implement as a true function, only as a macro. It is defined as

```
#include ⟨stdarg.h⟩
type va_arg(va_list ap, type);
```

Each call to this macro will extract the next argument from the argument list as a value of the specified type. The va_list argument must be the one initialized by va_start. If the next argument is not of the specified type, the behaviour is undefined. Take care here to avoid problems which could be caused by arithmetic conversions. Use of char or short as the second argument to va_arg is invariably an error: these types always promote up to one of signed int or unsigned int, and float converts to double. Note that it is implementation defined whether objects declared to have the types char, unsigned char, unsigned short and unsigned bitfields will promote to unsigned int, rather complicating the use of va_arg. This may be an area where some unexpected subtleties arise; only time will tell.

The behaviour is also undefined if va_arg is called when there are no further arguments.

The *type* argument must be a type name which can be converted into a pointer to such an object simply by appending a * to it (this is so the macro can work). Simple types such as char are fine (because char * is a pointer to a character) but array of char won't work (char [] does not turn into 'pointer to array of char' by appending a *). Fortunately, arrays can easily be processed by remembering that an array name used as an actual argument to a function call is converted into a pointer. The correct *type* for an argument of type 'array of char' would be char *.

When all the arguments have been processed, the va_end function should be called. This will prevent the va_list supplied from being used any further. If va_end is not used, the behaviour is undefined.

The entire argument list can be re-traversed by calling va_start again, after calling va_end. The va_end function is declared as

```
#include <stdarg.h>
void va_end(va_list ap);
```

The following example shows the use of va_start, va_arg, and va_end to implement a function that returns the biggest of its integer arguments.

```
#include <stdlib.h>
#include <stdarg.h>
#include <stdio.h>

int maxof(int, ...) ;
void f(void);

main(){
        f();
        exit(EXIT_SUCCESS);
}

int
maxof(int n_args, ...){
        register int i;
        int max, a;
        va_list ap;

        va_start(ap, n_args);
        max = va_arg(ap, int);
```

```
        for(i = 2; i <= n_args; i++) {
                if((a = va_arg(ap, int)) > max)
                        max = a;
        }
        va_end(ap);
        return max;
}

void
f(void) {
        int i = 5;
        int j[256];

        j[42] = 24;
        printf("%d\n",maxof(3, i, j[42], 0));
}
```

(Example 9.6)

## 9.10 Input and output

### 9.10.1 Introduction

One of the reasons that has prevented many programming languages from becoming widely used for 'real programming' is their poor support for I/O, a subject which has never seemed to excite language designers. C has avoided this problem, oddly enough, by having no I/O at all! The C language approach has always been to do I/O using library functions, which ensures that system designers can provide tailored I/O instead of being forced to change the language itself.

As C has evolved, a library package known as the 'Standard I/O Library' or stdio, has evolved with it and has proved to be both flexible and portable. This package has now become part of the Standard.

The old stdio package relied heavily on the UNIX model of file access, in particular the assumption that there is no distinction between unstructured binary files and files containing readable text. Many operating systems do maintain a distinction between the two, and to ensure that C programs can be written portably to run on both types of file model, the stdio package has been modified. There are changes in this area which affect many existing programs, although strenuous efforts were taken to limit the amount of damage.

Old C programs should still be able work unmodified in a UNIX environment.

### 9.10.2 The I/O model

The I/O model does not distinguish between the types of physical devices supporting the I/O. Each source or sink of data (file) is treated in the same way, and is viewed as a **stream** of bytes. Since the smallest object that can be represented in C is the character, access to a file is permitted at any character boundary. Any number of characters can be read or written from a movable point, known as the **file position indicator**. The characters will be read, or written, in sequence from this point, and the position indicator moved accordingly. The position indicator is initially set to the beginning of a file when it is opened, but can also be moved by means of positioning requests. (Where random access is not possible, the file position indicator is ignored.) Opening a file in append mode has an implementation defined effect on the stream's file position indicator.

The overall effect is to provide sequential reads or writes unless the stream was opened in append mode, or the file position indicator is explicitly moved.

There are two types of file, **text files** and **binary files**, which, within a program, are manipulated as **text streams** and **binary streams** once they have been opened for I/O. The stdio package does not permit operations on the contents of files 'directly', but only by viewing them as streams.

### Text streams

The Standard specifies what is meant by the term **text stream**, which essentially considers a file to contain lines of text. A line is a sequence of zero or more characters terminated by a newline character. It is quite possible that the actual representation of lines in the external environment is different from this and there may be transformations of the data stream on the way in and out of the program; a common requirement is to translate the '\n' line-terminator into the sequence '\r\n' on output, and do the reverse on input. Other translations may also be necessary.

Data read in from a text stream is guaranteed to compare equal to the data that was earlier written out to the file if the data consists only of complete lines of printable characters and the control characters horizontal-tab and newline, no newline character is immediately preceded by space characters and the last character is a newline.

It is guaranteed that, if the last character written to a text file is a newline, it will read back as the same.

It is implementation defined whether the last line written to a text file must terminate with a newline character; this is because on some implementations text files and binary files are the same.

Some implementations may strip the leading space from lines consisting only of a space followed by a newline, or strip trailing spaces at the end of a line!

An implementation must support text files with lines containing at least 254 characters, including the terminating newline.

Opening a text stream in update mode may result in a binary stream in some implementations.

Writing on a text stream may cause some implementations to truncate the file at that point – any data beyond the last byte of the current write being discarded.

### Binary streams

A binary stream is a sequence of characters that can be used to record a program's internal data, such as the contents of structures or arrays in binary form. Data read in from a binary stream will always compare equal to data written out earlier to the same stream, under the same implementation. In some circumstances, an implementation-defined number of NUL characters may be appended to a binary stream.

The contents of binary files are exceedingly machine specific, and not, in general, portable.

### Other streams
Other stream types may exist, but are implementation defined.

### 9.10.3  The stdio.h header file

To provide support for streams of the various kinds, a number of functions and macros exist. The ⟨stdio.h⟩ header file contains the various declarations necessary for the functions, together with the following macro and type declarations:

FILE
>   The type of an object used to contain stream control information. Users of stdio never need to know the contents of these objects, but simply manipulate pointers to them. It is not safe to copy these objects within the program; sometimes their addresses may be 'magic'.

fpos_t
>   A type of object that can be used to record unique values of a stream's file position indicator.

_IOFBF _IOLBF _IONBF
>   Values used to control the buffering of a stream in conjunction with the setvbuf function.

BUFSIZ
>   The size of the buffer used by the setbuf function. An integral constant expression whose value is at least 256.

EOF
>   A negative integral constant expression, indicating the end-of-file condition on a stream, that is, there is no more input.

FILENAME_MAX
>   The maximum length which a filename can have, if there is a limit, or otherwise the recommended size of an array intended to hold a file name.

FOPEN_MAX
>   The minimum number of files that the implementation guarantees may be held open concurrently; at least eight are guaranteed. Note that three predefined streams exist and may need to be closed if a program needs to open more than five files explicitly.

L_tmpnam
>   The maximum length of the string generated by tmpnam; an integral constant expression.

SEEK_CUR SEEK_END SEEK_SET
>    Integral constant expressions used to control the actions of fseek.

TMP_MAX
>    The minimum number of unique filenames generated by tmpnam; an integral
>    constant expression with a value of at least 25.

stdin stdout stderr
>    Predefined objects of type (FILE *) referring to the standard input, output and
>    error streams respectively. These streams are automatically opened when a
>    program starts execution.

### 9.10.4 Opening, closing and buffering of streams

*Opening*

A stream is connected to a file by means of the fopen, freopen or tmpfile functions.
These functions will, if successful, return a pointer to a FILE object.

Three streams are available without any special action; they are normally all
connected to the physical device associated with the executing program: usually your
terminal. They are referred to by the names stdin, the **standard input**, stdout, the
**standard output**, and stderr, the **standard error** streams. Normal keyboard input is
from stdin, normal terminal output is to stdout, and error messages are directed to
stderr. The separation of error messages from normal output messages allows the stdout
stream to be connected to something other than the terminal device, and still to have
error messages appear on the screen in front of you, rather than to be redirected to this
file. These files are only fully buffered if they do not refer to interactive devices.

As mentioned earlier, the file position indicator may or may not be movable,
depending on the underlying device. It is not possible, for example, to move the file
position indicator on stdin if that is connected to a terminal, as it usually is.

All non-temporary files must have a *filename*, which is a string. The rules for
what constitutes valid filenames are implementation defined. Whether a file can be
simultaneously open multiple times is also implementation defined. Opening a new
file may involve creating the file. Creating an existing file causes its previous contents
to be discarded.

*Closing*

Files are closed by explicitly calling fclose, exit or by returning from main. Any
buffered data is flushed. If a program stops for some other reason, the status of files
which it had open is undefined.

*Buffering*

There are three types of buffering:

*Unbuffered*

>    Minimum internal storage is used by stdio in an attempt to send or receive data
>    as soon as possible.

*Line buffered*
> Characters are processed on a line-by-line basis. This is commonly used in interactive environments, and internal buffers are flushed only when full or when a newline is processed.

*Fully buffered*
> Internal buffers are only flushed when full.

The buffering associated with a stream can always be flushed by using fflush explicitly. Support for the various types of buffering is implementation defined, and can be controlled within these limits using setbuf and setvbuf.

### 9.10.5  Direct file manipulation

A number of functions exist to operate on files directly.

```
#include ⟨stdio.h⟩

int remove(const char *filename);
int rename(const char *old, const char *new);
char *tmpnam(char *s);
FILE *tmpfile(void);
```

remove
> Causes a file to be removed. Subsequent attempts to open the file will fail, unless it is first created again. If the file is already open, the operation of remove is implementation defined. The return value is zero for success, any other value for failure.

rename
> Changes the name of the file identified by old to new. Subsequent attempts to open the original name will fail, unless another file is created with the old name. As with remove, rename returns zero for a successful operation, any other value indicating a failure.
>
> If a file with the new name exists prior to calling rename, the behaviour is implementation defined.
>
> If rename fails for any reason, the original file is unaffected.

tmpnam
> Generates a string that may be used as a filename and is guaranteed to be different from any existing filename. It may be called repeatedly, each time generating a new name. The constant TMP_MAX is used to specify how many times tmpnam may be called before it can no longer find a unique name. TMP_MAX will be at least 25. If tmpnam is called more than this number of times, its behaviour is undefined by the Standard, but many implementations offer no practical limit.
>
> If the argument s is set to NULL, then tmpnam uses an internal buffer to build the name, and returns a pointer to that. Subsequent calls may alter the same

internal buffer. The argument may instead point to an array of at least ⌐tmpnam characters, in which case the name will be filled into the supplied buffer. Such a filename may then be created, and used as a temporary file. Since the name is generated by the function, it is unlikely to be very useful in any other context. Temporary files of this nature are not removed, except by direct calls to the remove function. They are most often used to pass temporary data between two separate programs.

tmpfile

Creates a temporary binary file, opened for update, and returns a pointer to the stream of that file. The file will be removed when the stream is closed. If no file could be opened, tmpfile returns a null pointer.

### 9.10.6  Opening named files

Named files are opened by a call to the fopen function, whose declaration is this:

```
#include <stdio.h>
FILE *fopen(const char *pathname, const char *mode);
```

The pathname argument is the name of the file to open, such as that returned from tmpnam, or some program-specific filename.

Files can be opened in a variety of **modes**, such as *read* mode for reading data, *write* mode for writing data, and so on.

Note that if you only want to write data to a file, fopen will *create* the file if it does not already exist, or truncate it to zero length (losing its previous contents) if it did exist.

The Standard list of modes is shown in Table 9.3, although implementations may permit extra modes by appending extra characters at the end of the modes.

**Table 9.3**  File opening modes.

| Mode | Type of file | Read | Write | Create | Truncate |
|------|------|------|------|------|------|
| "r" | text | yes | no | no | no |
| "rb" | binary | yes | no | no | no |
| "r+" | text | yes | yes | no | no |
| "r+b" | binary | yes | yes | no | no |
| "rb+" | binary | yes | yes | no | no |
| "w" | text | no | yes | yes | yes |
| "wb" | binary | no | yes | yes | yes |
| "w+" | text | yes | yes | yes | yes |
| "w+b" | binary | yes | yes | yes | yes |
| "wb+" | binary | yes | yes | yes | yes |
| "a" | text | no | yes | yes | no |
| "ab" | binary | no | yes | yes | no |
| "a+" | text | yes | yes | yes | no |
| "a+b" | binary | no | yes | yes | no |
| "ab+" | binary | no | yes | yes | no |

Beware that some implementations of binary files may pad the last record with NULL characters, so opening them with append modes ab, ab+ or a+b could position the file pointer beyond the last data written.

If a file is opened in append mode, *all* writes will occur at the end of the file, regardless of attempts to move the file position indicator with fseek. The initial position of the file position indicator will be implementation defined.

Attempts to open a file in read mode, indicated by an 'r' as the first character in the mode string, will fail if the file does not already exist or can't be read.

Files opened for update ('+' as the second or third character of mode) may be both read and written, but a read may not immediately follow a write, or a write follow a read, without an intervening call to one (or more) of fflush, fseek, fsetpos or rewind. The only exception is that a write may immediately follow a read if EOF was read.

It may also be possible in some implementations to omit the b in the binary modes, using the same modes for text and binary files.

Streams opened by fopen are fully buffered only if they are not connected to an interactive device; this ensures that prompts and responses are handled properly.

If fopen fails to open a file, it returns a null pointer; otherwise, it returns a pointer to the object controlling the stream. The stdin, stdout and stderr objects are not necessarily modifiable and it may not be possible to use the value returned from fopen for assignment to one of them. For this reason, freopen is provided.

### 9.10.7 Freopen

The freopen function is used to take an existing stream pointer and associate it with another named file:

```
#include <stdio.h>
FILE *freopen(const char *pathname, const char *mode, FILE *stream);
```

The mode argument is the same as for fopen. The stream is closed first, and any errors from the close are ignored. On error, NULL is returned, otherwise the new value for stream is returned.

### 9.10.8 Closing files

An open file is closed using fclose.

```
#include <stdio.h>

int fclose(FILE *stream);
```

Any unwritten data buffered for stream is flushed out and any unread data is thrown away. If a buffer had been automatically allocated for the stream, it is freed. The file is then closed.

Zero is returned on success, EOF if any error occurs.

### 9.10.9 Setbuf, setvbuf

These two functions are used to change the buffering strategy for an open stream:

```
#include (stdio.h)

int setvbuf(FILE *stream, char *buf, int type, size_t size);
void setbuf(FILE *stream, char *buf);
```

**Table 9.4**   Type of buffering.

| Value | Effect |
|-------|--------|
| _IONBF | Do not buffer I/O |
| _IOFBF | Fully buffer I/O |
| _IOLBF | Line buffer: flush buffer when full, when newline is written or when a read is requested. |

They must be used *before* the file is either read from or written to. The type argument defines how the stream will be buffered (see Table 9.4). The buf argument can be a null pointer, in which case an array is automatically allocated to hold the buffered data. Otherwise, the user can provide a buffer, but should ensure that its lifetime is at least as long as that of the stream: a common mistake is to use automatic storage allocated inside a compound statement; in correct usage it is usual to obtain the storage from malloc instead. The size of the buffer is specified by the size argument.

A call of setbuf is exactly the same as a call of setvbuf with _IOFBF for the type argument, and BUFSIZ for the size argument. If buf is a null pointer, the value _IONBF is used for type instead.

No value is returned by setbuf; setvbuf returns zero on success, non-zero if invalid values are provided for type or size, or the request cannot be complied with.

### 9.10.10 Fflush

```
#include (stdio.h)

int fflush(FILE *stream);
```

If stream refers to a file opened for output or update, any unwritten data is 'written' out. Exactly what that means is a function of the host environment, and C cannot guarantee, for example, that data immediately reaches the surface of a disk which might be supporting the file. If the stream is associated with a file opened for input or update, any preceding ungetc operation is forgotten.

The most recent operation on the stream must have been an output operation; if not, the behaviour is undefined.

A call of fflush with an argument of zero flushes every output or update stream. Care is taken to avoid those streams that have not had an output as their last operation, thus avoiding the undefined behaviour mentioned above.

EOF is returned if an error occurs, otherwise zero.

## 9.11 Formatted I/O

There are a number of related functions used for formatted I/O, each one determining the format of the I/O from a **format string**. For output, the format string consists of plain text, which is output unchanged, and embedded *format specifications* which call for some special processing of one of the remaining arguments to the function. On input, the plain text must match what is seen in the input stream; the format specifications again specify what the meaning of remaining arguments is.

Each format specification is introduced by a % character, followed by the rest of the specification.

### 9.11.1 Output: the printf family

For those functions performing output, the format specification takes the following form, with optional parts enclosed in brackets:

%⟨ *flags*⟩⟨ *field width*⟩⟨ *precision*⟩⟨ *length*⟩ *conversion*

The meaning of *flags*, *field width*, *precision*, *length*, and *conversion* are given below, although tersely. For more detail, it is worth looking at what the Standard says.

*flags*

Zero or more of the following:
- –    Left justify the conversion within its field.
- +    A signed conversion will always start with a plus or minus sign.
- *space* If the first character of a signed conversion is not a sign, insert a space. Overridden by + if present.
- #    Forces an alternative form of output. The first digit of an octal conversion will always be a 0; inserts 0X in front of a non-zero hexadecimal conversion; forces a decimal point in all floating point conversions even if one is not necessary; does not remove trailing zeros from g and G conversions.

0   Pad d, i, o, u, x, X, e, E, f, F and G conversions on the left with zeros up to the field width. Overidden by the − flag. If a precision is specified for the d, i, o, u, x or X conversions, the flag is ignored. The behaviour is undefined for other conversions.

*field width*

A decimal integer specifying the minimum output field width. This will be exceeded if necessary. If an asterisk is used here, the next argument is converted to an integer and used for the value of the field width; if the value is negative it is treated as a − flag followed by a positive field width. Output that would be less than the field width is padded with spaces (zeros if the *field width* integer starts with a zero) to fit. The padding is on the left unless the left-adjustment flag is specified.

*precision*

This starts with a period '.'. It specifies the minimum number of digits for d, i, o, u, x, or X conversions; the number of digits after the decimal point for e, E, f conversions; the maximum number of digits for g and G conversions; the number of characters to be printed from a string for s conversion. The amount of padding overrides the *field width*. If an asterisk is used here, the next argument is converted to an integer and used for the precision. If the value is negative, it is treated as if it were missing. If only the period is present, the precision is taken to be zero.

*length*

h preceding a specifier to print an integral type causes it to be treated as if it were a short. (Note that the various sorts of short are always promoted to one of the flavours of int when passed as an argument.) l works like h but applies to a long integral argument. L is used to indicate that a long double argument is to be printed, and only applies to the floating-point specifiers. These cause undefined behaviour if they are used with the 'wrong' type of *conversion*.

*conversion*

See Table 9.5.

The functions that use these formats are described in Table 9.6. All need the inclusion of ⟨stdio.h⟩. Their declarations are as shown.

```
#include ⟨stdio.h⟩

int fprintf(FILE *stream, const char *format, ...);
int printf(const char *format, ...);
int sprintf(char *s, const char *format, ...);

#include ⟨stdarg.h⟩      /* as well as stdio.h */
int vfprintf(FILE *stream, const char *format, va_list arg);
int vprintf(const char *format, va_list arg);
int vsprintf(char *s, const char *format, va_list arg);
```

**Table 9.5** Conversions.

| Specifier | Effect | Default precision |
|---|---|---|
| d | signed decimal | 1 |
| i | signed decimal | 1 |
| u | unsigned decimal | 1 |
| o | unsigned octal | 1 |
| x | unsigned hexadecimal (0-f) | 1 |
| X | unsigned hexadecimal (0-F) | 1 |
| | *Precision* specifies minimum number of digits, expanded with leading zeros if necessary. Printing a value of zero with zero precision outputs no characters. | |
| f | Print a double with *precision* digits (rounded) after the decimal point. To suppress the decimal point use a *precision* of explicitly zero. Otherwise, at least one digit appears in front of the point. | 6 |
| e, E | Print a double in exponential format, rounded, with one digit before the decimal point, *precision* after it. A *precision* of zero suppresses the decimal point. There will be at least two digits in the exponent, which is printed as 1.23e15 in e format, or 1.23E15 in E format. | 6 |
| g, G | Use style f, or e (E with G) depending on the exponent. If the exponent is less than −4 or >= *precision*, f is not used. Trailing zeros are suppressed, a decimal point is only printed if there is a following digit. | unspecified |
| c | The int argument is converted to an unsigned char and the resultant character printed. | |
| s | Print a string up to *precision* digits long. If *precision* is not specified, or is greater than the length of the string, the string must be NUL terminated. | infinite |
| p | Display the value of a (void *) pointer in a system-dependent way. | |
| n | The argument must be a pointer to an integer. The number of characters output so far by this call will be written into the integer. | |
| % | A % | — |

All of these functions return the number of characters output, or a negative value on error. The trailing null is *not* counted by sprintf and vsprintf.

Implementations must permit at least 509 characters to be produced by any single conversion.

**Table 9.6**   Functions performing formatted output.

| Name | Purpose |
|------|---------|
| fprintf | General formatted output as described. Output is written to the file indicated by stream. |
| printf | Identical to fprintf with a first argument equal to stdout. |
| sprintf | Identical to fprintf except that the output is not written to a file, but written into the character array pointed to by s. |
| vfprintf | Formatted output as for fprintf, but with the variable argument list replaced by arg which must have been initialized by va_start. va_end is not called by this function. |
| vprintf | Identical to vfprintf with a first argument equal to stdout. |
| vsprintf | Formatted output as for sprintf, but with the variable argument list replaced by arg which must have been initialized by va_start. va_end is not called by this function. |

### 9.11.2 Input: the scanf family

A number of functions exist analogous to the printf family, but for the purposes of input instead. The most immediate difference between the two families is that the scanf group needs to be passed *pointers* to their arguments, so that the values read can be assigned to the proper destinations. Forgetting to pass a pointer is a very common error, and one which the compiler cannot detect – the variable argument list prevents it.

The format string is used to control interpretation of a stream of input data, which generally contains values to be assigned to the objects pointed to by the remaining arguments to scanf. The contents of the format string may contain:

*white space*

This causes the input stream to be read up to the next non-white-space character.

*ordinary character*

Anything except white-space or % characters. The next character in the input stream *must* match this character.

*conversion specification*

This is a % character, followed by an optional * character (which suppresses the conversion), followed by an optional nonzero decimal integer specifying the maximum field width, an optional h, l or L to control the length of the conversion and finally a non-optional conversion specifier. Note that use of h, l, or L will affect the type of pointer which must be used.

Except for the specifiers c, n and [, a field of input is a sequence of non-space characters starting at the first non-space character in the input. It terminates at the first conflicting character or when the input field width is reached.

The result is put into wherever the corresponding argument points, unless the assignment is suppressed using the * mentioned already. The following conversion specifiers may be used:

d i o u x

Convert a signed integer, a signed integer in a form acceptable to strtol, an octal integer, an unsigned integer and a hexadecimal integer respectively.

e f g

Convert a float (*not* a double).

s

Read a string, and add a null at the end. The string is terminated by white space on input (which is not read as part of the string).

[

Read a string. A list of characters, called the *scan set* follows the [. A ] delimits the list. Characters are read until (but not including) the first character which is not in the scan set. If the first character in the list is a circumflex ^, then the scan set includes any character *not* in the list. If the initial sequence is [^] or [], the ] is not a delimiter, but part of the list and another ] will be needed to end the list. If there is a minus sign (-) in the list, it must be either the first or the last character; otherwise the meaning is implementation defined.

c

Read a single character; white space is significant here. To read the first non-white space character, use %1s. A field width indicates that an array of characters is to be read.

p

Read a (void *) pointer previously written out using the %p of one of the printfs.

%

A % is expected in the input, no assignment is made.

n

Return as an integer the number of characters read by this call so far.

The size specifiers have the effect shown in Table 9.7. The functions are described below, with the following declarations:

```
#include ⟨stdio.h⟩

int fscanf(FILE *stream, const char *format, ...);
int sscanf(const char *s, const char *format, ...);
int scanf(const char *format, ...);
```

Fscanf takes its input from the designated stream, scanf is identical to fscanf with a first argument of stdin, and sscanf takes its input from the designated character array.

If an input failure occurs before any conversion, EOF is returned. Otherwise, the number of successful conversions is returned: this may be zero if no conversions are performed.

**Table 9.7**   Size specifiers.

| Specifier | Modifies | Converts |
|---|---|---|
| l | d i o u x | long int |
| h | d i o u x | short int |
| l | e f | double |
| L | e f | long double |

An input failure is caused by reading EOF or reaching the end of the input string (as appropriate). A conversion failure is caused by a failure to match the proper pattern for a particular conversion.

## 9.12  Character I/O

A number of functions provide for character oriented I/O. Their declarations are:

```
#include (stdio.h)
/* character input */
int fgetc(FILE *stream);
int getc(FILE *stream);
int getchar(void);
int ungetc(int c, FILE *stream);

/* character output */
int fputc(int c, FILE *stream);
int putc(int c, FILE *stream);
int putchar(int c);

/* string input */
char *fgets(char *s, int n, FILE *stream);
char *gets(char *s);

/* string output */
int fputs(const char *s, FILE *stream);
int puts(const char *s);
```

Their descriptions are as follows.

### Character input

These read an unsigned char from the input stream where specified, or otherwise stdin. In each case, the next character is obtained from the input stream. It is treated as an unsigned char and converted to an int, which is the return value. On End of File, the constant EOF is returned, and the end-of-file indicator is set for the associated stream. On error, EOF is returned, and the error indicator is set for the associated stream. Successive calls will obtain characters sequentially. The functions, if implemented as macros, may evaluate their stream argument more than once, so do not use side effects here.

There is also the supporting ungetc routine, which is used to push back a character on to a stream, causing it to become the next character to be read. This is not an output operation and can never cause the external contents of a file to be changed. A fflush, fseek, or rewind operation on the stream between the pushback and the read will cause the pushback to be forgotten. Only one character of pushback is guaranteed, and attempts to pushback EOF are ignored. In every case, pushing back a number of characters then reading or discarding them leaves the file position indicator unchanged. The file position indicator is decremented by every successful call to ungetc for a binary stream, but unspecified for a text stream, or a binary stream which is positioned at the beginning of the file.

### Character output
These are identical in description to the input functions already described, except performing output. They return the character written, or EOF on error. There is no equivalent to End of File for an output file.

### String output
These write strings to the output file; stream where specified, otherwise stdout. The terminating null is not written. Non-zero is returned on error, zero otherwise. *Beware*: puts appends a newline to the string output; fputs does not!

### String input
Fgets reads a string into the array pointed to by s from the stream stream. It stops on either EOF or the first newline (which it reads), and appends a null character. At most n-1 characters are read (leaving room for the null).

Gets works similarly for the stream stdin, but discards the newline!

Both return s if successful, or a null pointer otherwise. In each case, if EOF is encountered before any characters have been read, the array is unchanged and a null pointer is returned. A read error in the middle of a string leaves the array contents undefined and a null pointer is returned.

## 9.13 Unformatted I/O

This is simple: only two functions provide this facility, one for reading and one for writing:

```
#include ⟨stdio.h⟩

size_t fread(void *ptr, size_t size, size_t nelem, FILE *stream);
size_t fwrite(const void *ptr, size_t size, size_t nelem, FILE *stream);
```

In each case, the appropriate read or write is performed on the data pointed to by ptr. Up to nelem elements, of size size, are transferred. Failure to transfer the full number is an error only when writing; End of File can prevent the full number on input. The number of elements actually transferred is returned. To distinguish between End of File on input, or an error, use feof or ferror.

If size or nelem is zero, fread does nothing except to return zero.

An example may help:

```
#include <stdio.h>
#include <stdlib.h>

struct xx{
        int xx_int;
        float xx_float;
}ar[20];

main(){

        FILE *fp = fopen("testfile", "w");

        if(fwrite((const void *)ar,
                sizeof(ar[0]), 5, fp) != 5){

                fprintf(stderr,"Error writing\n");
                exit(EXIT_FAILURE);
        }

        rewind(fp);

        if(fread((void *)&ar[10],
                sizeof(ar[0]), 5, fp) != 5){

                if(ferror(fp)){
                        fprintf(stderr,"Error reading\n");
                        exit(EXIT_FAILURE);
                }
                if(feof(fp)){
                        fprintf(stderr,"End of File\n");
                        exit(EXIT_FAILURE);
                }
        }
        exit(EXIT_SUCCESS);
}
```
(Example 9.7)

## 9.14 Random access functions

The file I/O routines all work in the same way; unless the user takes explicit steps to change the file position indicator, files will be read and written sequentially. A read followed by a write followed by a read (if the file was opened in a mode to permit that) will cause the second read to start immediately following the end of the data just written. (Remember that stdio insists on the user inserting a buffer-flushing operation between each element of a read-write-read cycle.) To control this, the Random Access functions allow control over the implied read/write position in the file. The file position indicator is moved without the need for a read or a write, and indicates the byte to be the subject of the next operation on the file.

Three types of function exist which allow the file position indicator to be examined or changed. Their declarations and descriptions follow.

```
#include <stdio.h>

/* return file position indicator */
long ftell(FILE *stream);
int fgetpos(FILE *stream, fpos_t *pos);

/* set file position indicator to zero */
void rewind(FILE *stream);

/* set file position indicator */
int fseek(FILE *stream, long offset, int ptrname);
int fsetpos(FILE *stream, const fpos_t *pos);
```

Ftell returns the current value (measured in characters) of the file position indicator if stream refers to a binary file. For a text file, a 'magic' number is returned, which may only be used on a subsequent call to fseek to reposition to the current file position indicator. On failure, -1L is returned and errno is set.

Rewind sets the current file position indicator to the start of the file indicated by stream. The file's error indicator is reset by a call of rewind. No value is returned.

Fseek allows the file position indicator for stream to be set to an arbitrary value (for binary files), or for text files, only to a position obtained from ftell, as follows:

- In the general case, the file position indicator is set to offset bytes (characters) from a point in the file determined by the value of ptrname. Offset may be negative. The values of ptrname may be SEEK_SET, which sets the file position indicator relative to the beginning of the file, SEEK_CUR, which sets the file position indicator relative to its current value, and SEEK_END, which sets the file position indicator relative to the end of the file. The latter is not necessarily guaranteed to work properly on binary streams.

- For text files, offset must either be zero or a value returned from a previous call to ftell for the same stream, and the value of ptrname must be SEEK_SET.

- Fseek clears the end of file indicator for the given stream and erases the memory of any ungetc. It works for both input and output.

- Zero is returned for success, non-zero for a forbidden request.

Note that for ftell and fseek it must be possible to encode the value of the file position indicator into a long. This may not work for very long files, so the Standard introduces fgetpos and fsetpos which have been specified in a way that removes the problem.

Fgetpos stores the current file position indicator for stream in the object pointed to by pos. The value stored is 'magic' and only used to return to the specified position for the same stream using fsetpos.

Fsetpos works as described above, also clearing the stream's end-of-file indicator and forgetting the effects of any ungetc operations.

For both functions, on success, zero is returned; on failure, non-zero is returned and errno is set.

### 9.14.1 Error handling

The standard I/O functions maintain two indicators with each open stream to show the end-of-file and error status of the stream. These can be interrogated and set by the following functions:

```
#include ⟨stdio.h⟩

void clearerr(FILE *stream);
int feof(FILE *stream);
int ferror(FILE *stream);
void perror(const char *s);
```

Clearerr clears the error and EOF indicators for the stream.

Feof returns non-zero if the stream's EOF indicator is set, zero otherwise.

Ferror returns non-zero if the stream's error indicator is set, zero otherwise.

Perror prints a single-line error message on the program's standard output, prefixed by the string pointed to by s, with a colon and a space appended. The error message is determined by the value of errno and is intended to give some explanation of the condition causing the error. For example, this program produces the error message shown:

```
#include ⟨stdio.h⟩
#include ⟨stdlib.h⟩

main(){
        fclose(stdout);
        if(fgetc(stdout) >= 0){
                fprintf(stderr, "What — no error!\n");
                exit(EXIT_FAILURE);
        }
        perror("fgetc");
        exit(EXIT_SUCCESS);
}
```

```
/* Result */

fgetc: Bad file number
```
                                                              (Example 9.8)

Well, we didn't say that the message had to be very meaningful!

## 9.15  General utilities

These all involve the use of the header ⟨stdlib.h⟩, which declares a number of types
and macros and several functions of general use. The types and macros are as follows:

size_t
> Described at the start of this chapter (Section 9.1.3).

div_t
> This is the type of the structure returned by div.

ldiv_t
> This is the type of the structure returned by ldiv.

NULL
> Again, described at the start of this chapter.

EXIT_FAILURE
EXIT_SUCCESS
> These may be used as arguments to exit.

MB_CUR_MAX
> The maximum number of bytes in a multibyte character from the extended
> character set specified by the current locale.

RAND_MAX
> This is the maximum value returned by the rand function.

### 9.15.1  String conversion functions

Three functions take a string as an argument and convert it to a number of the type
shown below:

```
#include ⟨stdlib.h⟩

double atof(const char *nptr);
long atol(const char *nptr);
int atoi(const char *nptr);
```

For each of the functions, the number is converted and the result returned. None of
them guarantees to set errno (although they may do in some implementations), and the
results of a conversion which overflows or cannot be represented is undefined.

More sophisticated functions are:

```
#include <stdlib.h>

double strtod(const char *nptr, char **endptr);
long strtol(const char *nptr, char **endptr, int base);
unsigned long strtoul(const char *nptr, char **endptr, int base);
```

All three functions work in a similar way. Leading white space is skipped, then a *subject sequence*, resembling an appropriate constant, is found, followed by a sequence of unrecognized characters. The trailing null at the end of a string is always unrecognized. The subject sequence can be empty. The subject sequences are determined as follows:

strtod

> Optional + or −, followed by a digit sequence containing an optional decimal point character, followed by an optional exponent. No floating suffix will be recognized. If there is no decimal point present, it is assumed to follow the digit sequence.

strtol

> Optional + or −, followed by a digit sequence. The digits are taken from the decimal digits or an upper or lower case letter in the range a–z of the English alphabet; the letters are given the values 10–35 respectively. The base argument determines which values are permitted, and may be zero, or otherwise 2–36. Only 'digits' with a value less than that of base are recognized. A base of 16 permits the characters 0x or 0X to follow the optional sign. A base of zero permits the input of characters in the form of a C integer constant. No integer suffix will be recognized.

strtoul

> Identical to strtol but with no sign permitted.

If endptr is non-null, the address of the first unrecognized character is stored in the object that it points to. If the subject sequence is empty or has the wrong form, this is the value of nptr.

  If a conversion can be performed, the functions convert the number and return its value, taking into account a leading sign where permitted. Otherwise they return zero. On overflow or **error the** action is as follows:

strtod

> On overflow, returns ±HUGE_VAL according to the sign of the result; on underflow, returns zero. In either case, errno is set to ERANGE.

strtol

> On overflow, LONG_MAX or LONG_MIN is returned according to the sign of the result, errno is set to ERANGE.

strtoul

On overflow, ULONG_MAX is returned, errno is set to ERANGE.

If the locale is not the C locale, there may be other subject sequences recognised depending on the implementation.

### 9.15.2 Random number generation

Provision for pseudo-random number generation is made by the following functions.

```
#include ⟨stdlib.h⟩

int rand(void);
void srand(unsigned int seed);
```

Rand returns a pseudo-random number in the range 0 to RAND_MAX, which has a value of at least 32 767.

Srand allows a given starting point in the sequence to be chosen according to the value of seed. If srand is not called before rand, the value of the seed is taken to be 1. The same sequence of values will always be returned from rand for a given value of seed.

The Standard describes an algorithm which may be used to implement rand and srand. In practice, most implementations will probably use this algorithm.

### 9.15.3 Memory allocation

These functions are used to allocate and free storage. The storage so obtained is only guaranteed to be large enough to store an object of the specified type and aligned appropriately so as not to cause addressing exceptions. No further assumptions can be made.

```
#include ⟨stdlib.h⟩

void *malloc(size_t size);
void *calloc(size_t nmemb, size_t size);
void *realloc(void *ptr, size_t size);

void *free(void *ptr);
```

All of the memory allocation functions return a pointer to allocated storage of size size bytes. If there is no free storage, they return a null pointer. The differences between them are that calloc takes an argument nmemb which specifies the number of elements in an array, each of whose members is size bytes, and so allocates a larger piece of store (in general) than malloc. Also, the store allocated by malloc is not initialized, whereas calloc sets all bits in the storage to zero. This is not necessarily the equivalent representation of floating-point zero, or the null pointer.

Realloc is used to change the size of the thing pointed to by ptr, which may require some copying to be done and the old storage freed. The contents of the object pointed to by ptr is unchanged up to the smaller of the old and the new sizes. If ptr is null, the behaviour is identical to malloc with the appropriate size.

Free is used to free space previously obtained with one of the allocation routines. It is permissible to give free a null pointer as the argument, in which case nothing is done.

If an attempt is made to free store which was never allocated, or has already been freed, the behaviour is undefined. In many environments this causes an addressing exception which aborts the program, but this is not a reliable indicator.

## 9.15.4 Communication with the environment

A miscellany of functions is found here.

```
#include <stdlib.h>

void abort(void);
int atexit(void (*func)(void));
void exit(int status);
char *getenv(const char *name);
int system(const char *string);
```

abort

Causes abnormal program termination to occur, by raising the SIGABRT signal. Abnormal termination is only prevented if the signal is being caught, and the signal handler does not return. Otherwise, output files may be flushed and temporary files may be removed according to implementation definition, and an 'unsuccessful termination' status returned to the host environment. This function cannot return.

atexit

The argument func becomes a function to be called, without arguments, when the program terminates. Up to at least 32 such functions may be registered, and are called on program termination in reverse order of their registration. Zero is returned for success, non-zero for failure.

exit

Normal program termination occurs when this is called. First, all of the functions registered using atexit are called, but beware – by now, main is considered to have returned and *no* objects with automatic storage duration may safely be used. Then, all the open output streams are flushed, then closed, and all temporary files created by tmpfile are removed. Finally, the program returns control to the host environment, returning an implementation-defined form of successful or unsuccessful termination status depending on whether the argument to exit was EXIT_SUCCESS or EXIT_FAILURE respectively. For compatibility with Old C, zero can be used in place of EXIT_SUCCESS, but other values have implementation-defined effects. Exit *cannot* return.

getenv

The implementation-defined *environment list* is searched to find an item which corresponds to the string pointed to by name. A pointer to the item is returned – it points to an array which must not be modified by the program, but may be overwritten by a subsequent call to getenv. A null pointer is returned if no item matches.

The purpose and implementation of the environment list depends on the host environment.

system

An implementation-defined *command processor* is passed the string string. A null pointer will cause a return of zero if no command processor exists, non-zero otherwise. A non-null pointer causes the command to be processed. The effect of the command and the value returned are implementation defined.

### 9.15.5  Searching and sorting

Two functions exist in this category: one for searching an already sorted list, the other for sorting an unsorted list. They are completely general, handling arrays of arbitrary size with elements of arbitrary size.

To enable them to compare two elements, the user provides a comparison function, which is called with pointers to two of the elements as its arguments. It returns a value less than, equal to or greater than zero depending on whether the first pointer points to an element considered to be less than, equal to or greater than the object pointed to by the second pointer, respectively.

```
#include (stdlib.h)

void *bsearch(const void *key, const void *base,
        size_t nmemb, size_t size,
        int (*compar)(const void *, const void *));

void *qsort(const void *base, size_t nmemb,
        size_t size,
        int (*compar)(const void *, const void *));
```

For both functions, nmemb is the number of elements in the array, size is the size in bytes of an array element and compar is the function to be called to compare them. Base is a pointer to the base of the array.

Qsort will sort the array into ascending order.

Bsearch assumes that the array is already sorted and returns a pointer to any element it finds that compares equal to the object pointed to by key. A null pointer is returned if no match is found.

### 9.15.6 Integer arithmetic functions

These provide ways of finding the absolute value of an integral argument and the quotient and remainder of a division, for both int and long types.

```
#include <stdlib.h>

int abs(int j);
long labs(long j);

div_t div(int numerator, int denominator);
ldiv_t ldiv(long numerator, long denominator);
```

abs
labs

These return the absolute value of their argument – choose the appropriate one for your needs. The behaviour is undefined if the value cannot be represented – this can happen in two's complement systems where the most negative number has no positive equivalent.

div
ldiv

These divide the numerator by the denominator and return a structure of the indicated type. In each case the structure will contain a member called quot which contains the quotient of the division truncated towards zero, and a member called rem which will contain the remainder. The type of each member is int for div and long for ldiv. Provided that the result can be represented, quot * denominator + rem == numerator.

### 9.15.7 Functions using multibyte characters

The LC_CTYPE category of the current locale affects the behaviour of these functions. For an encoding that is state-dependent, each function is put in its initial state by a call in which its character pointer argument, s, is a null pointer. The internal state of the function is altered as necessary by subsequent calls when s is not a null pointer. If s is a null pointer, the functions return a non-zero value if encodings are state-dependent, otherwise zero. If the LC_CTYPE category is changed, the shift state of the functions will become indeterminate.

The functions are:

```
#include (stdlib.h)

int mblen(const char *s, size_t n);
int mbtowc(wchar_t *pwc, const char *s, size_t n);
int wctomb(char *s, wchar_t wchar);
size_t mbstowcs(wchar_t *pwcs, const char *s, size_t n);
size_t wcstombs(char *s, const wchar_t *pwcs, size_t n);
```

mblen

Returns the number of bytes that are contained in the multibyte character pointed to by s, or -1 if the first n bytes do not form a valid multibyte character. If s points to the null character, zero is returned.

mbtowc

Converts the multibyte character pointed to by s to the corresponding code of type wchar_t and stores the result in the object pointed to by pwc, unless pwc is a null pointer. Returns the number of bytes successfully converted, or -1 if the first n bytes do not form a valid multibyte character. No more than n bytes pointed to by s are examined. The value returned will not be more than n or MB_CUR_MAX.

wctomb

Converts the code whose value is in wchar to a sequence of bytes representing the corresponding multibyte character, and stores the result in the array pointed to by s, if s is not a null pointer. Returns the number of bytes that are contained in the multibyte character, or -1 if the value in wchar does not correspond to a valid multibyte character. At most, MB_CUR_MAX bytes are processed.

mbstowcs

Converts the sequence of multibyte characters, beginning in the initial shift state, in the array pointed to by s, into a sequence of corresponding codes which are then stored in the array pointed to by pwcs. Not more than n values will be placed in pwcs. Returns -1 if an invalid multibyte character is encountered, otherwise returns the number of array elements modified, excluding the terminating null-code.
    If the two objects overlap, the behaviour is undefined.

wcstombs

Converts the sequence of codes pointed to by pwcs to a sequence of multibyte characters, beginning in the initial shift state, which are then stored in the array pointed to by s. Conversion stops when either a null-code is encountered or n bytes have been written to s. Returns -1 if a code is encountered which does not correspond to a valid multibyte character, otherwise the number of bytes written, excluding the terminating null-code.
    If the two objects overlap, the behaviour is undefined.

## 9.16 String handling

Numerous functions exist to handle strings. In C, a string is an array of characters
terminated by a null. In all cases, the functions expect a pointer to the first character
in the string. The header ⟨string.h⟩ declares these functions.

### 9.16.1 Copying

The functions for this purpose are:

```
#include ⟨string.h⟩

void *memcpy(void *s1, const void *s2, size_t n);
void *memmove (void *s1, const void *s2, size_t n);
char *strcpy(char *s1, const char *s2);
char *strncpy(char *s1, const char *s2, size_t n);
char *strcat(char *s1, const char *s2);
char *strncat(char *s1, const char *s2, size_t n);
```

memcpy

> This copies n bytes from the place pointed to by s2 to the place pointed to by s1.
> If the objects overlap, the result is undefined. The value of s1 is returned.

memmove

> Identical to memcpy, but works even for overlapping objects. It may be mar-
> ginally slower, though.

strcpy
strncpy

> Both of these copy the string pointed to by s2 into the string pointed to by s1,
> including the trailing null. Strncpy will copy at most n characters, and pad with
> trailing nulls if s2 is shorter than n characters. If the strings overlap, the
> behaviour is undefined. They return s1.

strcat
strncat

> Both append the string in s2 to s1, overwriting the null at the end of s1. A final
> null is always written. At most n characters are copied from s2 by strncat,
> which means that for safety the destination string should have room for its
> original length (not counting the null) plus n + 1 characters. They return s1.

### 9.16.2 String and byte comparison

These comparison functions are used to compare arrays of bytes. This obviously
includes the traditional C strings, which are an array of char (bytes) with a terminating
null. All of these functions work by comparing a byte at a time, and stopping either

when two bytes differ (in which case they return the sign of the difference between the two bytes), or the arrays are considered to be equal: no differences were found, and the length of the arrays was equal to the specified amount, or the null was found at the end of a string comparison.

For all except strxfrm, the value returned is less than, equal to or greater than zero depending on whether the first object was considered to be less than, equal to or greater than the second.

```
#include ⟨string.h⟩

int memcmp(const void *s1, const void *s2, size_t n);
int strcmp(const char *s1, const char *s2);
int strncmp(const char *s1, const char *s2, size_t n);
size_t strxfrm(char *to, const char *from, size_t maxsize);
int strcoll(const char *s1, const char *s2);
```

memcmp

Compares the first n characters in the objects pointed to by s1 and s2. It is very dodgy to compare structures in this way, because unions or 'holes' caused by alignment padding can contain junk.

strcmp

Compares the two strings. This is one of the most commonly used of the string-handling functions.

strncmp

As for strcmp, but compares at most n characters.

strxfrm

The string in from is converted (by some magic), and placed wherever to points. At most maxsize characters (including the trailing null) are written into the destination. The magic guarantees that two such transformed strings will give the same comparison with each other for the user's current locale when using strcmp, as when strcoll is applied to the original two strings.

In all cases, the length of the resulting string (not counting its terminating null) is returned. If the value is equal to or greater than maxsize, the contents of *to is undefined. If maxsize is zero, s1 may be a null pointer.

If the two objects overlap, the behaviour is undefined.

strcoll

This function compares the two strings according to the collating sequence specified by the current locale.

### 9.16.3 Character and string searching functions

```
#include ⟨string.h⟩

void *memchr(const void *s, int c, size_t n);
char *strchr(const char *s, int c);
```

```
size_t strcspn(const char *s1, const char *s2);
char *strpbrk(const char *s1, const char *s2);
char *strrchr(const char *s, int c);
size_t strspn(const char *s1, const char *s2);
char *strstr(const char *s1, const char *s2);
char *strtok(const char *s1, const char *s2);
```

memchr

Returns a pointer to the first occurrence in the initial n characters of *s of the (unsigned char)c. Returns null if there is no such occurrence.

strchr

Returns a pointer to the first occurrence of (char)c in *s, including the null in the search. Returns null if there is no such occurrence.

strcspn

Returns the length of the initial part of the string s1 which contains no characters from s2. The terminating null is not considered to be part of s2.

strpbrk

Returns a pointer to the first character in s1 which is any of the characters in s2, or null if there is none.

strrchr

Returns a pointer to the last occurrence in s1 of (char)c counting the null as part of s1, or null if there is none.

strspn

Returns the length of the initial part of s1 consisting entirely of characters from s1.

strstr

Returns a pointer to the first occurrence in s1 of the string s2, or null if there is none.

strtok

Breaks the string in s1 into 'tokens', each delimited by one of the characters from s2 and returns a pointer to the first token, or null if there is none. Subsequent calls with (char *)0 as the value of s1 return the next token in sequence, with the extra fun that s2 (and hence the delimiters) may differ on each subsequent call. A null pointer is returned if no tokens remain.

## 9.16.4 Miscellaneous functions

```
#include <string.h>

void *memset(void *s, int c, size_t n);
char *strerror(int errnum);
size_t strlen(const char *s);
```

memset

> Sets the n bytes pointed to by s to the value of (unsigned char)c. Returns s.

strlen

> Returns the length of the string s not counting the terminating null. This is a very widely used function.

strerror

> Returns a pointer to a string describing the error number errnum. This string may be changed by subsequent calls to strerror. Useful for finding out what the values in errno mean.

## 9.17 Date and time

These functions deal with either 'elapsed' or 'calendar' time. They share the ⟨time.h⟩ header, which declares the functions as necessary and also the following:

CLOCKS_PER_SEC

> This is the number of 'ticks' per second returned by the clock function.

clock_t
time_t

> These are arithmetic types used to represent different forms of time.

struct tm

> This structure is used to hold the values representing a calendar time. It contains the following members, with the meanings as shown.

```
int tm_sec      /* seconds after minute [0-61] (61 allows for 2 leap-seconds)*/
int tm_min      /* minutes after hour [0-59] */
int tm_hour     /* hours after midnight [0-23] */
int tm_mday     /* day of the month [1-31] */
int tm_mon      /* month of year [0-11] */
int tm_year     /* current year-1900 */
int tm_wday     /* days since Sunday [0-6] */
int tm_yday     /* days since January 1st [0-365] */
int tm_isdst    /* daylight savings indicator */
```

The tm_isdst member is positive if daylight savings time is in effect, zero if not and negative if that information is not available.

The time manipulation functions are the following:

```
#include ⟨time.h⟩

clock_t clock(void);
double difftime(time_t time1, time_t time2);
time_t mktime(struct tm *timeptr);
time_t time(time_t *timer);
```

```
char *asctime(const struct tm *timeptr);
char *ctime(const time_t *timer);
struct tm *gmtime(const time_t *timer);
struct tm *localtime(const time_t *timer);
size_t strftime(char *s, size_t maxsize,
        const char *format,
        const struct tm *timeptr);
```

The functions asctime, ctime, gmtime, localtime, and strftime all share static data structures, either of type struct tm or char [], and calls to one of them may overwrite the data stored by a previous call to one of the others. If this is likely to cause problems, their users should take care to copy any values needed.

clock

Returns the best available approximation to the time used by the current invocation of the program, in 'ticks'. (clock_t) - 1 is returned if no value is available. To find the actual time used by a run of a program, it is necessary to find the difference between the value at the start of the run and the time of interest – there is an implementation-defined constant factor which biases the value returned from clock. To determine the time in seconds, the value returned should be divided by CLOCKS_PER_SEC.

difftime

This returns the difference in seconds between two calendar times.

mktime

This returns the calendar time corresponding to the values in a structure pointed to by timeptr, or (time_t) - 1 if the value cannot be represented.

The tm_wday and tm_yday members of the structure are ignored, the other members are not restricted to their usual values. On successful conversion, the members of the structure are all set to appropriate values within their normal ranges. This function is useful to find out what value of a time_t corresponds to a known date and time.

time

Returns the best approximation to the current calendar time in an unspecified encoding. (time_t) - 1 is returned if the time is not available.

asctime

Converts the time in the structure pointed to by timeptr into a string of the form

```
Sun Sep 16 01:03:52 1973\n\0
```

the example being taken from the Standard. The Standard defines the algorithm used, but the important point to notice is that all the fields within that string are of constant width and relevant to most English-speaking communities. The string is stored in a static structure which may be overwritten by a subsequent call to one of the other time-manipulation functions (see above).

ctime

Equivalent to asctime(localtime(timer)). See asctime for the return value.

gmtime

> Returns a pointer to a struct tm set to represent the calendar time pointed to by timer. The time is expressed in terms of Coordinated Universal Time (UTC) (formerly Greenwich Mean Time). A null pointer is returned if UTC is not available.

localtime

> Converts the time pointed to by timer into local time and puts the results into a struct tm, returning a pointer to that structure.

strftime

> Fills the character array pointed to by s with at most maxsize characters. The format string is used to format the time represented in the structure pointed to timeptr. Characters in the format string (including the terminating null) are copied unchanged into the array, unless one of the following format directives is found – then the value specified below is copied into the destination, *as appropriate to the locale.*

| | |
|---|---|
| %a | abbreviated weekday name |
| %A | full weekday name |
| %b | abbreviated month name |
| %B | full month name |
| %c | date and time representation |
| %d | decimal day of month number 01–31 |
| %H | hour 00–23 (24 hour format) |
| %I | hour 01–12 (12 hour format) |
| %j | day of year 001–366 |
| %m | month 01–12 |
| %M | minute 00–59 |
| %p | local equivalent of 'AM' or 'PM' |
| %S | second 00–61 |
| %U | week number in year 00–53 (Sunday is first day of week) |
| %w | weekday, 0–6 (Sunday is 0) |
| %W | week number in year 00–53 (Monday is first day of week) |
| %x | local date representation |
| %X | local time representation |
| %y | year without century prefix 00–99 |
| %Y | year with century prefix |
| %Z | timezone name, or no characters if no timezone exists |
| %% | a % character |

Any unrecognized character following a % format indicator gives undefined behaviour.

The total number of characters copied into *s is returned, excluding the null. If there was not room (as determined by maxsize) for the trailing null, zero is returned.

## ■ 9.18 SUMMARY

It will almost certainly be the standardization of the run-time library that has the most effect on the portability of C programs. Prospective users of C really should read through this chapter carefully and familiarize themselves with its contents. The lack of a widely implemented, portable library was historically the biggest single barrier to portability.

If you are writing programs for embedded systems, bad luck! The library is not defined for stand-alone applications, but in practice we can expect suppliers to produce a stand-alone library package too. It will probably come without the file handling, but there is no reason why, say, the string-handling functions should not work just as well in hosted and unhosted environments.

# CHAPTER 10

# Complete Programs in C

## 10.1  Putting it all together

Having considered the language and the libraries defined by the Standard, all that now remains is to demonstrate what complete programs look like. This chapter contains some example programs which illustrate how to combine these elements to build programs.

However, just before these examples are presented there is one more aspect of the C language to discuss.

## 10.2  Arguments to main

For those writing programs which will run in a hosted environment, arguments to main provide a useful opportunity to give parameters to programs. Typically, this facility is used to direct the way the program goes about its task. It's particularly common to provide file names to a program through its arguments.

The declaration of main looks like this:

```
int main(int argc, char *argv[]);
```

This indicates that main is a function returning an integer. In hosted environments such as DOS or UNIX, this value or **exit status** is passed back to the command line interpreter. Under UNIX, for example, the exit status is used to indicate that a program completed successfully (a zero value) or some error occurred (a non-zero value). The Standard has adopted this convention; exit(0) is used to return 'success' to its host environment, any other value is used to indicate failure. If the host environment itself uses a different numbering convention, exit will do the necessary translation. Since the translation is implementation-defined, it is now considered better practice to use the values defined in ⟨stdlib.h⟩: EXIT_SUCCESS and EXIT_FAILURE.

There are at least two arguments to main, argc and argv. The first of these is a count of the arguments supplied to the program and the second is an array of pointers to the strings which are those arguments – its type is (almost) 'array of pointer to char'. These arguments are passed to the program by the host system's command line interpreter or job control language.

The declaration of the argv argument is often a novice programmer's first encounter with pointers to arrays of pointers and can prove intimidating. However, it is really quite simple to understand. Since argv is used to refer to an array of strings, its declaration will look like this:

```
char *argv[]
```

Remember too that when it is passed to a function, the name of an array is converted to the address of its first element. This means that we can also declare argv as char **argv; the two declarations are equivalent in this context.

Indeed, you will often see the declaration of main expressed in these terms. This declaration is exactly equivalent to that shown above:

```
int main(int argc, char **argv);
```

When a program starts, the arguments to main will have been initialized to meet the following conditions:

- argc is greater than zero.
- argv[argc] is a null pointer.
- argv[0] through to argv[argc-1] are pointers to strings whose meaning will be determined by the program.
- argv[0] will be a string containing the program's name or a null string if that is not available. Remaining elements of argv represent the arguments supplied to the program. In cases where there is only support for single-case characters, the contents of these strings will be supplied to the program in lower-case.

To illustrate these points, here is a simple program which writes the arguments supplied to main on the program's standard output:

```
#include ⟨stdio.h⟩
#include ⟨stdlib.h⟩

int
main(int argc, char **argv){
        while ( argc-- ){
                printf("%s\n", *argv++);
        }
        exit(EXIT_SUCCESS);
}
```
(Example 10.1)

If the program name is show_args and it has arguments abcde, text, and hello when it is run, the state of the arguments and the value of argv can be illustrated as shown in Figure 10.1.

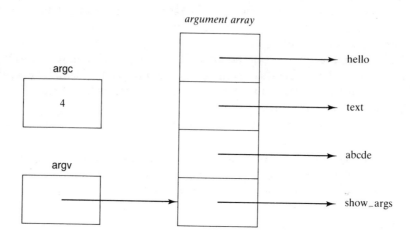

**Figure 10.1**   Arguments to a program.

Each time that argv is incremented, it is stepped one item further along the array of arguments. Thus after the first iteration of the loop, argv will point to the pointer which in turn points to the abcde argument. This is shown in Figure 10.2.

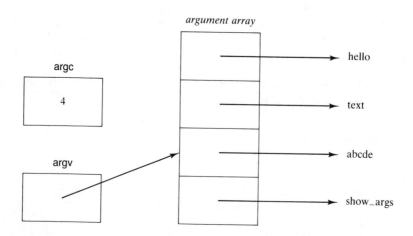

**Figure 10.2**

On the system where this program was tested, a program is run by typing its name and then the arguments, separated by spaces. This is what happened (the $ is a prompt):

```
$ show_args abcde text hello
show_args
abcde
text
hello
$
```

## 10.3  Interpreting program arguments

The loop used to examine the program arguments in the example above is a common C idiom which you will see in many other programs. An additional common idiom is to use 'options' to control the behaviour of the program (these are also sometimes called switches or flags). Arguments which start with a '-' are taken to introduce one or more single-letter option indicators, which can be run together or provided separately:

```
progname -abxu file1 file2
progname -a -b -x -u file1 file2
```

The idea is that each of the options selects a particular aspect from the program's repertoire of features. An extension to that idea is to allow options to take arguments; if the -x option is specified to take an argument, then this is how it might be used:

```
progname -x arg file1
```

so that the arg argument is associated with the option. The options function below automates the processing of this style of use, with the additional (common but preferably considered obsolescent) support for the provision of option arguments immediately following the option letter, as in:

```
progname -xarg file1
```

In either of the above cases, the options routine returns the character 'x' and sets a global pointer, OptArg, to point to the value arg.

To use this routine, a program must supply a list of valid option letters in the form of a string; when a letter in this string is followed by a ':' this indicates that the option letter is to be followed by an argument. When the program is run, it is then simply a question of repeatedly calling the options routine until no more option letters remain to be found.

It seems to be a fact of life that functions which scan text strings looking for various combinations or patterns within them end up being hard to read; if it's any consolation they aren't all that easy to write either. The code that implements the options is definitely one of the breed, although by no means one of the worst:

```
/*
 * options() parses option letters and option arguments from the argv list.
 * Successive calls return successive option letters which match one of
 * those in the legal list. Option letters may require option arguments
 * as indicated by a ':' following the letter in the legal list.
 * For example, a legal list of "ab:c" implies that a, b and c are
 * all valid options and that b takes an option argument. The option
 * argument is passed back to the calling function in the value
 * of the global OptArg pointer. The OptIndex gives the next string
 * in the argv[] array that has not already been processed by options().
 *
 * options() returns -1 if there are no more option letters or if
 * double SwitchChar is found. Double SwitchChar forces options()
 * to finish processing options.
 *
 * options() returns '?' if an option not in the legal set is
 * encountered or an option needing an argument is found without an
 * argument following it.
 *
 */


#include <stdio.h>
#include <string.h>

static const char SwitchChar = '-';
static const char Unknown = '?';


int OptIndex = 1;                    /* first option should be argv[1] */
char *OptArg = NULL;    /* global option argument pointer */


int
options(int argc, char *argv[], const char *legal){
        static char *posn = "";  /* position in argv[OptIndex] */
        char *legal_index = NULL;
        int letter = 0;

        if(!*posn){
                /* no more args, no SwitchChar or no option letter ? */
                if((OptIndex >= argc) ||
                        (*(posn = argv[OptIndex]) != SwitchChar) ||
                        !*++posn)
                                return -1;
```

```
                /* find double SwitchChar ? */
                if(*posn == SwitchChar) {
                        OptIndex++;
                        return -1;
                }
        }
        letter = *posn++;
        if(!(legal_index = strchr(legal, letter))){
                if(!*posn)
                        OptIndex++;
                return Unknown;
        }
        if(*++legal_index != ':'){
                /* no option argument */
                OptArg = NULL;
                if(!*posn)
                        OptIndex++;
        } else {
                if(*posn)
                        /* no space between opt and opt arg */
                        OptArg = posn;
                else
                        if(argc <= ++OptIndex){
                                posn = "";
                                return Unknown;
                        } else
                                OptArg = argv[OptIndex];
                posn = "";
                OptIndex++;
        }
        return letter;
}
```

(Example 10.2)

## 10.4 A pattern matching program

This section presents a complete program which makes use of option letters as program arguments to control the way it performs its job.

The program first processes any arguments that resemble options; the first argument which is not an option is remembered for use as a 'search string'. Any remaining arguments are used to specify file names which are to be read as input to the program; if no file names are provided, the program reads from its standard input instead. If a match for the search string is found in a line of input text, that whole line is printed on the standard output.

The options function is used to process all option letters supplied to the program. This program recognises five options: -c, -i, -l, -n, and -v. None of these options is required to be followed by an option argument. When the program is run with one or more of these options its behaviour is modified as follows:

- -c   the program prints a count of the total number of matching lines it found in the input file(s). No lines of text are printed.
- -i   when searching for a match, the case of letters in both the input lines and string is ignored.
- -l   each line of text printed on the output is prefixed with the line number being examined in the current input file.
- -n   each line of text printed on the output is prefixed with the name of the file that contained the line.
- -v   the program prints only lines which do *not* match the string supplied.

When the program finishes, it returns an exit status to indicate one of the following situations:

- EXIT_SUCCESS at least one match was found.
- EXIT_FAILURE no match was found, or some error occurred.

The program makes extensive use of standard library functions to do all of the hard work. For example, all of the file handling is performed by calls to stdio functions. Notice too that the real heart of the program, the string matching, is simply handled by a call to the strstr library function.

Here is the code for the whole program. Of course, to get this to work you would need to compile it together with the code for the options routine presented above.

```
/*
 * Simple program to print lines from a text file which contain
 * the "word" supplied on the command line.
 *
 */

#include <stdio.h>
#include <stdlib.h>
#include <string.h>
#include <ctype.h>

/*
 * Declarations for the pattern program
 *
 */

#define CFLAG 0x001    /* only count the number of matching lines */
#define IFLAG 0x002    /* ignore case of letters */
#define LFLAG 0x004    /* show line numbers */
#define NFLAG 0x008    /* show input file names */
#define VFLAG 0x010    /* show lines which do NOT match */
```

```
extern int OptIndex;    /* current index into argv[] */
extern char *OptArg;    /* global option argument pointer */

/*
 * Fetch command line switches from arguments to main()
 */

int options(int, char **, const char *);

/*
 * Record the required options ready to control program behaviour
 */

unsigned set_flags(int, char **, const char *);

/*
 * Check each line of the input file for a match
 */

int look_in(const char *, const char *, unsigned);

/*
 * Print a line from the input file on the standard output
 * in the format specified by the command line switches
 */

void print_line(unsigned mask, const char *fname,
                int lnno, const char *text);

static const char
                /* Legal options for pattern */
        *OptString = "cilnv",
                /* message when options or arguments incorrect */
        *errmssg = "usage: pattern [-cilnv] word [filename]\n";

int
main(int argc, char *argv[]){
        unsigned flags = 0;
        int success = 0;
        char *search_string;

        if(argc < 2){
                fprintf(stderr, errmssg);
                exit(EXIT_FAILURE);
        }

        flags = set_flags(argc, argv, OptString);

        if(argv[OptIndex])
                search_string = argv[OptIndex++];
```

```c
        else {
                fprintf(stderr, errmssg);
                exit(EXIT_FAILURE);
        }

        if(flags & IFLAG){
                /* ignore case by dealing only with lowercase */
                char *p;
                for(p = search_string ; *p ; p++)
                        if(isupper(*p))
                                *p = tolower(*p);
        }

        if(argv[OptIndex] == NULL){
                /* no file name given, so use stdin */
                 success = look_in(NULL, search_string, flags);
        } else while(argv[OptIndex] != NULL)
                success += look_in(argv[OptIndex++],
                                search_string, flags);

        if(flags & CFLAG)
                printf("%d\n", success);

        exit(success ? EXIT_SUCCESS : EXIT_FAILURE);
}


unsigned
set_flags(int argc, char **argv, const char *opts){
        unsigned flags = 0;
        int ch = 0;

        while((ch = options(argc, argv, opts)) != -1){
                switch(ch) {
                        case 'c':
                                flags |= CFLAG;
                                break;
                        case 'i':
                                flags |= IFLAG;
                                break;
                        case 'l':
                                flags |= LFLAG;
                                break;
                        case 'n':
                                flags |= NFLAG;
                                break;
                        case 'v':
                                flags |= VFLAG;
                                break;
```

```
                        case '?':
                                fprintf(stderr, errmssg);
                                exit(EXIT_FAILURE);
                }
        }
        return flags;
}

int
look_in(const char *infile, const char *pat, unsigned flgs){
        FILE *in;
        /*
         * line[0] stores the input line as read,
         * line[1] is converted to lower-case if necessary
         */
        char line[2][BUFSIZ];
        int lineno = 0;
        int matches = 0;

        if(infile){
                if((in = fopen(infile, "r")) == NULL){
                        perror("pattern");
                        return 0;
                }
        } else
                in = stdin;

        while(fgets(line[0], BUFSIZ, in)){
                char *line_to_use = line[0];
                lineno++;
                if(flgs & IFLAG){
                        /* ignore case */
                        char *p;
                        strcpy(line[1], line[0]);
                        for(p = line[1] ; *p ; *p++)
                                if(isupper(*p))
                                        *p = tolower(*p);
                        line_to_use = line[1];
                }

                if(strstr(line_to_use, pat)){
                        matches++;
                        if(!(flgs & VFLAG))
                                print_line(flgs, infile, lineno, line[0]);
                } else if(flgs & VFLAG)
                        print_line(flgs, infile, lineno, line[0]);
        }
        fclose(in);
        return matches;
}
```

```
void
print_line(unsigned mask, const char *fname,
                  int lnno, const char *text){
        if(mask & CFLAG)
               return;
        if(mask & NFLAG)
               printf("%s:", *fname ? fname : "stdin");
        if(mask & LFLAG)
               printf(" %d :", lnno);
        printf("%s", text);
}
```
                                                            (Example 10.3)

## 10.5 A more ambitious example

Finally here is a set of programs designed to cooperate and manipulate a single data file in a coherent, robust fashion.

The programs are intended to help keep track of a ladder of players who compete against each other at some game, squash or chess perhaps.

Each player has a rank from one to $n$, where $n$ is the number of players who play, one being the highest rank on the ladder. Players lower down the ladder may challenge players above them and, if the lower ranked player wins, he or she moves up taking the rank of the player who loses. The loser in such a situation, and any other players between challenger and loser, are then moved down one rank. If a challenger does not win, the rankings on the ladder remain unchanged.

To provide some measure of equilibrium in the rankings, a player may challenge any higher ranked player, but only wins over players ranked three (or less) higher will allow the challenger to move up the rankings. This ensures that new players added to the bottom of the ladder are forced to play more than one game to reach the top of the ladder!

There are three basic tasks which are required to record all the information needed to keep such a ladder going:

- Printing the ladder
- Addition of new players
- Recording of results.

The design to be used here provides a separate program to perform each of these tasks. Having made this decision it is clear that a number of operations needed by each program will be common to all three. For example, all three will need to read player records from the data file, at least two will need to write player records into the data file.

This suggests that a good approach would be to design a 'library' of functions which manipulate player records and the data file which may in turn be combined to make up the programs which maintain the ladder.

Before this can be done it will be necessary to define the data structure which represents player records. The minimum information necessary to record for each player consists of player name and rank. However, to allow for more interesting statistics to be compiled about the ladder let us choose to keep also a record of games won, games lost and the time when the last game was played. Clearly this disparate set of information is best collected together in a structure.

The player structure declaration together with the declarations of the player library functions are combined together in the player.h header file. The data file is maintained as lines of text, each line corresponding to a record; this requires input and output conversions to be performed but is a useful technique if the conversions don't cost too much in performance terms.

```
/*
 *
 * Declarations and definitions for functions which manipulate player
 * records which form the basis of the ladder
 *
 */

#include (stddef.h)
#include (stdio.h)
#include (stdlib.h)
#include (time.h)

#define NAMELEN 12              /* max. for player name length */
#define LENBUF 256             /* max. for input buffer length */
#define CHALLENGE_RANGE 3      /* number of higher ranked players who may
                                * be challenged to move up in rank
                                */

extern char *OptArg;

typedef struct {
        char    name[NAMELEN + 1];
        int     rank;
        int     wins;
        int     losses;
        time_t  last_game;
} player;

#define NULLPLAYER (player *)0

extern const char *LadderFile;
extern const char *WrFmt;       /* used when writing records */
extern const char *RdFmt;       /* used when reading records */
```

```
/*
 * Declarations for routines used to manipulate the player records
 * and the ladder file which are defined in player.c
 *
 */

int     valid_records(FILE *);
int     read_records(FILE *, int, player *);
int     write_records( FILE *, player *, int);
player *find_by_name(char *, player *, int);
player *find_by_rank(int, player *, int);
void    push_down(player *, int, int, int);
int     print_records( player *, int);
void    copy_player(player *, player *);
int     compare_name(player *, player *);
int     compare_rank(player *, player *);
void    sort_players(player *, int);
```
                                                              (Example 10.4)

Here is the code for the player.c file implementing the generic functions which
manipulate player records and the data file. These functions can be combined with
more specific routines to make up the three programs required to maintain the ladder.

Notice that to manipulate the player records, each program is required to read
the entire data file into a dynamically allocated array. Before this array is written back
to the data file, it is assumed that the records it contains will have been sorted into
rank order. If the records do not remain sorted, the push_down function will produce
some 'interesting' results!

```
/*
 * Generic functions to manipulate the ladder data file and
 * player records.
 *
 */

#include "player.h"

const char *LadderFile = "ladder";
const char *WrFmt = "%s %d     %d      %d     %ld\n";
const char *RdFmt = "%s %d     %d      %d     %ld";

/* note use of string-joining */
const char *HeaderLine =
        "Player Rank Won Lost Last Game\n"
        "=================================================\n";

const char *PrtFmt = "%-12s%4d %4d %4d %s\n";

/* return the number of records in the data file */
```

```c
int
valid_records(FILE *fp)
{
        int i = 0;
        long plrs = 0L;
        long tmp = ftell(fp);
        char buf[LENBUF];

        fseek(fp, 0L, SEEK_SET);
        for(i = 0; fgets(buf, LENBUF, fp) != NULL ; i++)
                ;

        /* Restore the file pointer to original state */

        fseek(fp, tmp, SEEK_SET);

        return i;
}

/* read num player records from fp into the array them */

int
read_records(FILE *fp, int num, player *them){
        int i = 0;
        long tmp = ftell(fp);

        if(num == 0)
                return 0;

        fseek(fp, 0L, SEEK_SET);

        for(i = 0 ; i < num ; i++){
                if(fscanf(fp, RdFmt, (them[i]).name,
                                &((them[i]).rank),
                                &((them[i]).wins),
                                &((them[i]).losses),
                                &((them[i]).last_game)) != 5)
                        break;          /* error on fscanf! */
        }

        fseek(fp, tmp, SEEK_SET);
        return i;
}

/* write num player records to the file fp from the array them */

int
write_records(FILE *fp, player *them, int num){
        int i = 0;
```

```
        fseek(fp, OL, SEEK_SET);

        for(i = 0 ; i < num ; i++) {
                if(fprintf(fp, WrFmt, (them[i]).name,
                                (them[i]).rank,
                                (them[i]).wins,
                                (them[i]).losses,
                                (them[i]).last_game) < 0)
                break;          /* error on fprintf! */
        }
        return i;
}

/*
 * return a pointer to the player in array them
 * whose name matches name
 */

player
*find_by_name(char * name, player *them, int num){
        player *pp = them;
        int i = 0;

        for(i = 0; i < num; i++, pp++)
                if(strcmp(name, pp->name) == 0)
                        return pp;

        return NULLPLAYER;
}

/*
 * return a pointer to the player in array them
 * whose rank matches rank
 */

player
*find_by_rank(int rank, player *them, int num){
        player *pp = them;
        int i = 0;

        for(i = 0; i < num; i++, pp++)
                if(rank == pp->rank)
                        return pp;

        return NULLPLAYER;
}

/*
 * reduce by one the ranking of all players in array them
 * whose ranks are now between start and end
 */
```

```
void
push_down(player *them, int number, int start, int end){
        int i;
        player *pp;

        for(i = end; i >= start; i--){
        if((pp = find_by_rank(i, them, number)) == NULLPLAYER){
                fprintf(stderr,
                "error: could not find player ranked %d\n", i);
                free(them);
                exit(EXIT_FAILURE);
        } else
                (pp->rank)++;
        }
}


/* pretty print num player records from the array them */


int
print_records(player *them, int num){
        int i = 0;

        printf(HeaderLine);

        for(i = 0 ; i < num ; i++){
                if(printf(PrtFmt,
                        (them[i]).name, (them[i]).rank,
                        (them[i]).wins, (them[i]).losses,
                        asctime(localtime(&(them[i]).last_game))) < 0)
                break;            /* error on printf! */
        }
        return i;
}


/* copy the values from player from to player to */


void
copy_player(player *to, player *from){
        if((to == NULLPLAYER) || (from == NULLPLAYER))
                return;

        *to = *from;
        return;
}


/* compare the names of player first and player second */
```

```
int
compare_name(player *first, player *second){
        return strcmp(first->name, second->name);
}

/* compare the ranks of player first and player second */

int
compare_rank(player *first, player *second){
        return(first->rank - second->rank);
}

/* sort num player records in the array them */

void
sort_players(player *them, int num){
        qsort(them, num, sizeof(player), compare_rank);
}
```
(Example 10.5)

This code, when tested, was compiled into an object file which was then linked (together with an object file containing the code for the options function) with one of the following three programs for the ladder maintenance utilities.

Here is the code for the simplest of those utilities, showlddr which is contained in the file showlddr.c.

This program takes a single option, -f, which you will notice takes an option argument. The purpose of this argument is to allow you to print a ladder data file with a name other than the default file name, ladder.

The player records in the data file should be stored pre-sorted but, just to be safe, showlddr sorts them before it prints them out.

```
/*
 * Program to print the current ladder status.
 *
 */

#include "player.h"

const char *ValidOpts = "f:";
const char *Usage = "usage: showlddr [-f ladder_file]\n";
char *OtherFile;

int
main(int argc, char *argv[]){
        int number;
        char ch;
        player *them;
        const char *fname;
        FILE *fp;
```

```
    if(argc == 3){
            while((ch = options(argc, argv, ValidOpts)) != -1){
                    switch(ch){
                            case 'f':
                                    OtherFile = OptArg;
                                    break;
                            case '?':
                                    fprintf(stderr, Usage);
                                    break;
                    }
            }
    } else if(argc > 1){
            fprintf(stderr, Usage);
            exit(EXIT_FAILURE);
    }

    fname = (OtherFile == 0)? LadderFile : OtherFile;
    fp = fopen(fname, "r+");

    if(fp == NULL){
            perror("showlddr");
            exit(EXIT_FAILURE);
    }

    number = valid_records(fp);
    them = (player *)malloc((sizeof(player) * number));

    if(them == NULL){
            fprintf(stderr,"showlddr: out of memory\n");
            exit(EXIT_FAILURE);
    }

    if(read_records(fp, number, them) != number){
            fprintf(stderr, "showlddr: error while reading"
                                        " player records\n");
            free(them);
            fclose(fp);
            exit(EXIT_FAILURE);
    }

    fclose(fp);
    sort_players(them, number);

    if(print_records(them, number) != number){
            fprintf(stderr, "showlddr: error while printing"
                                        " player records\n");
            free(them);
            exit(EXIT_FAILURE);
    }

    free(them);
    exit(EXIT_SUCCESS);
}
```

**(Example 10.6)**

Of course the showlddr program works only if there is an existing data file containing player records in the correct format. The program newplyr creates such a file if one does not already exist and then adds a new player record, in the correct format, to that file.

Typically, new players are added at the bottom of the rankings but for the odd occasion where this really may not make sense, newplyr also allows a player to be inserted into the middle of the rankings.

A player may only appear once on the ladder (unless a pseudonym is used!) and there can only be one player at any one rank. Thus the program checks for duplicate entries and if the new player is to be inserted into a middling rank, moves other players already on the ladder out of the way.

As with the showlddr program, newplyr recognises a -f option as a request to add the new player to a file named by the option argument rather than the default file, ladder. In addition, newplyr requires two options, -n and -r, each with option arguments to specify both the new player's name and initial ranking respectively.

```c
/*
 * Program to add a new player to the ladder.
 * You are expected to assign a realistic
 * ranking value to the player.
 *
 */

#include "player.h"

const char *ValidOpts = "n:r:f:";
char *OtherFile;
static const char *Usage = "usage: newplyr -r rank -n name [-f file]\n";

/* Forward declaration of function defined in this file */

void record(player *extra);

int
main(int argc, char *argv[]){
        char ch;
        player dummy, *new = &dummy;

        if(argc < 5){
                fprintf(stderr, Usage);
                exit(EXIT_FAILURE);
        }

        while((ch = options(argc, argv, ValidOpts)) != -1){
                switch(ch){
                case 'f':
                        OtherFile = OptArg;
                        break;
```

```
                    case 'n':
                            strncpy(new->name, OptArg, NAMELEN);
                            new->name[NAMELEN] = 0;
                            if(strcmp(new->name, OptArg) != 0)
                            fprintf(stderr,
                                    "Warning: name truncated to %s\n", new->name);
                            break;
                    case 'r':
                            if((new->rank = atoi(OptArg)) == 0){
                            fprintf(stderr, Usage);
                            exit(EXIT_FAILURE);
                            }
                            break;
                    case '?':
                            fprintf(stderr, Usage);
                            break;
                    }
            }

            if((new->rank == 0)){
                    fprintf(stderr, "newplyr: bad value for rank\n");
                    exit(EXIT_FAILURE);
            }

            if(strlen(new->name) == 0){
                    fprintf(stderr,
                            "newplyr: needs a valid name for new player\n");
                    exit(EXIT_FAILURE);
            }

            new->wins = new->losses = 0;
            time(& new->last_game); /* make now the time of the "last game" */
            record(new);
            exit(EXIT_SUCCESS);
    }

void
record(player *extra){
        int number, new_number, i;
        player *them;
        const char *fname = (OtherFile == 0) ? LadderFile : OtherFile;
        FILE *fp;

        fp = fopen(fname, "r+");

        if(fp == NULL){
                if((fp = fopen(fname, "w")) == NULL){
                        perror("newplyr");
                        exit(EXIT_FAILURE);
                }
        }
```

```c
number = valid_records(fp);
new_number = number + 1;


if((extra->rank <= 0) || (extra->rank > new_number)){
        fprintf(stderr,
                "newplyr: rank must be between 1 and %d\n",
                new_number);
        exit(EXIT_FAILURE);
}


them = (player *)malloc((sizeof(player) * new_number));


if(them == NULL){
        fprintf(stderr,"newplyr: out of memory\n");
        exit(EXIT_FAILURE);
}


if(read_records(fp, number, them) != number){
        fprintf(stderr,
                "newplyr: error while reading player records\n");
        free(them);
        exit(EXIT_FAILURE);
}


if(find_by_name(extra->name, them, number) != NULLPLAYER){
        fprintf(stderr,
                "newplyr: %s is already on the ladder\n",
                        extra->name);
        free(them);
        exit(EXIT_FAILURE);
}


copy_player(&them[number], extra);


if(extra->rank != new_number)
        push_down(them, number, extra->rank, number);


sort_players(them, new_number);


if((fp = freopen(fname, "w+", fp)) == NULL){
        perror("newplyr");
        free(them);
        exit(EXIT_FAILURE);
}
```

```
        if(write_records(fp, them, new_number) != new_number){
                fprintf(stderr,
                        "newplyr: error while writing player records\n");
                fclose(fp);
                free(them);
                exit(EXIT_FAILURE);
        }
        fclose(fp);
        free(them);
}
```
                                                              **(Example 10.7)**

The only remaining utility required is one for recording the results of games played.
The result program performs this task.

As with the previous two utilities, result will accept a -f option together with a
file name to specify an alternative to the default player record file.

Unlike the newplyr utility, result interactively prompts the user for the names of
the winning and losing players. The program insists that the names supplied should
be those of existing players.

Given a valid pair of names, a check is then made to see if the loser is higher
ranked than winner and whether or not the winner is ranked close enough for the
victory to alter the rankings.

If a change in the standings is in order, the victor takes the loser's rank and the
loser (as well as any other player on an intervening rank) is demoted one rank.

Here is the code for the result utility.

```
/*
 * Program to record a result in the ladder
 *
 */

#include "player.h"

/* Forward declarations for functions defined in this file */

char *read_name(char *, char *);
void move_winner(player *, player *, player *, int);

const char *ValidOpts = "f:";
const char *Usage = "usage: result [-f file]\n";
char *OtherFile;

int
main(int argc, char *argv[]){
        player *winner, *loser, *them;
        int number;
        FILE *fp;
        const char *fname;
        char buf[LENBUF], ch;
```

```
        if(argc == 3){
                while((ch = options(argc, argv, ValidOpts)) != -1){
                        switch(ch){
                                case 'f':
                                        OtherFile = OptArg;
                                        break;
                                case '?':
                                        fprintf(stderr, Usage);
                                        break;
                        }
                }
        } else if(argc > 1){
                fprintf(stderr, Usage);
                exit(EXIT_FAILURE);
        }


        fname = (OtherFile == 0)? LadderFile : OtherFile;
        fp = fopen(fname, "r+");


        if(fp == NULL){
                perror("result");
                exit(EXIT_FAILURE);
        }


        number = valid_records(fp);
        them = (player *)malloc((sizeof(player) * number));


        if(them == NULL){
                fprintf(stderr,"result: out of memory\n");
                exit(EXIT_FAILURE);
        }


        if(read_records(fp, number, them) != number){
                fprintf(stderr,
                        "result: error while reading player records\n");
                fclose(fp);
                free(them);
                exit(EXIT_FAILURE);
        }


        fclose(fp);


        if((winner = find_by_name(read_name(buf, "winner"), them, number))
                == NULLPLAYER){
                fprintf(stderr,"result: no such player %s\n",buf);
                free(them);
                exit(EXIT_FAILURE);
        }
```

```c
        if((loser = find_by_name(read_name(buf, "loser"), them, number))
                == NULLPLAYER){
                fprintf(stderr,"result: no such player %s\n",buf);
                free(them);
                exit(EXIT_FAILURE);
        }

        winner->wins++;
        loser->losses++;

        winner->last_game = loser->last_game = time(0);

        if(loser->rank < winner->rank)
                if((winner->rank - loser->rank) <= CHALLENGE_RANGE)
                        move_winner(winner, loser, them, number);

        if((fp = freopen(fname, "w+", fp)) == NULL){
                perror("result");
                free(them);
                exit(EXIT_FAILURE);
        }

        if(write_records(fp, them, number) != number){
                fprintf(stderr,"result: error while writing player records\n");
                free(them);
                exit(EXIT_FAILURE);
        }
        fclose(fp);
        free(them);
        exit(EXIT_SUCCESS);
}

void
move_winner(player *ww, player *ll, player *them, int number){
        int loser_rank = ll->rank;

        if((ll->rank - ww->rank) > 3)
                return;

        push_down(them, number, ll->rank, (ww->rank - 1));
        ww->rank = loser_rank;
        sort_players(them, number);
        return;
}

char
*read_name(char *buf, char *whom){
        for(;;){
                char *cp;
                printf("Enter name of %s : ",whom);
                if(fgets(buf, LENBUF, stdin) == NULL)
                        continue;
```

```
                        /* delete newline */
                        cp = &buf[strlen(buf) - 1];
                        if(*cp == '\n')
                                *cp = 0;
                        /* at least one char? */
                        if(cp != buf)
                                return buf;
                }
        }
```

(Example 10.8)

## 10.6 Afterword

The programs shown in this chapter should help you to get a feel for what middle-of-the-road C programs look like, using the language and libraries defined in the Standard.

What do we mean by 'middle-of-the-road'? Simply this: they have been designed, implemented, tested and documented in a way appropriate for small, self-contained programs that have no real need to show high levels of robustness and reliability. Many programs don't need to meet demanding criteria; to do more to them would be over-engineering. Clearly, it is entirely dependent on the eventual purpose for which the program is intended.

There are situations which place very high demands on the software that is in use; programs to meet these requirements are very carefully engineered and have much higher amounts of effort put into reviewing, testing and the control of access to the source code than would be appropriate for simple illustrative example programs. C is also used in these application areas. The source code of programs that meet such high requirements tends to look distinctively different; the language is the same, but the amount of error checking and correction is typically much higher. We have *not* tried to illustrate that type of program.

Whichever environment you work in, we hope that this book has helped you in your understanding of C. Good luck!

# Answers to Exercises

## Chapter 1

### Exercise 1.2

```
#include <stdio.h>
#include <stdlib.h>


main(){
        int this_number, divisor, not_prime;
        int last_prime;


        this_number = 3;
        last_prime = 3;
        printf("1, 3 is a prime pair\n");
        while(this_number < 10000){
                divisor = this_number / 2;
                not_prime = 0;
                while(divisor > 1){
                        if(this_number % divisor == 0){
                                not_prime = 1;
                                divisor = 0;
                        }
                        else
                                divisor = divisor - 1;
                }


                if(not_prime == 0){
                        if(this_number == last_prime + 2)
                                printf("%d, %d is a prime pair\n",
                                        last_prime, this_number);
                        last_prime = this_number;
                }
                this_number = this_number + 1;
        }
        exit(EXIT_SUCCESS);
}
```

## Exercise 1.3

```
#include (stdio.h)
#include (stdlib.h)

main(){
        printf("Type in a string: ");
        printf("The value was: %d\n", getnum());
        exit(EXIT_SUCCESS);
}

getnum(){
        int c, value;;

        value = 0;
        c = getchar();
        while(c != '\n'){
                value = 10 * value + c - '0';
                c = getchar();
        }
        return (value);
}
```

## Exercise 1.4

```
#include (stdio.h)
#include (stdlib.h)

/* array size */
#define NUMBER   10

main(){
        int arr[NUMBER], count, lo, hi;

        count = 0;
        while(count < NUMBER){
                printf("Type in a string: ");
                arr[count] = getnum();
                count = count + 1;
        }
        lo = 0;
        while(lo < NUMBER - 1){
                hi = lo + 1;
                while(hi < NUMBER){
                        int tmp;
                        if(arr[lo] > arr[hi]){
                                tmp = arr[lo];
                                arr[lo] = arr[hi];
                                arr[hi] = tmp;
                        }
                        hi = hi + 1;
                }
                lo = lo + 1;
        }
```

```
        /* now print them */
        count = 0;
        while(count < NUMBER){
                printf("%d\n", arr[count]);
                count = count + 1;
        }
        exit(EXIT_SUCCESS);
}

getnum(){
        int c, value;

        value = 0;
        c = getchar();
        while(c != '\n'){
                value = 10 * value + c - '0';
                c = getchar();
        }
        return (value);
}
```

## Exercise 1.5

```
#include ⟨stdio.h⟩
#include ⟨stdlib.h⟩

/*
 * To print an int in binary, hex, decimal,
 * we build an array of characters and print it out
 * in order.
 * The values are found least significant digit first,
 * and printed most significant digit first.
 */
#define NDIG     32      /* assume max no. of digits */

int getnum(void);

main(){
        int val, i, count;
        char chars[NDIG];

        i = getnum();

        /* print in binary */
        val = i;
        count = 0;
        do{
                chars[count] = val % 2;
                val = val / 2;
                count = count + 1;
        }while(val);
        count = count - 1; /* just incremented above */
```

```
        while(count >= 0){
                printf("%d", chars[count]);
                count = count - 1;
        }
        printf("\n");
        /* print in decimal */
        val = i;
        count = 0;
        do{
                chars[count] = val % 10;
                val = val / 10;
                count = count + 1;
        }while(val);
        count = count - 1; /* just incremented above */
        while(count >= 0){
                printf("%d", chars[count]);
                count = count - 1;
        }
        printf("\n");
        /* print in hex */
        val = i;
        count = 0;
        do{
                chars[count] = val % 16;
                val = val / 16;
                count = count + 1;
        }while(val);
        count = count - 1; /* just incremented above */
        while(count >= 0){
                if(chars[count] < 10){
                        printf("%d", chars[count]);
                }
                else{
                        /* assume 'A' - 'F' consecutive */
                        chars[count] = chars[count] - 10 + 'A';
                        printf("%c", chars[count]);
                }
                count = count - 1;
        }
        printf("\n");
        exit(EXIT_SUCCESS);
}

getnum(){
        int c, value;;
        value = 0;
        c = getchar();
        while(c != '\n'){
                value = 10 * value + c - '0';
                c = getchar();
        }
        return (value);
}
```

# Chapter 2

### Exercise 2.1

Trigraphs are used when the input device used, or the host system's native character set, do not support enough distinct characters for the full C language.

### Exercise 2.2

Trigraphs would not be used in a system that has enough distinct characters to allocate a separate one to each of the C language symbols. For maximum portability, one might see a trigraph representation of a C program being distributed, on the grounds that most systems which do not use ASCII will be able to read ASCII coded data and translate it into their native codeset. A Standard C compiler could then compile such a program directly.

### Exercise 2.3

White space characters are not equivalent to each other inside strings and character constants. Newline is special to the preprocessor.

### Exercise 2.4

To continue a long line. Especially in systems that have an upper limit on physical line length.

### Exercise 2.5

They become joined.

### Exercise 2.6

Because the */ which apparently terminates the inner comment actually terminates the outer comment.

### Exercise 2.7

31 characters for internal variables, six for external variables. The six character names must not rely on distinction between upper and lower case, either.

### Exercise 2.8

A declaration introduces a name and a type for something. It does not necessarily reserve any storage.

## Exercise 2.9

A definition is a declaration that also reserves storage.

## Exercise 2.10

It is always the case that the largest range of values can be held in a long double, although it may not actually be any different from one of the smaller floating point types.

## Exercise 2.11

The same answer holds true for the type with the greatest precision: long double. C does not permit the language implementor to use the same number of bits for, say, double and long double, then to allocate more bits for precision in one type and more for range in the other.

## Exercise 2.12

There can never be problems assigning a shorter floating point type to a longer one.

## Exercise 2.13

Assigning a longer floating type to a shorter one can result in overflow and undefined behaviour.

## Exercise 2.14

Undefined behaviour is completely unpredictable. *Anything* may happen. Often, nothing seems to happen except that erroneous arithmetic values are produced.

## Exercise 2.15

(a)     Signed int (by the integral promotions).
(b)     This cannot be predicted without knowing about the implementation. If an int can hold all of the values of an unsigned char the result will be int, again by the integral promotions. Otherwise, it will have to be unsigned int.
(c)     Unsigned int.
(d)     Long.
(e)     Unsigned long.
(f)     Long.
(g)     Float.
(h)     Float.
(i)     Long double.

## Exercise 2.16

(a)     i1 % i2
(b)     i1 % (int)f1
(c)     If either operand is negative, the sign is implementation defined, otherwise it is positive. This means that, even if both operands are negative, you can't predict the sign.
(d)     Two – unary negate, binary subtract.
(e)     i1 &= 0xf;
(f)     i1 |= 0xf;
(g)     i1 &= ~0xf;
(h)     i1 = ((i2 >> 4) & 0xf) | ((i2 & 0xf) << 4);
(i)     The result is unpredictable. You must never use the same variable more than once in an expression if the expression changes its value.

## Exercise 2.17

(a)     ```
        (c = (( u * f) + 2.6L);
        (int = ((float) + long double);
        (int = (long double));
        (int);
        ```

Note: the integral promotion of char to int might be to unsigned int, depending on the implementation.

(b)     ```
        (u += (((--f) / u) % 3));
        (unsigned += ((float / unsigned) % int));
        (unsigned += (float % int));
        (unsigned += float);
        (unsigned);
        ```

(c)     ```
        (i <<= (u * (÷ (++f))));
        (int <<= (unsigned * (- float)));
        (int <<= (unsigned * float));
        (int <<= float);
        (int);
        ```

The rules for the shift operators state the right-hand operand is always converted to int. However, this does not affect the result, whose type is always determined by the type of the left-hand operand. This is doubly so for the current example, since an assignment operator is being used.

(d)     ```
        (u = (((i + 3) + 4) + 3.1));
        (unsigned = (((int + int) + int) + double))
        (unsigned = ((int + int) + double));
        (unsigned = (int + double));
        (unsigned = double);
        (unsigned);
        ```

(e)      
```
(u = (((3.1 + i) + 3 ) + 4));
(unsigned = (((double + int) + int) + int));
(unsigned = ((double + int) + int));
(unsigned = (double + int));
(unsigned = double);
(unsigned);
```

(f)      
```
(c = ((i << (- (--f))) & 0xf));
(char = ((int << (- (--float))) & int ));
(char = ((int << (- float)) & int ));
(char = ((int << float) & int));
(char = (int & int));
(char);
```

# Chapter 3

### Exercise 3.1

They all give an int result with a value of 1 for true and 0 for false.

### Exercise 3.2

They all give an int result with a value of 1 for true and 0 for false.

### Exercise 3.3

They guarantee an order of evaluation: left to right, and stop as soon as the overall result can be determined.

### Exercise 3.4

Break can be used to turn a switch statement into a set of exclusive choices of action.

### Exercise 3.5

Continue has no special meaning in a switch statement, but only to an outer do, while or for statement.

### Exercise 3.6

Inside a while statement, the use of continue may cause the update of the loop control variable to be missed. It is, of course, the responsibility of the programmer to get this right.

## Exercise 3.7

Because the scope of a label doesn't extend outside the function that it lives in, you can't use goto to jump from one function to another. Using the longjmp library routine, described in Chapter 9, a form of function-to-function jump is supported, but not a completely general one.

# Chapter 4

## Exercise 4.1

```
#include (stdio.h)
#include (stdlib.h)

main(){
        int i, abs_val(int);;

        for(i = -10; i <= 10; i++){
                printf("abs of %d is %d\n", i, abs_val(i));
        }
        exit(EXIT_SUCCESS);
}

int
abs_val(int x){

        if(x < 0){
                return(-x);
        }
        return(x);
}
```

## Exercises 4.2 and 4.3

There are two files that together form the answer to these exercises. This is the first for Exercise 4.3.

```
#include (stdio.h)
#include (stdlib.h)

int curr_line(void), curr_col(void);
void output(char);

main(){
        printf("line %d\n", curr_line());
        printf("column %d\n", curr_col());

        output('a');
        printf("column %d\n", curr_col());

        output('\n');
        printf("line %d\n", curr_line());
        printf("column %d\n", curr_col());
        exit(EXIT_SUCCESS);
}
```

The second file contains the functions and static variables for Exercise 4.2.

```
#include <stdio.h>

int curr_line(void), curr_col(void);
void output(char);

static int lineno=1, colno=1;

int
curr_line(void){
        return(lineno);
}

int
curr_col(void){
        return(colno);
}

void
output(char a){
        putchar(a);
        colno++;
        if(a == '\n'){
                colno = 1;
                lineno++;
        }
}
```

## Exercise 4.4

The recursive function:

```
#include <stdio.h>
#include <stdlib.h>

void recur(void);

main(){
        recur();
        exit(EXIT_SUCCESS);
}

void
recur(void){
        static ntimes;

        ntimes++;
        if(ntimes < 100){
                recur();
        }
        printf("%d\n", ntimes);
        ntimes--;
}
```

## Exercise 4.5

And finally, the largest of all of the answers.

```
#include <stdio.h>
#include <stdlib.h>

#define PI 3.141592
#define INCREMENT (PI/20)
#define DELTA .0001

double sine(double), cosine(double);
static unsigned int fact(unsigned int n);
static double pow(double x, unsigned int n);

main(){
        double arg = 0;

        for(arg = 0; arg <= PI; arg += INCREMENT){
                printf("value %f\tsine %f\tcosine %f\n", arg,
                        sine(arg), cosine(arg));
        }
        exit(EXIT_SUCCESS);
}

static unsigned int
fact(unsigned int n){
        unsigned int answer;

        answer = 1;
        while(n > 1)
                answer *= n--;

        return(answer);
}

static double
pow(double x, unsigned int n){
        double answer;

        answer = 1;
        while(n){
                answer *= x;
                n--;
        }
        return(answer);
}

double
sine(double x){
        double difference, thisval, lastval;
        unsigned int term;
        int sign;
```

```
        sign = -1;
        term = 3;

        thisval = x;
        do{
                lastval = thisval;
                thisval = lastval + pow(x, term) / fact(term)
                        * sign;
                term += 2;
                sign = -sign;
                difference = thisval - lastval;
                if(difference < 0)
                        difference = -difference;
        }while(difference > DELTA && term < 16);

        return(thisval);
}

double
cosine(double x){
        double difference, thisval, lastval;
        unsigned int term;
        int sign;

        sign = -1;
        term = 2;

        thisval = 1;
        do{
                lastval = thisval;
                thisval = lastval + pow(x, term) / fact(term)
                        * sign;
                term += 2;
                sign = -sign;
                difference = thisval - lastval;
                if(difference < 0)
                        difference = -difference;
        }while(difference > DELTA && term < 16);

        return(thisval);
}
```

# Chapter 5

## Exercise 5.1

0-9.

## Exercise 5.2

Nothing. It is guaranteed to be a valid address and can be used to check a pointer against the end of the array.

## Exercise 5.3

Only when they point into the same array, or to the same object.

## Exercise 5.4

It can safely be used to hold the value of a pointer to any sort of object.

## Exercise 5.5

(a)
```
int
st_eq(const char *s1, const char * s2){

        while(*s1 && *s2 && (*s1 == *s2)){
                s1++; s2++;
        }

        return(*s1 - *s2);
}
```

(b)
```
const char *
find_c(char c, const char *cp){

        while(*cp && *cp != c)
                cp++;
        if(*cp){
                return(cp);
        }

        return(0);
}
```

(c)
```
const char *
sub_st(const char *target, const char *sample){

        /*
         * Try for a substring starting with
         * each character in sample.
         */
        while(*sample){
                const char *targ_p, *sample_p;

                targ_p = target;
                sample_p = sample;
                /* string compare */
                while(*targ_p && *sample_p
                            && (*targ_p == *sample_p)){
                        targ_p++; sample_p++;
                }
                /*
                 * If at end of target, have substring!
                 */
```

```
                        if(*targ_p == 0)
                                return(sample);
                        /* otherwise try next place */
                        sample++;
                }
                return(0);       /* no match */
        }
```

## Exercise 5.6

No answer can be given.

# Chapter 6

## Exercise 6.1

```
        struct {
                int a, b;
        };
```

## Exercise 6.2

Without a tag or any variables defined, the structure declaration is of little use. It cannot be referred to later.

## Exercise 6.3

```
        struct int_struc{
                int a, b;
        }x, y;
```

## Exercise 6.4

```
        struct int_struc z;
```

## Exercise 6.5

```
        p = &z;
        p->a = 0;
```

## Exercise 6.6

Explicitly, for example

```
        struct x;
```

or implicitly,

```
struct x *p;
```

when no outer declaration exists.

### Exercise 6.7

It is not treated as a pointer, but as a short-hand way of initializing the individual array elements.

### Exercise 6.8

Nothing unusual at all, the string is treated as a literal constant of type const char *.

### Exercise 6.9

Yes. It is easier!

## Chapter 7

### Exercise 7.1

```
#define MAXLEN 100
```

### Exercise 7.2

In expressions, there may be precedence problems. A safer definition would be #define VALUE (100 + MAXLEN).

### Exercise 7.3

```
#define REM(a, b) ((a)%(b))
```

### Exercise 7.4

```
#define REM(a, b) ((long)(a)%(long)(b))
```

### Exercise 7.5

It generally signifies a library header file.

**Exercise 7.6**

It generally signifies a private header file.

**Exercise 7.7**

By using the conditional compilation directives. Examples are shown in the text.

**Exercise 7.8**

It uses `long int` in place of `int` and `unsigned long int`, in place of `unsigned int` using the arithmetic environment provided by the translator, not the target. It must provide at least the ranges described in ⟨`limits.h`⟩.

# Index